ISLAND TREASURE

ISLAND TREASURE

THE SEARCH FOR SIR CLOUDESLEY SHOVELL'S FLAGSHIP 'ASSOCIATION'

Roland Morris

HUTCHINSON OF LONDON

HUTCHINSON & CO (*Publishers*) LTD
178–202 Great Portland Street, London W1

London Melbourne Sydney Auckland
Bombay Toronto Johannesburg New York

First published 1969

This book has been set in Scotch Roman,
printed in Great Britain on Cartridge paper
by Anchor Press, and bound by
Wm. Brendon, both of Tiptree, Essex

09 089400 6

CONTENTS

Who was he? what was he? Soldier or seaman? Someone of 'good family' perhaps? or was he one of 'the people'—a 'cockswain', a 'joyner' or gunner maybe? Certain it is he was in his early twenties when he met his death—trapped below decks in the flagship 'Association' at the time of her foundering. His remains were discovered twelve fathoms down, at the foot of the Outer Gilstone Ledges in the Islands of Scilly.

No matter who, or what, he was, I dedicate my book to the especial memory of this young man, and to that of all the hundreds of others who died with him on that October night of 1707.

All the drawings are the work of the author, except for the Admiralty chart of the Western Rocks, which is reproduced by courtesy of the Controller of H.M. Stationery Office and of the Hydrographer of the Navy (*pp* 42-3), and all the photographs were either taken by the author or by members of his staff, except for those of the chart by Edmund Gostelo, reproduced by courtesy of the Public Record Office (*pp* 2-3, 4-5, 28, 62); the wreck of the *Bessemer City,* Studio St. Ives Ltd. (*p* 7); the iron gun from the *Anson,* Western Morning News Co. Ltd. (*p* 19); from the *Anson,* the iron gun raised from Mount's Bay and the *Greencastle,* Richards Bros, Penzance (*pp* 17, 20, 24, 30, 135) the sternboard of the *Association,* by courtesy of the British Travel Association (*p* 71); and the three bronze guns from *Association* on the quay at St. Mary's, F. E. Gibson, Scilly Isles (*p* 156). The letter from Sir Cloudesley Shovell (*p* 64) is reproduced by courtesy of Plymouth City Library.

The author acknowledges permission to quote from the *Eastern Evening News* (*pp* 215–16) and *Western Morning News* (*pp* 18-20, 21-2); and owes particular thanks to Mr John Page, editor of *Cornishman* (*pp* 116-18, 126–7), and Mr. Tregarthen Mumford, editor of the *Scillonian Magazine* (*pp* 177-8, 191-3).

1

SHRIMPS AND COGNAC

Before one sets out on an undersea treasure hunt one should be armed with a chart. If possible, a chart smelling strongly of tobacco and tar, a chart stained here and there with rum and such; a chart tied up in an oilcloth for a certainty.

Well, I got my chart all right; the marks on it were so clear I could scarce believe my luck or my eyes. Like young Jim's, it was a chart of an island, several islands in fact, with 'latitude and longitude; with soundings, names of hills and bays and inlets, and every particular that would be needed to bring a ship to a safe anchorage upon their shores'. The larger island was about three miles long and two across, shaped, you might say, like a fat snail. The islands had several fine landlocked harbours, the biggest island had a hill in the centre marked—no, not Spy-glass but Telegraph. There were no instructions, no crosses marked in red ink, there were no words: 'Bulk of treasure here', or anything in that way. But, by thunder! there was something much clearer, much more cunning, far more crafty—the treasure ship itself was sketched in right alongside the very rock she had struck on! Could luck be more favourable than that? Athwart the drawing of the rock, in a small neat hand was written these words:

On this Gilston Sir Clodesly was lost

And beneath the likeness of the ship, a ship inundated by many

A
Map of the Ylands
of SCILLY.
Shewing all the Rocks
And Ledges, with the
Soundings & Barings,
And ye Exact Places where
The Association Eagle
Rumny & Fierbrand was
Lost. These Islands are
In Number 43 and but 6
Of them Inhabited.
Sidney Godolphin ye Gover
Edmund Gostelo F.
SEMPER EADEM
BROAD SOUND
S W chan
Gunner
Creebawethen
Bishop and Clerks
Creebinnack
B
O

St HELLENS SOUND
TRAN SOUND
St Martins
Tresco
ROAD
St Maryes
CRO SOUND
St MARYES SOUND

waves, with but the mainmast surviving and with a large ensign drooping over her high stern, was the further information:

Association lost

The chart, for such it was, bore the information: *A map of the Islands of Scilly. Shewing all the rocks and Ledges, with the Soundings & Barings, And ye Exact Places where the 'Association', 'Eagle', 'Rumney' and 'Firebrand' was lost. These Islands are in Number 43 and but 1 Of them Inhabited. Sidney Kedolfin ye Governour.* Let me say right away, this chart was not some creased and faded parchment, some tattered much-thumbed document, which had lain hidden in a seagoing slop chest, away from prying eyes.

No matter, it was something equally exciting: it was a mellowing photograph of a chart drawn by Edmund Gostelo sometime between 1707 and 1711, which, up to the time my eyes lit on it in an old Cornish manor, I never knew existed.

The Islands of Scilly—I know them well; why, living as I do at Penzance, which is in Mount's Bay at the lower end of Cornwall, you could almost say they were on my very doorstep. As the cormorants fly they are but forty miles out in the Atlantic, a few points, if you will, sou' of westerly. Land of the daffodil and narcissus, they are strange, exotic islands, each set in its own surround of fine white sand, each hedged

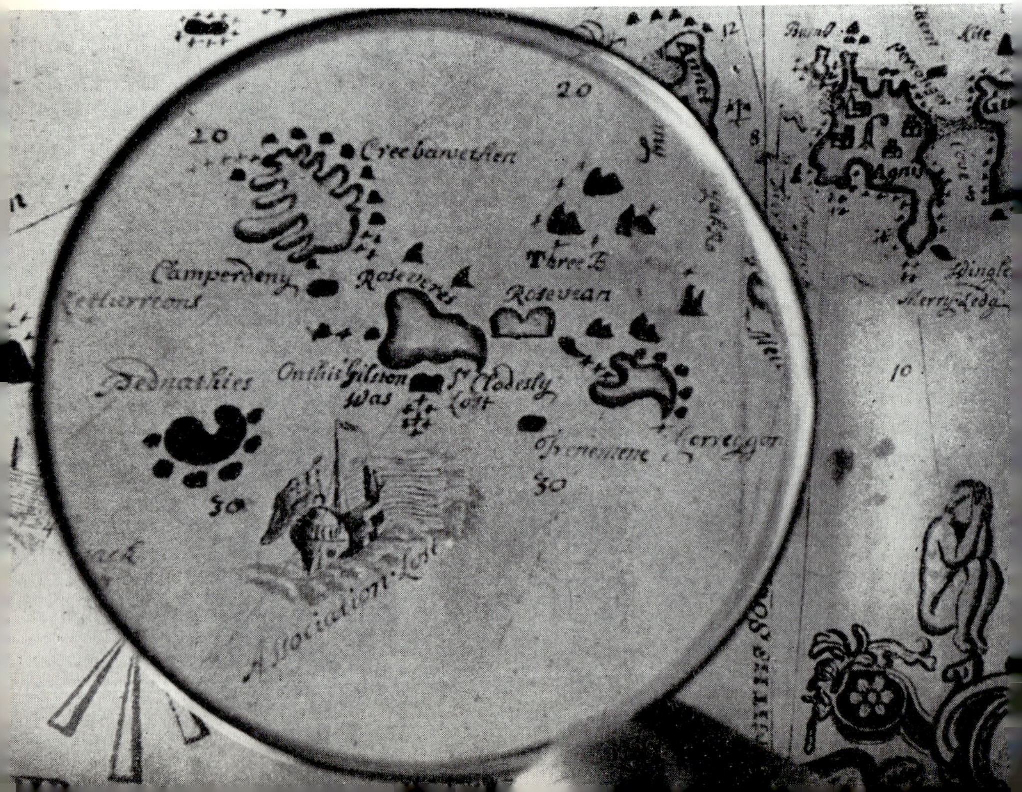

about with fuchsia, tamarisk and escallonia. Here cactuses thrive on the dry walls and giant tropical trees flourish as contentedly as if they were in their own native soil. What finer place—what more exciting place than this—in which to search for sunken treasure?

Since my childhood days I have read, and read again, every book, every article relating to Admiral Sir Cloudesley Shovell and his famous wrecks. These, along with two Spanish treasure ships which foundered, long ago, in Mount's Bay, have never failed to intrigue me. Like so many records of old-time Cornwall, a time when roguery flourished and records were frowned upon, the records of these Spanish wrecks are vague indeed: '*foundered in ye region of Gunwaloe*' they say; I wonder, what region? North: south: west? The sites of such wrecks may well take months, even years, to locate. The ship's journals, and records, relating to Sir Cloudesley's wrecks are full of errors and inaccuracies, so much so, until the chart came into my possession, I was doubtful of finding any one of them.

I first started diving in the clear, cold waters of the Scilly Isles during the 1940 war. One of my more pleasant tasks was to assist in overhauling the moorings, which held the large red rubber buoys, placed in Porthcressa and St. Mary's Pool.

These were the mooring buoys provided for the big Sunderland flying boats which were stationed there at that time.

In my off-duty periods I would take a launch over to that most beautiful of all islands, the one with the long, white, deserted beaches—St. Martin's; here I would stay and visit with my very good friend, Eric Goddard.

Eric was a flower farmer and, like many Scillonians, was a splendid seaman. Eric had previously worked with me on the wreck of the American *Bessemer City*, which had struck on the north Cornish coast, to the west of St. Ives. The wreck lay on a reef 200 yards from the high cliff coastline. We gained access to her by rigging an overhead taut wire from the cliff-top; she was to last but a few days.

Lloyd's of London wanted us to salvage the ship's Sperry Master Gyro and its intricate attachments and recorders; this was a valuable and delicate instrument, and in those days scarce and hard to come by.

I could (and may yet!) write a complete book on the subject of that *Bessemer City* wreck. She had been a magnificent ship, loaded with motor-cycles, timber, zinc ingots, fur coats and over 2,000 tons of tinned fruit and other foods. Quite illegally, so far as the Customs were concerned, I paid our crew at the rate of forty-eight tins of Sockeye salmon per day. Several tons of tinned peaches were washed overboard; by the time they had reached the St. Ives beaches they had fermented; literally hundreds of people went down with dysentery. So heavy was the demand for it, Cornish cream was obtainable only if ordered several days in advance!

This was Eric Goddard's first wreck. During his lifetime he never ceased to refer to it. You see, it was such a good wreck, and, by the very nature of its being out at sea, such a very private wreck; for no-one could venture out to it for the first few days, other than ourselves, and a great deal can happen in just a few days. Sadly, Eric has passed on; he had never quite recovered from the strain of being involved, himself, in shipwreck. He had been an apprentice in the ill-fated *Trevessa* which sank without warning, in the middle of the Indian Ocean. He was in the first officer's open lifeboat, which covered 1,747 miles in twenty-five grilling days, during which all suffered terrible hardship and exposure, from which six men died during the passage.

Eric and I, on either side of his kitchen table, with a great

The wreck of the American 'Bessemer City'

bowl of shrimps between us, would talk 'wrecks' well into the night. It was in Eric's cottage, during one of these late-night sessions, that I made a vow:

'When I can afford the time and the money,' I had said, 'I'll have a dip on old Sir Cloudesley's guns and gold.' In my mind's eye I could see myself in the blue-green depths, staring through my thick front glass at a rotting oaken chest: gold plate, and jewels as big as Christmas-tree decorations had spilled out from its dark interior. Mark this—Eric's cognac was just as 'moorish', as they say in Cornwall, as his shrimps!

Faced with a bold statement such as the one I had just made, Eric would gain time by rolling himself a cigarette. He could do this intricate task with one hand, as can many boatmen, who are loth to let their tillers go free.

'You'll never do it,' said Eric, referring to my vow. 'I know the Gilstone well, you'll never get down in your rig-out, there's too much current.'

And he was right. The next day, to prove his point, he took

ABOVE *The wreck of the 8000-ton S. S. 'Liberty' near Pendeen Light. Work on her was difficult as men and materials had to be transported by overhead wires. Note the spare bronze propeller at the stern.* BELOW *Excessive damage to the structure from breaking seas was avoided by cutting the wreck open to form a 'bridge'*

me in his boat to the site of the treasure wreck. We chug-chugged our way over some seven or eight sea miles of sparkling, brilliantly hued water, straight through Broad Sound. But, sure enough, at the Gilstone it was another world, it was far from calm; a tide rip riffled the water as if a shoal of giant fish were fighting for their lives just beneath the surface.

This was the first time I had seen the barbarous Gilstone and its two ruthless ledges, and certain I was it was no place for a hard-top diver.

'Fair enough,' said I, feeling a trifle discomfited, 'we'll have to go treasure hunting some other way, that's all.' And in the fullness of time that 'some other way' was to pay off.

Round about 1959 I decided I had finished with steel shipwreck. I had during my lifetime cut many steel ships into a surprising number of very small pieces. Now it was all over; I had just completed slicing up the 8,000-ton *Liberty* wreck on the Cornish, Pendeen coast; that was the last, I said.

So I put away my oxy'-cutting gear and my green-eyed goggles, no longer would I hear the familiar clang of one oxy'-bottle against another. No longer would I get sizzling little globules of white-hot metal searching their way down into the thick stockings of my rubber thigh boots.

I put away my underwater gear; my copper helmet, my brass corselet and my metal boots. No longer would I hear the 'seep-seep' of air coming down from above, of air warmed by pressure, air tinged with whatever aroma that happened to be near the intake of my diving pump—tobacco smoke, perhaps, or maybe pilchards frying. No longer would I have a sticky bluebottle let loose in my helmet just before my front glass was screwed in place. No longer would I get the slap on my helmet top to let me know all was well, and I could drop away into the depths.

There it was—I had finished with wrecks of steel plate and their 'treasure' of non-ferrous metal: gleaming condensers, sparkling bronze propellers, rosy-hued copper winch pipes and silver-hued white metal bearings; a fair description if you were thinking of the money these items would fetch.

No, I was turning my back on all that, no more underwater salvage for me, I had something better, something much more exciting, in mind, I was going up one; I was going in for the luxury class of underwater activity—marine exploration—or Marine Archaelogical Survey, as some people call it very grandly. It was to be nothing more than a hobby with me, I most certainly did not expect it to pay off. In Cornwall these days one cannot expect salvage in a small way to pay for itself; this is sad indeed. One way for the young in heart to turn a pretty underwater penny is to go 'craying'—that is to hunt crayfish, lobster and crab. This arduous trade, in Cornish waters, has produced some of the finest divers in the world, but even they have to turn to other things in winter.

Cornish winters can be mild and sunny—I have seen bees working late bramble blossom on Christmas Day—but even if the sun be shining, that will not deter the great, slow Atlantic swells coming in from mid-ocean storms; the sea can be rough for days on end.

It is essential, therefore to have a 'second string' if one works on or under the water. My own particular winter work was the congenial task of preserving old-time cottages, converting their interiors to snug little dwellings, and very satisfying it could be.

But now here I was, changing my way of life completely, from a diver I was to become—a restaurateur, of all things. Did I know anything about catering? Not a thing, but at least I could convert an old derelict building into a restaurant, that would be a fine start. When I was younger my desire was to own an inn, an old-world English inn, with bowed beams and flagged floors. But one just cannot set to and convert any old place into an inn, there are untold restrictions; with a restaurant you can do as you like. So when an old property came up for sale in Penzance, an old house near the sea, with low beams, thick walls and great cellars, an old building which in the misty past had been a beerhouse, I knew I had found the snug berth I had always had in mind.

Three years it took to get that place to my liking. I had one advantage over most, there was no lack of material with which to bring it back to something like its original appearance.

Relics of old-time ships

During my salvage life I had saved something of interest, or of use, from every wreck I had worked on. Great timbers of oak, green-heart, teak and pitch-pine; wood carvings, stanchions, curved beams and ornate mouldings. Moreover, from an early age I had been an avid collector of marine artefacts and shipwreck souvenirs. Ship's fittings from wrecks, famous and infamous; ships' wheels, bells, lamps, binnacles, logs, gratings, figureheads, all had been stacked away for my place of retreat when the time came.

Well, now all these relics of old-time ships had been inveigled, coaxed, even forced, to take up their respective positions in the old building. All that was required now was a sign; in the olden days when it was a beerhouse and sailor's doss house it was called 'The Admiral's'; later, when it became a respectable lodging house, its name was changed to 'Benbow House'. That was enough for me. I called it the 'Admiral Benbow', and I ask you, what better could you have?

With the restaurant running sweetly I could now turn my attention, more and more, to gold and guns.

I assembled together a team of four young divers from the several who were available at that time. They were to prove an excellent crew; they were Geoffrey Upton, Ivor Trevellyan, Derek Blundell and John Punter; all had had vast diving experience, one or two of them in the Mediterranean.

It was decided that before we ventured over to the Scilly Isles to tackle 'Enterprise G. & G.', as we called our protracted guns and gold effort, we would organise a dummy run on a wreck that was much nearer to hand. This might show up any snags in the method which we meant to adopt in raising heavy objects by means of 'air-lifts'—inflatable air-bags.

The wreck I had chosen for our first combined venture was that of the forty-four-gun frigate *Anson*. She had come ashore in Mount's Bay in December 1807, a century and two months later than the wreck of the treasure ship *Association*.

At the time of the disaster *Anson* had become embayed. She was at the mercy of a sou'westerly gale, she had swung to her anchors for one whole night, but eventually her cables parted: she ran aground on Looe Bar near Porthlevan with the loss of over sixty lives. Battered by tremendous seas, the great ship quickly broke in pieces, but not before many men, greatly daring, had scrambled on board at low water and had salvaged 'watches, jewellery and articles of considerable value' from her great cabin. The bulk of the treasure must have been considerable; the old records say that it was taken, under a strong guard, to the Old Inn at Porthlevan; here 'one of the beams of the bedroom floor was permanently bowed by the unusual weight of the chests'.

I had dived down on the *Anson* wreck in the past. It had not been very rewarding, all I had seen at that time was half a dozen great iron cannon embedded in the sandy bottom.

On every wreck I have dived and worked on I have never failed to obtain, from the owners, permission to do so. *Anson* was no exception. In 1961 I bought the sole rights of her from the British Admiralty; these cost the princely sum of ten pounds and the contract was to last seven years. With the Rights went the usual Agreement which is drawn up in such cases; in this instance I had to agree to pay the Admiralty thirty per cent of the value of any specie found, which is about right for this class of salvage. I also had to agree to the Conditions of Sale (Wrecks) which absolved the Admiralty from any liability whatsoever concerning the wreck.

Many years ago, I cut up several ex-German submarines. These were the small First World War U-boats of about 800 tons and they lay about on the rocks at Falmouth like a flock of stranded whales. Many years after, a bather gashed a leg on an underwater projection in the vicinity of these wrecks.

H.M.S. 'Anson' ran aground on Looe Bar near Porthlevan, with the loss of over sixty lives

As it happened, I had sold them previous to this or I might well have been liable. Fisherman, also, can snag their nets or trawls on a wreck. So the Rights of a wreck can work two ways: while they are supposed to give you certain benefits, they can also be a serious hazard. The Agreement goes on to say:

'After the date of acceptance of tender the wreck will be at the purchaser's risk, and be deemed to be his property and in his possession and control, and all responsibility in connection with the wreck will rest with the purchaser.'

All very fair and above board, as it should be, but for the first time my purchase of the Right of Wreck was going to land me in trouble, as we shall see later.

Were there guns or gold in the *Anson* wreck? we asked ourselves, and by 'guns' we meant bronze, not iron. We had every intention of salvaging a few of the three-ton iron monsters. These lay in shallow water, on the seaward side of the giant surf that continually pounds the bar. There well might be bronze cannon to be found under the iron ones. Our interest lay deep in the sand; in our opinion the complete bottom of the wrecked ship lay engulfed in sand, like an enormous shallow dish, holding in its curved sides the thou-

Ex-German submarines lay about on the rocks at Falmouth like a flock of stranded whales

sand-and-one objects that could have filtered down into the bilges. Gold?—gold coins? Very problematical, we decided. Gold coins have been found on the beach, in the vicinity of the wreck, for as long as local people can remember, but in spite of this we thought the early salvors must surely have taken the greater part of any bulk of coin, they were no fools.

No, we based no hopes of treasure in this wreck, the whole thing was a challenge, we kept reminding ourselves, a try-out; salving in sand was always a gamble anyway. Nevertheless, we were all keeping our fingers crossed for the luck of finding at least one fat, shining bronze cannon.

Next to gold coins, a diver's dream, anywhere in the world is to raise at least one bronze cannon during his lifetime. A cannon preferably fitted with gay, gambolling dolphin lifting-eyes, a cannon graceful and sleek, a long, lean thing of beauty, decorated in that cunning manner which only old-time cannon-makers could have devised. Possibly it is too much to ask, to be able to bring back such a thing from oblivion into the world of human beings once again: to be looked at and admired: for ever more!

2

SHIFTING SANDS AND IRON MONSTERS

We started work on the *Anson* wreck in August 1961. Somehow the news of our salvage attempt had leaked out. The local newspaper had splashed headlines reading: 'Skin divers Search for Gold Bullion', 'Heavy Lifting Gear to be Rushed to Scene of Wreck', both mere figments of some reporter's imagination. On our first morning we left the small harbour of Porthlevan with all the necessary gear for a preliminary reconnaissance. It was early, the sun had not long risen, the sea, which had a 'bit of a lop on it', was deserted with the exception of one small trawler; this appeared to be hovering about the very spot for which we were making.

The wreck site was about two miles distant along the sandbar, and but a few yards out from the beach. On the bar a big surf constantly runs, so we aimed to anchor just to the seaward side of the breakers. As we approached the trawler we could see that the two men on board were awaiting our arrival.

'It's Silas Oats in the *Guide Me*,' said someone, 'what's he doing out here?'

We were soon to find out. With the two boats dipping and rolling within yards of each other, with the blue sea catching the early sun on our one side and the white surf foaming and thundering on the other, we began a shouted conversation.

This was my first meeting with Cap'n Silas Oats; I saw a tall, lean, good-looking young man with whom, over the years, I was to become good friends, but at that moment our relationship was anything but cordial.

It appeared that a keen local historian, roused by the announcement in the Press that we were about to start work on the *Anson* wreck, had hoped to secure the services of Cap'n Silas in order to start a counter-operation.

For a while it looked as if we had reached an impasse. When I explained that there was a vast difference between historical research and the tricky work of salvage, Cap'n Silas began to take more notice of what I was saying. For Silas is a salvage man through and through; soon it became obvious that he was wavering. As he tilted his peaked cap, his skipper's cap with the fouled anchor motif, to scratch the back of his head in hesitation, I gave him the news that I had purchased the wreck from the Admiralty.

'My goodness!' said Silas, his eyes gleaming, 'you've bought her?'

'Lock, stock and barrel,' said I, 'for a period of seven years; we to keep seventy per cent of any specie we find.'

'Specie?' asked Silas softly. Coming from him it sounded like a password to an Aladdin's cave.

'You know, coin—silver and gold,' I said.

And that is how we came to gain a captain; in Cap'n Silas Oats' little wheelhouse, over the spot where *Anson* lay buried, he swore allegiance to us and our operations, we shook hands all round, opened our coffee flasks and drank to our future success.

Round about this time we were joined by a Porthlevan diver, by name Tony Sampson, bringing the team of divers up to five.

On our first dive we discovered eleven guns of iron, each about nine feet long and of about three tons in weight. We found what we had long suspected—that the guns were 'cemented' together with an extremely hard calcified mixture of rust deposit and gravel. This deposit, anything from one inch to six inches thick, can be just as much a benefit as a dire hindrance. It coats everything; so that the guns were not only stuck to each other, they were glued to the sea-bed, over a large area of which the stuff had spread. That was its hindrance. The benefit, derived from the deposit, is that it

preserves everything it holds in its grasp. Crack it off a cannon-ball, for instance, and the shot will roll out in a perfect state of preservation, like a nut from its shell.

Before attempting to lift anything from the sea-bed I had occasion to visit the Porthleven Harbour Office. Here I made tentative enquiries about landing salvaged material. I was met with a cold reception; I was told that a well-known gentleman of the village held permission to recover relics of an historical value from the site; I seemed to have heard this somewhere before.

'And anyway, Mr. Morris, you just cannot go and disturb this wreck without any kind of word from the Authorities, you know.'

'No, no, I quite understand that,' said I. 'You see, I have taken the precaution of buying the wreck.'

'You've bought it?'

'Yes, from the owners, from the Admiralty.'

'But this is hard to believe, Mr. Morris, do you mind if we check?'

Of course I did not mind; I could have told them that I had bought many a wreck; I could have told them (I wonder if they would have believed me?) that at one time I had bought a complete chunk of the Mulberry Harbour, weighing in all some three hundred tons, for thirty one-pound notes. I could have told them that one day my phone rang and on it someone was shouting wildly:

'Come quickly, Rowley! There's a darn geet thing come floatin' in! Well, shay's like a—what shall I say?—like a monstrous iron crickot pitch! Ess, like a crickot pitch made of iron!'

At the time there was no one available to accompany me. I flung myself into a car and drove quickly to a cliff situated between Prah Sands and Prussia Cove. Arriving, breathless, on top of the cliff, I was amazed to look down on a great oblong of floating steel. A great square-bowed, square-sterned, straight-sided vessel with no superstructure, but with just a huge expanse of deck and a hand winch at each corner.

There was not a soul in sight as I scrambled down the cliff to the water's edge. The great structure was floating peacefully five feet from the rocks. I leapt on board marvelling at its construction; it was made up of hundreds of tanks, connected with each other by big ball joints. The vessel undulated in sympathy with the movement of the sea.

From the nearest winch I unrove a length of wire rope; leaping ashore with this I made it secure round a rock and jumped on board again. Putting the winch in low gear I warped that great floating mass close under the cliffs. Although there was no one to bear witness, I raised an arm up high and shouted: 'I, Roland Morris, claim salvage on this —er well—on *this!*' and stamped a foot on the steel-plated deck.

I think if I had told those Porthlevan Harbour officials that story they would never have believed me, and, although it is absolutely true, you could not have blamed them. I left that office feeling a trifle disgruntled. The report in the local paper[1] of next day explains why:

'An important part in salvaging the wrecked Frigate H.M.S. *Anson* which has been on the sea bed off Porthlevan

[1] The *Western Morning News*, 24th August 1961.

ABOVE *To the strains of the local brass band the iron monster from the 'Anson' was lifted from the sea.* BELOW *One of the three-ton iron guns seen being carefully loaded onto a lorry: seven such guns were recovered*

since 1807 begins today. But, if any of the vessel's cannon are raised they will not be taken to the port.

'Porthlevan, only a cannon's shot from the scene of the wreck, is the obvious centre for any salvage brought from the wreck, but a shock awaited salvager Mr. Roland Morris when

Other artefacts recovered from the 'Anson' included grape shot, still in its original canvas and twine wrapping

he went to the Harbour Office to arrange the landing of the ship's guns. Mr. Morris was told:

' "Yes, certainly you can bring them in, but we must warn you that they will be impounded by the Receiver of Wreck and kept under lock and key until such time as we think it is fit for them to be released." '

This was high-handed stuff; I told them I would not bother them, I would land my salvage elsewhere.

However, the very next day, the Receiver of Wreck from Penzance came to see me; he was courteous and very helpful; he had read of my predicament, he said:

'Of course you can land your salvage when and where you please, no-one can stop you, and for a very good reason—you are the owner of the wreck.'

The thick deposit which covered the wreck site was to prove an expensive delay to our getting to grips with the wreck itself. But in the end we moved most of it; not with pickaxes, not with crowbars, but with hammer blows from small charges of explosives.

Mention explosives to an archaeologist and he will recoil in horror, as well he might if he is ignorant of their use. It is more likely he thinks in terms of vast upheavals of water, devastating blast effects and the like. The truth is, an explosive charge can be set to give a blow as gentle as that of a toffee hammer wielded by a child.

This was a long and tedious task, the stuff lay like hard macadam over everything. It formed a hard, false sea-bed over soft sand; small wonder that the guns had not sunk deeper over the years, they were held suspended like cherries stuck on an iced sponge-cake.

The lifting of our first big forty-two-pounder gun coincided with the harbour sports at Porthlevan; to the strains of the local brass band, to the shouts of gaily clad holidaymakers, the iron monster was lifted by crane from the sea, the selfsame sea into which it had plunged some 154 years previously. But what a difference in its surroundings! Now sunshine and gaiety—then stormracked skies and cries of drowning men.

The wreck could only be worked when the shifting sands of the sandbank allowed. Months would go by with the wreck lying completely covered. It might show for a week, or two weeks, then disappear once more. We had recovered seven three-ton guns and many small artefacts by the end of 1963. That year, before leaving the wreck for the winter, we placed a series of special underwater charges suggested to us by I.C.I. We sank two-inch diameter tubes deep into the hard sand; these were packed with a slow-burning blasting powder. With the loosening effect of this, aided by gales and high seas throughout the winter, we expected to find the wreck site well raked over by the following spring.

In 1964 the sand stayed over the wreck until July. It seems we were not the only ones who anxiously awaited the wreck's appearance. I awoke one morning to learn that our wreck had been 'raided' by other divers. In the *Western Morning News* it was reported:

'A team of Royal Naval divers from the R.N.A.S. *Culdrose* last evening salvaged part of the rudder equipment of the wreck of the Naval Frigate *Anson*. The rudder piece is made of copper or bronze and weighs about a quarter of a ton. When the naval team, who are members of H.M.S. *Seahawk* Sub-Aqua Club, discovered the piece they got a line on it and with one of the members below water conducting the operation, the rest of the team and holidaymakers on the beach towed the rudder section on to the sands.

'A salvage team from the R.N.A.S. with a crane then towed the piece to the top of the beach and last night it was taken to the Royal Naval Air Station.

'The entire operation was conducted under the direct attention of the C.O. of *Culdrose*, Capt. P. S. Beale who was on the beach with Mrs. Beale. Capt. Beale said last night that the Royal Naval team intended to pursue their salvage operations and recover other cannon which had been seen on the sea bed.

'Lieut-Commander Alan Baldwin, who was in charge of the diving team, said that the visibility below the sea had been fairly good. The bottom was clean and sandy and the piece of rudder had been sticking out of the sand from where the team had dug it out. He had seen two sets of four cannon on the sea bed, some distance from each other, and he intends to start salvage operations again today!'

'Over my dead body!' I exclaimed furiously. I got in touch with my solicitor, he got in touch with the Naval Air Station and told them to belay everything.

And stop they did, much to the disappointment of the London Press who had got hold of the story: '*Anson* guns in action again', said one paper, '*Anson* ghost sails into action', said another; they would have liked a ding-dong battle, for news was scarce, and summer is the time for 'silly' news. If I had been earning my living as a salvager, and not as a restaurateur, there would most certainly have been a battle, for my team felt pretty badly about the invasion.

The Penzance Receiver of Wreck, on hearing of the incident—the Press gave it great publicity—immediately ordered the Air Station to deliver the artefact to the 'Admiral Benbow', where by the terms of my contract it rightly belonged.

The 'rudder piece', as the Press described it, was indeed a fine rudder pintle of which the *Anson* would have had six. In its original form it was shaped like a huge letter 'V', with its sides, some six-feet in length, curving outwards. One of these curved pieces was broken off. A book on wreck hunting, which I have read with much pleasure, goes to great lengths to explain how this pintle, which it says was attached to the rudder, came to be bent at the time of the wreck.

Actually, the pintle was never attached to the rudder, it was spiked to the stern of the vessel, that is why it is not bent—but curved to suit the sweep of the hull. The draft plans which I have of *Anson* show this very clearly.

At the time of the recovery of this fine relic it was stated that 'a magnificent copper spike nail' was found. Seemingly that is one of the many *Anson* relics of which the 'Benbow' will never boast!

After this contretemps, not wanting to put a halt to so much enthusiasm, I gave my blessing to the Culdrose Sub-Aqua Club's request that they be allowed to recover two guns, my only stipulation being that I be handed all small articles found in the process. Whether they came across anything in that line I was not to know, but they certainly recovered the guns.

One of these stands outside the splendid little Helston Museum; the gun has been mounted on a carriage, an unfortunate carriage, the proportions of which would curl the toes of any old-time gunner; the carriage bears a plaque. Well, even if we are not mentioned it is nice to know that we helped!

Two of the big iron *Anson* guns salved by us happily remain in Porthlevan for all to see. They have been sunk muzzle down in the quay-road; they form unique and imposing 'posts' at each side of the entrance to the Boatbuilding Yard and Harbour Office.

One of our last tasks on the *Anson* wreck before we left it for ever was to salvage a splendid example of a carronade. We had delved deep enough into the sand to reach timber; at this point the carronade showed itself. A carronade is a swivelling gun, the breach of which is raised or lowered by means of a screw-threaded shaft. This one was five feet long and weighed about fifteen hundredweight: it was in perfect condition and without a doubt was the gem of our finds.

On the day we made this discovery we were using two divers, Derek Blundell and John Punter, with Gordon Baker as boatman; the launch was the small *African Queen* of Porthlevan. On the beach, anxiously awaiting our departure, were assembled the many members of the Air Station Sub-Aqua Club. They were waiting there to recover one of the guns I have mentioned; this gun lay on the sea-bed, unencumbered, untrammelled, on the brink of our great underwater sand-pit.

Spread over the beach was the club's equipment; besides a small field kitchen there was a tractor, with steel wired winch, a five-ton crane, a five-ton lorry and a trailer with a bank of enormous compressed air cylinders. A most impressive display. It was as well our divers did not keep the others waiting. We lifted our carronade in half an hour flat, which I thought was pretty good.

A day or two after, when my solicitor rang up to ask if everything was now under control, I told him we had finished our stint on the *Anson* wreck:

'We will go on to bigger and better things,' said I.

'Anything I can do to help?' he asked.

'Yes, please get me the rights to work on the wrecks of the *Association*, the *Eagle*, the *Romney* and the *Firebrand*,' I said. 'Oh, and let's include the *Phoenix* and the *Collossus* for luck.'

'Right,' said he, 'I'll get on with it.'

With our work on *Anson* concluded, with prospects of our operations moving over to the Islands of Scilly, business commitments became all-important to those of the team

The carronade from the 'Anson': five feet long and weighing about fifteen hundredweight

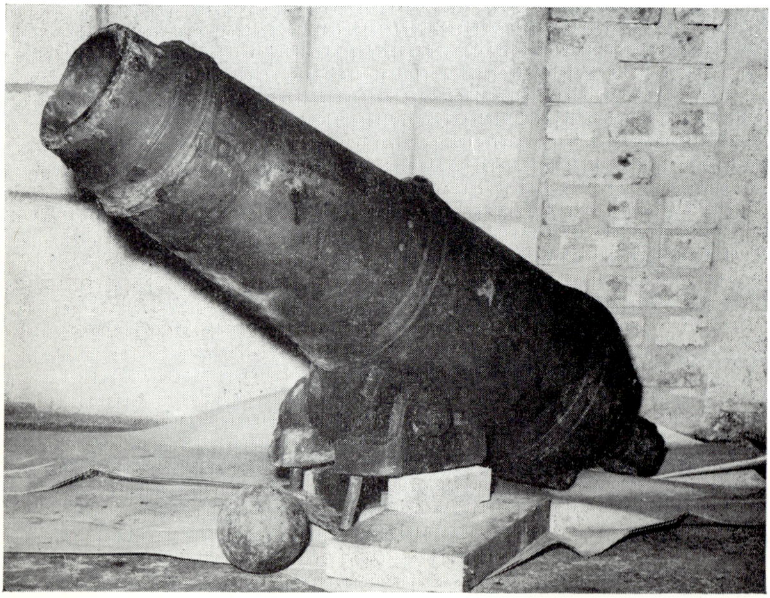

who could not leave the mainland; because of this we lost Derek, John, Tony and Ivor.

Silas graduated to larger and yet larger salvage vessels and, on his own account, sailed off up Channel; he was to gain fame in the autumn of 1967 when he found the long-lost, long-submerged, ill-fated British submarine *MI*.

My solicitor had said that he would get on with the *Association* Agreement, and get on with it he must have done, for in next to no time at all I received a signed and sealed Document which stated:

'WHEREAS the salvor proposes to dive on and carry out underwater salvage operations on the wrecks of four of Sir Cloudesley Shovell's Squadron, namely the *Association*, *Eagle*, *Romney* and *Firebrand*, which are known to lie in the area of the Gilstone in the Scilly Isles, together with the *Phoenix* beached between Tresco and St. Martin's where they were wrecked in 1707, and the *Collossus* wrecked on the Southern Wells near Samson, Scilly Isles, in 1798.
'AND WHEREAS the said vessels, with their gear, tackle, equipment and accoutrements belonged, at the time of their loss, to the Admiralty, to whose powers, rights and titles the Secretary of State for Defence has succeeded.'

This time we were to deal with the Ministry of Defence, and not the Admiralty. This time there would be no 'sole rights', instead the rights would be shared with others:

'The salvor is not given any exclusive right to dive and carry out underwater salvage operations on the aforesaid vessels, and the Secretary of State for Defence hereby reserves the right to grant similar rights to any other salvor and salvors.'

It looked as if my brush with the R.N.A.S. Sub-Aqua Club may have had repercussions.

Nevertheless I was very grateful to be allowed to work on such celebrated wrecks. The only trouble that I could see in this type of Agreement was that everything depended on the identity of the vessels being proven.

What if the wrecks were not proved to be those of the Admiral's squadron? In that case they could be treated as ‘owners unknown’ wrecks, on which every diver in the kingdom could have a go. Any object thus found on the wrecks would, as in the normal procedure of marine salvage, be handed to the Receiver of Wreck. (A fascinating title I always think. Don’t make the error, though, of calling this important personage the Receiver of Wrecks, as so many people do. He cannot take ‘wrecks’ into custody—he simply handles wreckage, or, a more intriguing word, ‘wreck’.) The object would be held for a specified time, during which any claims as to its rightful ownership would be investigated. If none was forthcoming the object could be sold by tender.

In the happy event of any of Sir Cloudesley’s wrecks being positively identified then the salvor’s lot would become a much easier one, for in that case divers who had not entered into an agreement could be barred from the area. Moreover, if the owner were known (in this case the Ministry of Defence) then only detailed lists of salvaged goods need be taken to the Receiver; not the objects themselves, some of which might well be two or three tons in weight. The Agreement says:

> ‘The salvor shall, from time to time, deliver to the Receiver full and detailed lists of all objects found, showing: the description and identification of the objects, where found’.

So, it seemed to me, it behoved all those who had contracts to set to and find evidence of identity as quickly as possible.

The percentage of award in the Agreement had been revised. Instead of the usual seventy-thirty per cent arrangement, with the salvor taking the larger cut, the *Association* Agreement laid out a fifty-fifty transaction:

> ‘The Secretary of State for Defence shall be absolutely entitled to one half of, or one half of the market value of, any of the aforesaid objects *which prove to be made of, or to include, gold, silver, jewellery, precious stones or other objects of unusual intrinsic value.*’

So that bronze guns and other ‘equipment and accoutrements’ raised by the salvor become his *sole* property, once the wreck is identified. The percentage is low compared with the rate given by the authorities in other countries. In Florida, for instance, in exchange for twenty-five per cent of any treasure, or value of artefacts recovered, the State Internal Improvement Fund will give every assistance, and grant *bona-fide* salvors exclusive Salvage Search Leases. I do not wish to appear mercenary when I say that the Ministry of Defence awards are too low. Increasing numbers of skin-divers are exploring the sea-bed every year, so that without any doubt valuable and important finds are going to be made, and there is danger that these finds may be hushed up unless the rewards make handing over the recovered goods worth while.

The Ministry of Defence had even warned the Naval men that if the wreck at the Gilstone were positively identified as a British Naval ship they, as servants of the Crown, would not expect to share in any reward should anything of value be recovered by their efforts. Any treasure located and raised would become the property of the Crown. In spite of this announcement, I am sure some way will be found to encourage these divers to further efforts. I am not suggesting for one minute that the Navy men are undertaking the *Association* operation for anything other than training and adventure, but I know that they give up a great part of their leave on this project and that prolonged diving can become real hard work. I am sure that when they heard of the Prime Minister's plea that their work at Scilly might be extended in duration they would also have liked to have heard that they had been given an extension of leave to follow, as a reward for a task well performed.

In its legal jargon the Agreement went on to outline many other fundamental points of contract, for instance:

'The Secretary of State for Defence shall have an absolute right of pre-emption in respect of any of the aforesaid objects which in his opinion is of national or historical interest at an agreed market price, or in default of agreement, at such price as shall be determined by an independent Arbitrator whose appointment shall be agreed upon by the parties hereto, and whose decision as to value should be final and binding upon the Parties hereto.'

All of which is very necessary, and very right and proper.

Although our Agreement allowed us to work on Sir Cloudes-

Another detail from Edmund Gostelo's chart showing the St. Mary's Gilstone and Perhellick—'here Sr Clodesly was Found and Buryed'—modern Porth Hellick

ley's ships in 1966, we were not prepared to go to the Islands until the summer of 1967.

During the summer of 1966, even as we worked out our plans for the following year, we learnt of other divers searching for the *Association* wreck. We were delighted, but at the same time puzzled by the fact that they could not find her. Then we heard that they were busy searching in the area of the wrong Gilstone! For there are two sets of Gilstone Ledges in the Scillies; one lying to the south of St. Mary's Island and the other—where the *Association* lies—out amongst the west'-ard rocks. What might well have been a red herring for the searching divers is the fact that in the vicinity of the St. Mary's Gilstone there lies a quantity of old cannon from some unknown wreck.

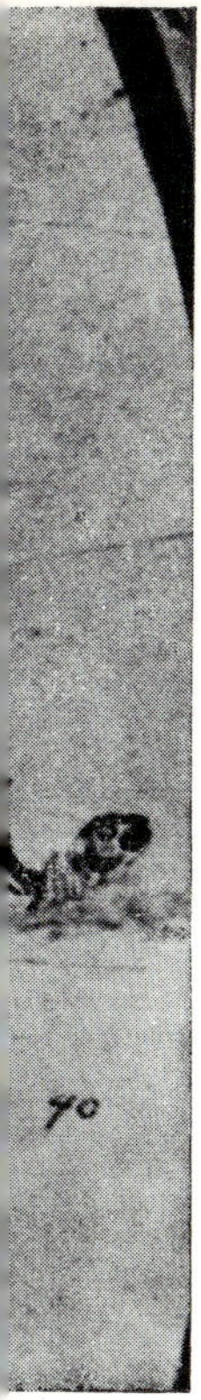

Then came reports, from the Islands, of a find of many cups and plates made of pewter. We thought that this pewter could not have come from the *Association*; pewter pest shows early in Cornish waters. In less than fifty years submergence the metal becomes bloated with nodular blebs and boils. On being brought into contact with air the gnarled tumours crack and flake, and disintegrate into bluish powder.

Later we heard that a wreck site had been located by yet another party of divers—from the Fleet Air Arm—near the west'ard Gilstone. This news sent our blood pressure soaring, our anxiety complex became almost unmanageable, for this was exactly the area where we were intending to dive on our arrival in the Islands, planned for the last week of July 1967. Just as I had had my old chart, with its picture of the *Association* striking on the outer Gilstone, they had got hold of yet another showing a rock called the Shovel, at the very same spot.

I might add here, in view of the comments that were to be made . . . and still are . . . that although the Fleet Air Arm boys probably had no *civil* agreement such as mine to allow them to work on the *Association* site, I consider that their first confirmation of the location of the wreck gives them as much right as anyone to be there. As a lifelong salvage man, my view has in fact always been that the actual finders of a wreck should have the sole rights to work it. Commercially it would be impossible to work in any other way than under an Exclusive Contract. But here the case was a deal more complex. Not to speak of official agreements existing with myself and one other party, there was the fact that the approximate location of the wreck had been known to 'natives' of the district such as myself time out of mind, and that 'pirate' expeditions were ready to pounce and exploit the work of serious salvors at every chance. Even so, well as I knew some of the 'Navy boys', I was never really to become used to working at the Gilstone while they were there, and tried as discreetly as possible to give them a free field during their visits. As regards the other party mentioned as sharing my Non-Exclusive Agreement, there was no worry: there was no chance of our treading on the flippers of the Blue Sea Divers, who hailed from Bromley in London. Even some time before the arrangement of the Agreement itself in early 1966, they had been hunting for *Association* all of six miles away from Sir Cloudesley's Gilstone, misled as non-local people might well be by the other group of rocks of the same name. This despite an account by George Gordon, in the *Daily Sketch* for 6th June 1966, of how the group 'spurred on by the chance discovery two years ago of one of the cannons from Sir Cloudesley's Flagship, the *Association*, is attempting to recover the treasure. Mike Ross and Bob Rogers, both aged twenty-two, were engaged in underwater photography when, they say, they spotted the cannon *with the name of the ship marked on it . . .*'

I believe that the wreck of the *Association* will become famous in the history of diving, not particularly because of

The six-foot iron gun, lead musket shot and a clay pipe from an old-time wreck in Mount's Bay

its guns and gold, but because it will have been the one which made the authorities change their minds and—what is more—their salvage laws. We were to give our 'non-exclusive rights', in themselves something quite new in underwater exploration, a thorough try-out to see if they would work, but in the end they gave no protection to the participants, and allowed non-agreement divers to reap a bonanza at the expense of the wreck site.

During the early part of that month we raised an iron gun from an old-time wreck in Mount's Bay. It was some six feet long; although it was in a 'soft' state we thought we could preserve it. We rolled it in a bed of cement powder for several days but to no avail. Decomposition was too far advanced, taking it from the sea was the last thing it wanted, it started to shed great chunks of its barrel. A quantity of lead musket shot, the bowl of a clay pipe and a sounding stone were recovered from the same wreck site.

While we were engaged on this small project news came from the Islands that Fleet Air Arm divers, who we knew were working at the west'ard Gilstone site, had raised a twenty-seven-hundredweight bronze cannon. I looked at our pathetic disintegrating iron gun and hoped fervently that our next underwater trophy would be made of something much more durable.

Naturally, we were more than interested in the method used by the Fleet Air Arm divers in raising their gun; it seems that oil drums were first attached to the gun, but these proving to have insufficient lift, a large flotation bag (used for salving ditched helicopters) was radioed for. This was flown out to the scene and dropped by helicopter on to the site. Some trouble was experienced with this huge bag, however, as at one stage it broke away from the underwater gun; rushing to the surface at ever-increasing speed and thrust, as released air-filled containers will do, it leapt from the surface and into the air, narrowly missing coming up beneath the rubber inflatable dinghies. Some pretty nasty injuries could have occurred if this had happened, as the dinghies were filled with men. When the gun was finally lifted, by the combined oil drums and flotation bag, it was towed to the 120-ton inshore minesweeper *Puttenham* with the aid of the Scillonian launch *Sea King*.

The news of the recovery of this gun, coming so close to the

Geoff Upton at the wheel of the twenty-foot assault storm-boat

opening of our own project, gave us a tremendous fillip. We were puzzled, though, by the reported weight of the salved gun—twenty-seven hundredweight—and by the fact that the divers had experienced difficulty in raising this comparatively moderate weight by oil drums. We ourselves hoped to do some useful work by this method of lift.

The mystery of the stubborn gun was solved later; instead of the twenty-seven hundredweight estimated, it actually weighed in the region of three tons.

At the end of July our two divers from the mainland, Geoffrey Upton and David Regalado, arrived in the Islands. With them went all their host of equipment. Geoff took his twenty-foot assault storm boat, which was in the charge of diver-boatman Michael Reynolds. This storm boat can be used as a diving platform, and was to prove its worth time and time again. It is powered by a '500' Mercury outboard, with a second outboard—a Seagull—as stand-by.

At St. Mary's Island, Geoff, David and Michael were met by Doug Rowe and Terry Parr, the two divers who were already stationed at Scilly, and who were to complete our team. At the time, Doug and Terry were working on several underwater steel wrecks.

A couple of days later, exhausted by chasing long-promised, long-overdue equipment, I saw my car swung aboard the R.M.V. *Scillonian*, its decks a gay kaleidoscope of some four to five hundred passengers. An hour later, 2,000 feet above the Scillies and after a twenty-minute flight, I was dropping down from a blue sky in a B.E.A. helicopter. The Islands lay below; sand-fringed, irregular shapes of green; green islands set in a calm tropical blue sea. I looked way down to the sou'west, away out to the hazy west'ard rocks; I tried to pick out the Gilstone Ledges; the sea out there was a deep green flecked with silver, the rocks were encircled with white.

The 'copter landed softly on the smooth tarmac: 'You may unfasten your safety belts'—the treasure hunt was on!

3

OUTRIDERS TO THE DEVIL—THE 'GILSTONE'

Many, many times have I had the pleasure of travelling to the Islands of Scilly. I have achieved this by several forms of transport; in the past I have made the trip in the graceful *Lady of the Isles*, a steamer at one time on the Scilly run. I was on her when she was working out her retirement as a salvage vessel. And I have, of course, crossed over to Scilly, in fair weather and foul, in the regular island-owned steamers which have plied to and from the Scillies over the years.

I have taken my own boat across more than once; on one memorable occasion, travelling single-handed, I took the inordinate time of nine hours to complete the trip. I was paying far too much attention to sunbathing on the cabin top rather than to navigation. With engine cut and mains'il just drawing I glistered alone over a glassy sea in the company of a veritable fleet of Portuguese men-o'-war, all with their little sails bent and their long tentacular filaments trailing deep below them in the clear water. As the setting sun caught the western sky aflame I found to my consternation that the Islands were not in sight. Peering against the glare of the sunset I strained my eyes in vain; I even climbed the mast to get a better view, but to no avail. Only when the sun sank below the sizzling horizon did the blue-grey Islands rear up out of the sea. I was way down south of them, the glare of the sunset had hidden them from my sight.

My fastest trip to the Islands was made during the darkness of an early winter's morning in a 500 h.p. boat called the *Raider*. Geoff, Doug and I left Penzance at 5 a.m., we reached St. Mary's at 7.30 a.m., were having coffee in Mike Hick's cottage at 8 a.m. and at 9 a.m. we were working at the Gilstone, but I will tell you more of that incident later.

Travelling to the Islands by air is a thrill, for what is sweeter than a gull's-eye view of an island set in the sea?

When it was first inaugurated the air service was undertaken by small eight-seater biplanes; now the big helicopters take one judderingly, but efficiently, across in no time at all.

No matter how one gets there, the thrill is in actually setting foot on island soil. For at that moment the mainland becomes a thousand miles away. One gets a feeling of reprieve; reprieve from punishment by noise, by traffic congestion and by the rush and tear of mainland life. The only rush and bustle at Scilly occurs when 'last orders' is called in the crowded bars on summer nights. The only traffic congestion met with is the pleasant watery one when the pleasure launches get away to the 'off' islands. This is a twice-daily event, after breakfast and after lunch, when the gaily dressed —or undressed—'visitors' line the pier and await the launch, or boatman, of their choice.

One of our first, most pleasing, duties was to go along to the Customs and Excise and make ourselves known to the Receiver of Wreck, Mr. 'Bill' Saunby. When we met him Mr. Saunby was dressed in shorts, sandals and lightweight sports shirt; his sun-tanned face and legs, combined with his well-trimmed, greying goatee beard, gave him a spruce continental appearance. Indeed, standing in the Customs Office, looking out through the big windows over the harbour beach to the blue waters of St. Mary's Pool, we could very well have been in some foreign port. With the tropical-tree-clad island of Tresco lying dark green on the far side of St. Mary's Road, with the white beaches of the island of St. Martins gleaming on the eastern horizon, I could well imagine myself in the Canary Islands, though the beaches of Scilly, made up as they are of fine white sand, are far superior to those of the Canaries.

Mr. Saunby was most courteous and helpful; would we like to view the spoils brought up by the sub-aqua divers of R.N. Air Command who had only just left the Islands? We most certainly would! In the long shed attached to H.M. Custom House at St. Mary's lay the nine foot six inch bronze gun of French origin. It was a massive, superb piece of ordnance. We smoothed our hands reverently over its heavy decorations; the name Le Duc de Beaufort was emblazoned over crossed anchors. In the centre of the decorative motif were the Royal Arms of France and the Royal Arms of Navarre. Entwined in the collars surrounding the Royal Arms were the Orders of St. Michael and the Order of St. Esprit (the Order of the Holy Ghost).

There it lay—this majestic culverin—silent, almost brooding, the bronze-green metal looking dense and heavy. Silent now, after 260 years' immersion in the ebullition of the sea—and before that, what tumult had it seen?—what insurrection?—what havoc?—what battle? Most certainly it had seen action, for these were fine guns, they had the same bore as English iron cannon and, what is more, they had a far longer life; yes, certainly it had seen action, but where? Vigo Bay in 1702 perhaps, when the combined English and Dutch fleets captured or destroyed seventeen French galleons? No man can now tell; we as onlookers, our eyes roaming from muzzle to breech, could only use our imagination. My mind was taken up by the men, way back over three hundred years ago, who designed and who cast this sleek weapon. The men who reamed out its bore, probably with the aid of crude machinery driven by water power. And then I thought of all the people, stretching away forward into the limitless future, who would view this gun and who, like me, would set their imagination working—to their great pleasure. Also in the Customs shed, by the side of the gun, lay several large bronze pulley wheels, or sheaves, obviously from immensely large blocks, perhaps large enough to take a rope two inches in diameter. There were two or three thick circular timber discs of the same size as the sheaves. There was a small breech-loading cannon, an even smaller swivel gun and other interesting oddments, all of which gave convincing proof of the diving ability of the underwater men of R.N. Air Command.

We left that Customs shed vowing that if, by chance, there happened to be another bronze gun lying fathoms deep at the Gilstone, then we would capture it—*per ardua* and, perhaps, by good fortune.

Our next contact had to be with that most important of all

people—our guide and pilot, Michael Hicks. Mike is a powerfully built man with a sun-tanned and weather-beaten face, dark eyes and dark curly hair; he owns and runs the launch *Sea King*. It is the *Sea King* which runs the gauntlet of the heavy seas and tearing currents that frequent the Western Isles and enables the relief of the Bishop light to be undertaken at regular intervals. It is Mike, with his *Sea King*, who excels in thrilling the holidaymakers by his seamanship in ploughing through high seas in the region of the western rocks; sometimes sluicing past giant rocks, over which the surf is pounding, with but feet to spare. The holidaymakers invariably return from these trips very thrilled, very wet and very boastful.

It was early afternoon, the sun was striking hot, the harbour was a picture of placid blue water, white yachts and colourful holiday clothes. We looked over the harbour wall, the water sparkled in Broad Sound, white balls of fluffy cloud rode the sky, a grey heron, long-billed and long-necked, stood on equally long legs on a rock twenty-five yards from us; it spread open its wings—jagged edged—it held them thus to dry in the sun.

Mike Hicks was further down the pier, waving his arms and directing the holiday crowd to their various boats.

'Hi!' he called, as we came up to him.

'Hi!' said we, 'it's a lovely day!'

'Couldn't be better!' said Mike, grinning, and, as is his wont, swaying to and fro on his feet as if a boat were under him.

'How's it looking for the Gilstone today?' we asked.

'Well,' said Mike. He rubbed his nose with the back of his hand, then turned to a lady who was making enquiries. 'No, ma'am, not this one, you'll want the *Nemo* for St. Martin's and the east'ard isles.' We tried again: 'Any chance of getting to the Gilstone today? Have you got time?'

Mike looked at us quizzically. 'It's not the time I want but the weather,' he said; 'there's a lot of white water showing at the west'ard isles, it's no weather for diving.'

'Darn it!' said I, 'we'd like to get cracking as soon as possible.'

'Well,' said Mike, 'I can tell you this, you won't do any diving today, nor will you do any while the wind's sou'westerly, that's for a certainty.'

And we knew full well that there was no argument; if Mike

said the sea conditions were rough at the Gilstone, then rough they were, and that was the all of it.

That evening, as the setting sun put on its grand finale to a perfect summer's day performance, we congregated in the Mermaid Inn.

'Now look,' said Mike, making his favourite opening remark. He held up a large glass containing his invariable drink —iced Coca Cola. Every so often he would jerk the glass so that the ice would clink, to emphasise some point he was making: 'Now look, I don't want to keep you from the Gilstone, I'd take you there in any weather, but not to go diving. What if you went diving from my launch and someone gets drowned? My name would be mud from then on! No, I'll take you there when the sea is favourable, and you can rely on that.'

'Yes, but, Mike . . . ' said I, 'these divers of mine, Geoff and David, are crayfish divers, they would never earn a living if they had to wait for calm water. As for Doug and Terry, they are scrap-metal divers, and the same thing applies.'

'Well,' said Mike, 'you mark my words, someone's going to get killed out there before long. I've seen some near shaves as it is and all the diving I've seen so far has been done in calm weather.'

'Meaning the Navy?' I asked.

'Never you mind,' said Mike. 'The Navy were blessed with fine sea conditions for most of their time, if it came up rough they laid off.'

I must admit I was a bit nonplussed. I knew from my visit to the Gilstone of many years before that it was a treacherous, current-ridden place where extreme caution had to be exercised at all times. I knew this and Mike knew it, but what Mike was not acquainted with was the fact that divers can operate in rough surface conditions. What Mike did not know at that time was that a rough sea on the top does not necessarily mean a rough time four fathoms or more below. Obviously Mike Hicks had the safety of the divers at heart, and this was to be applauded; the safety of the divers was top priority number one at all times and must remain so. But the Gilstone and its reefs were seven miles out in the Atlantic. We thought we ought to go out there and see the conditions for ourselves; the divers could then give the final verdict.

The economics of the situation were simple: at Scilly my divers were earning ten pounds a day, or seventy pounds a week. And why should they not? They could earn that much, and more, at their crayfish or scrap-metal work. Delay in salvage is like pouring water into a sieve, it is the greatest hazard of all.

Before I had crossed over to the Islands I had made a small agreement with a London newspaper. The paper was the week-end Colour Supplement of the *Daily Telegraph.* The agreement was that I should allow them prior use of all my colour photographs of the treasure hunt, the fee to me being one hundred pounds. On the second night of my stay at Tregarthen's Hotel I was called to the phone; it was the *Daily Telegraph.* Did I know that I was going to encounter competition? No, I did not know. Well, a very large London syndicate were sending down a very well-equipped salvage vessel. This up-to-the-minute craft, whose arrival was imminent, was carrying, among other things, the very latest in underwater suction gear, for—you know—sucking up stuff from the sea-bottom. Did I understand?

'Yes, yes,' said I, 'I understand very well.'

'How do you feel about it?' asked the voice.

'I think I feel a little sad,' said I.

'Sad?' asked the *Telegraph* man.

'Well yes, sad because it looks as if we, who have worked undisturbed on Cornish wrecks for many years, are going to be plagued with hordes of foreign divers from now on.'

'*Foreign* divers?'

'You wouldn't understand,' I said,

'Do you fear you'll be swamped?' asked the voice.

'They may swamp us with equipment,' I said, 'but they'll never swamp us with experience, especially of local conditions.'

'How do you feel about our photo agreement?' came the voice.

'Oh I see . . . ' I said, 'do you want to get out of it?'

'Well, we rather think that a bigger concern might produce better results and have better opportunities of taking photographs.'

'Right! the agreement is null and void as from this minute.' I said, 'I will return your cheque today.'

And though I did not know it at the time, that was the start of our good luck. After all, if the continued bad sea conditions were to make our venture expensive, then to keep within compass, I should have to look at my 'cheese parings and candle ends'. Many of the—literally hundreds—of photographs which I myself took throughout the operation turned out to be worth good money later on and this helped considerably to defray expenses.

I learnt that a cheque for a hundred pounds, as far as good photos are concerned, is mere chick-feed.

Meanwhile, as we waited impatiently in the beautiful July weather for the sea to subside, the Press were busy. One big London paper quoted me as saying: 'The treasures I seek are the pewter pots, muskets, trinkets and cutlasses that antique dealers throughout the world are clamouring for.' It went on to quote a Scilly Council member as saying: 'If this new expedition to salvage the wreck uncovers real antiques I hope that they will make a gesture and present some to our museum.' Not only was it ridiculous to expect muskets and cutlasses to survive 260 years' immersion in this sea area, it was equally ridiculous to suppose that we could hand them over, even if we had found them, as if they were our property to do with as we liked. The local newspapers, who should have known better, were also busy: 'Are the western rocks at the Isles of Scilly going to become a frogman's "Klondike" following the recent discovery of over fifty old cannon lying on the sea bed close to Gilstone Reef?' one of them asked. It went on: 'If so, it is likely the treasure hunt will have the traditional ingredients of gold rushes—greed, irresponsibility and death—and in the end no fortune.'

The paper mentioned the Deputy Keeper of the National Maritime Museum as being concerned 'that the activities of treasure-seeking divers, some of them prepared to use explosives, will cause irreparable damage to wrecks of great historical interest. In the Mediterranean old wrecks are fully protected, but in British waters only ordinary salvage laws apply.'

It could hardly be said, at this time, that we had many allies showering us with encouragement in our treasure-hunting endeavour, other, of course, than our many friends on the Islands. The Press, with one or two exceptions, were a sour lot; as our treasure hunt progressed they were to become a nuisance.

As day followed day, with the wind settled in the sou'west, with the sun beating down from cloudless skies, with permanent rough seas at the west'ard rocks, we all grew restive.

Came the day when we took some friends across from St. Mary's to Tresco in the storm-boat. It was a beautiful day, the air was warm, the sea, in the shelter of the islands, was as it should be during the last few days of July—blue and green, and twinkling with silver in the sun.

As we zipped across the Sound, with the outboard throwing back two curving white plumes of wake, the islands and islets slid smoothly into fresh positions with relation to each other, like moving bodies in a water-bound cosmos.

We motored slowly up to a white and deserted beach at Tresco where our two friends waded ashore. This left Geoff, David, Mike Reynolds and myself in the boat.

'Come on,' said Geoff, 'we've got all our gear aboard, what-say we go out to the Gilstone?'

'Good idea!' said I.

Without further ado we set off, with the wind and the sun in our faces.

Down through St. Mary's Road we thrummed; there was an atmosphere of anticipation aboard. We decided not to risk navigating the Western Rocks even though we had a chart with us; instead we took Smith Sound between Annet and St. Agnes and came out into the open sea south of the Islands. Skirting the Melledgan and Gorregan rocks, we started to round Pednathise Head, and here our smooth water left us. The Gilstone and its Ledges lay several hundred yards away from us, we could see only too plainly that they lay in a welter of broken water and heaving seas. Mike Hicks had been right, for only that morning he had reported white water at the west'ard rocks.

It was far too rough in the open water for the divers to change into their diving gear, so the storm-boat was taken back into the shelter of Gorregan. Here, with the gulls wheeling and crying over us like lost souls, Geoff and David stripped down to their underpants, dusted their bodies liberally with—no, not French chalk as is usual but—run away, you little boys, this is not for your ears—something much more suitable, a famous baby powder! Now, looking like Cornish china-clay workers, they pulled on their skin-tight rubber diving suits. Compressed air 'sets' were slung to their backs, face masks and valves were placed at the ready, and we were off once again.

Taking a big sweep down to the sou'west we approached

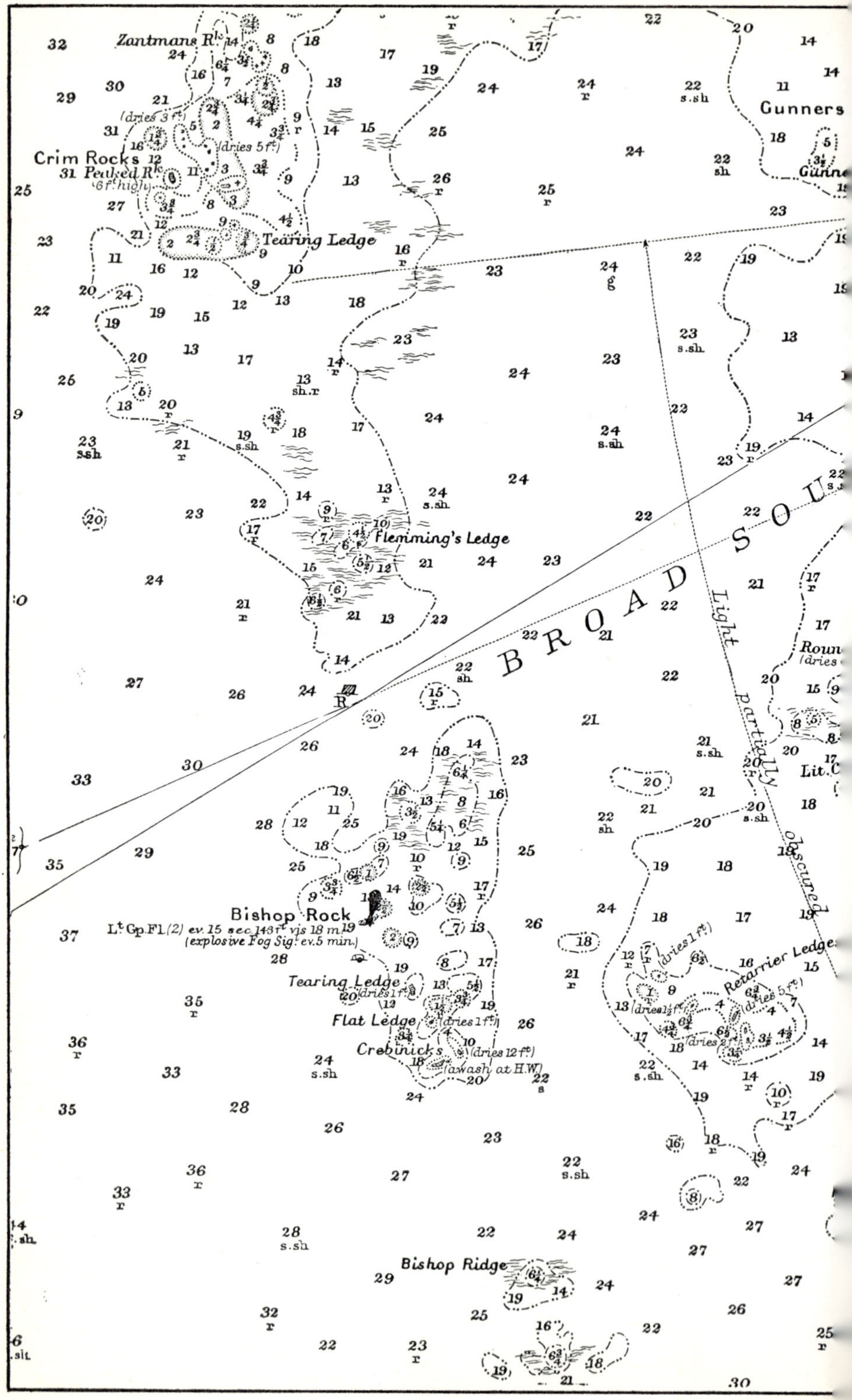

The Western Rocks, reproduced from Admiralty Chart No. 34

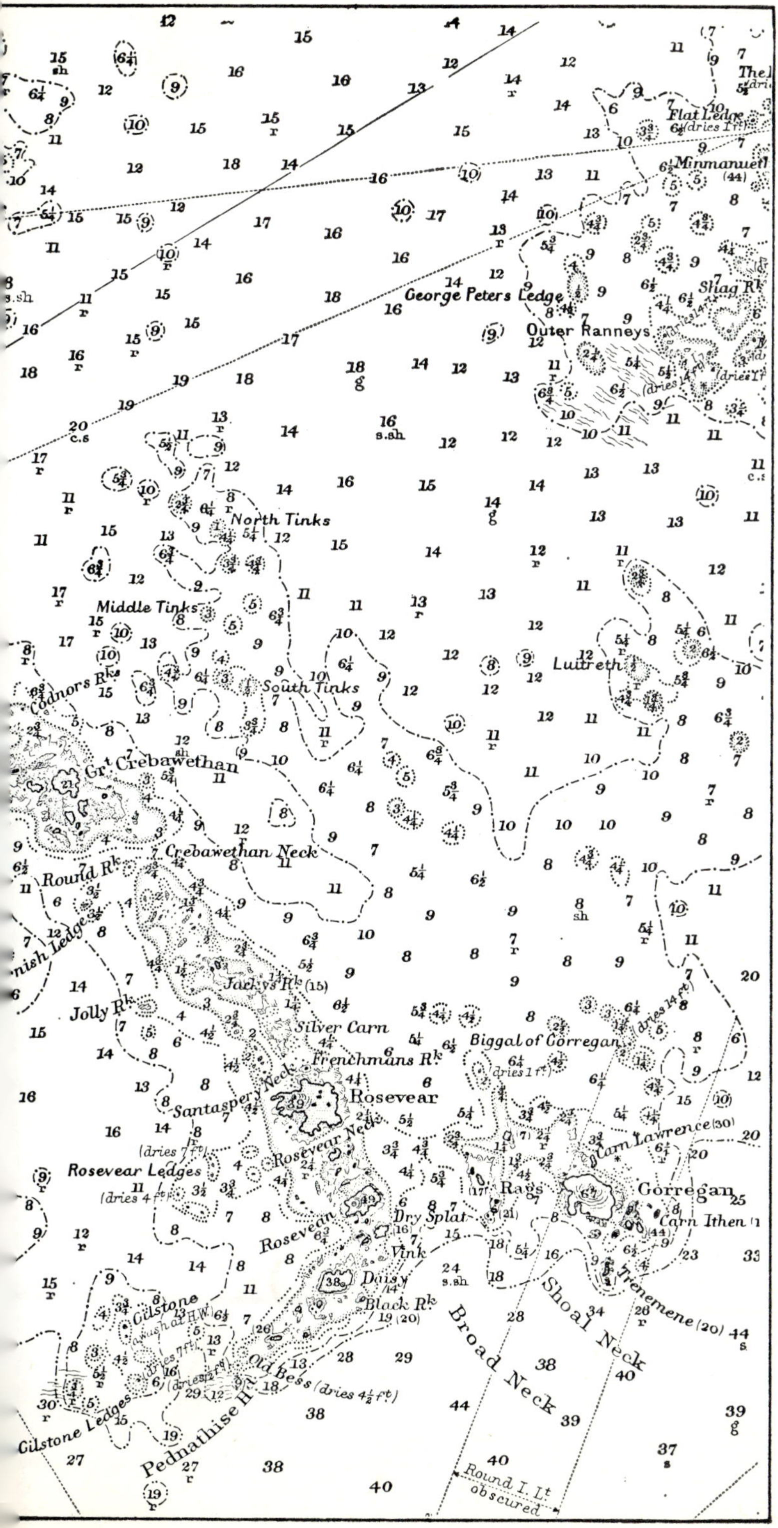
Flat Ledge
(dries 1 ft)
Minmanuel
George Peters Ledge
Outer Ranneys
Slag Rk
(dries 4 ft)
North Tinks
Middle Tinks
South Tinks
Codnors Rks
Lutreth
Gt Crebawethan
Crebawethan Neck
Round Rk
Jacky's Rk (15)
Silver Carn
Jolly Rk
Frenchmans Rk
Biggal of Corregan
(dries 14 ft)
(dries 1 ft)
Santaspery Neck
Rosevear
Rosevear Neck
(dries 7 ft)
Rosevear Ledges
(dries 4 ft)
Carn Lawrence (30)
Rags
Gorregan
Carn Ithen
Dry Splat
Vink
Daisy
Black Rk
Broad Neck
Shoal Neck
Tremenene (20)
Gilstone
awash at H.W.
(dries 7 ft)
Old Bess (dries 4½ ft)
Gilstone Ledges
Pednathise Hd
Round I. Lt obscured

the Gilstone from that point of the compass, just as Sir Cloudesley had done on that fatal night all those years ago.

The sun had hazed over by now, the sea was grey and sullen. The Gilstone itself, the shape and colour of a bowler hat, was being continually washed over by creaming seas. But it was not the Gilstone Rock that inspired our respect, though goodness knows that in itself gave one food enough for thought. No—it was the Outer Ledge that was the villain of the piece. For many minutes at a time it would lie quiet, giving no indication of its presence, then suddenly, without warning, it would erupt into malevolent action. Now a ghastly, forbidding picture would be presented; now the sea would slowly open and close like some giant, evil, slobbering mouth. In a great circle the waters would roll back, revealing, at the bottom of a deep pit of swirling water, a jagged black rock not unlike the beak of a monstrous squid. Roaring with anger the huge 'mouth' would close together, a great pointed tongue of water would rear into the air, to curl over and subside in a slaver

The Outer Ledge at the Gilstone: suddenly, without warning, the sea erupts into malevolent action, the tongue of water being twenty to thirty feet high

of foam and spray. Then, with all sign of the disturbance gone, the oily swell of the Atlantic would again ride silently over the spot, just as if nothing out of the way had happened.

Our usual diving procedure is always to use a shot-line and buoy for the divers, and if possible to moor the diving boat to the buoy. In this way we do not have the dangerous situation of divers surfacing here, there, and everywhere as we have seen others do so often. Moreover, with a shot-line as a fixed location, divers tend to memorise the underwater terrain very much more quickly. But today's unplanned operation was to be a 'recce' dive; we had no sinkers or buoys with us, the plan therefore was to put the divers down close to the Gilstone Rock, sheer off and watch for them to surface in a sou'westerly direction from the rock; the duration of each dive to be twenty minutes, the number of dives to be three.

The dive went well; the sea was rough, very rough, but neither Geoff nor David was at all deterred, they had dived in far worse conditions. Though they reported pretty hectic underwater currents in certain places, the topside conditions generally were not felt on the bottom.

While the divers were below, Michael Reynolds and I had plenty of time to study the area of the west'ard rocks. Away to our nor'west stood the imposing Bishop Light; this is a magnificent structure and it is as well that it is, for it has to withstand the unbelievable might of the Atlantic storms. The depth of water round about the Bishop is all of 150 feet, yet coarse sand from the sea-bed there has been found on the lighthouse gallery 120 feet above sea-level!

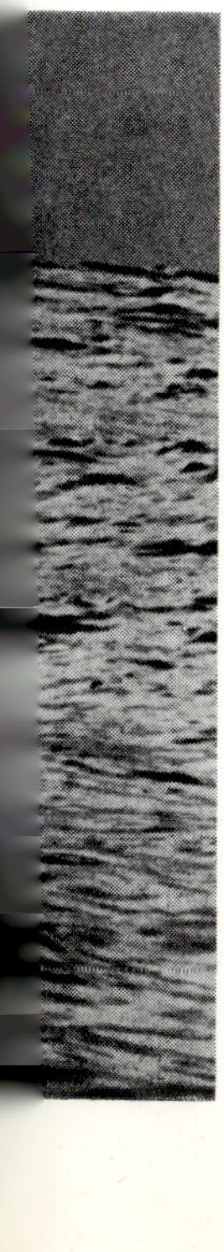

Admiral Sir Cloudesley could not have entered into a worse trap than those outer sou'western rocks of the Scillies. The area of the Gilstone is a forlorn, God-forsaken place, ringed about with half-tide rocks and saw-edged reefs. Look nor'-west, due north, nor'east or due east and all you can see, sprinkled everywhere, is rocks—pinnacles and ridges of rock. If the ship below us had not foundered on the Gilstone she could well have driven on to a similar fate on one of a hundred different rocks in her path.

From where we were being flung about in the storm-boat we could make out, between breaks in the far rock ridges, the white tower which replaced the old-time lighthouse of St. Agnes. Why the Admiral and his men in *Association* did not

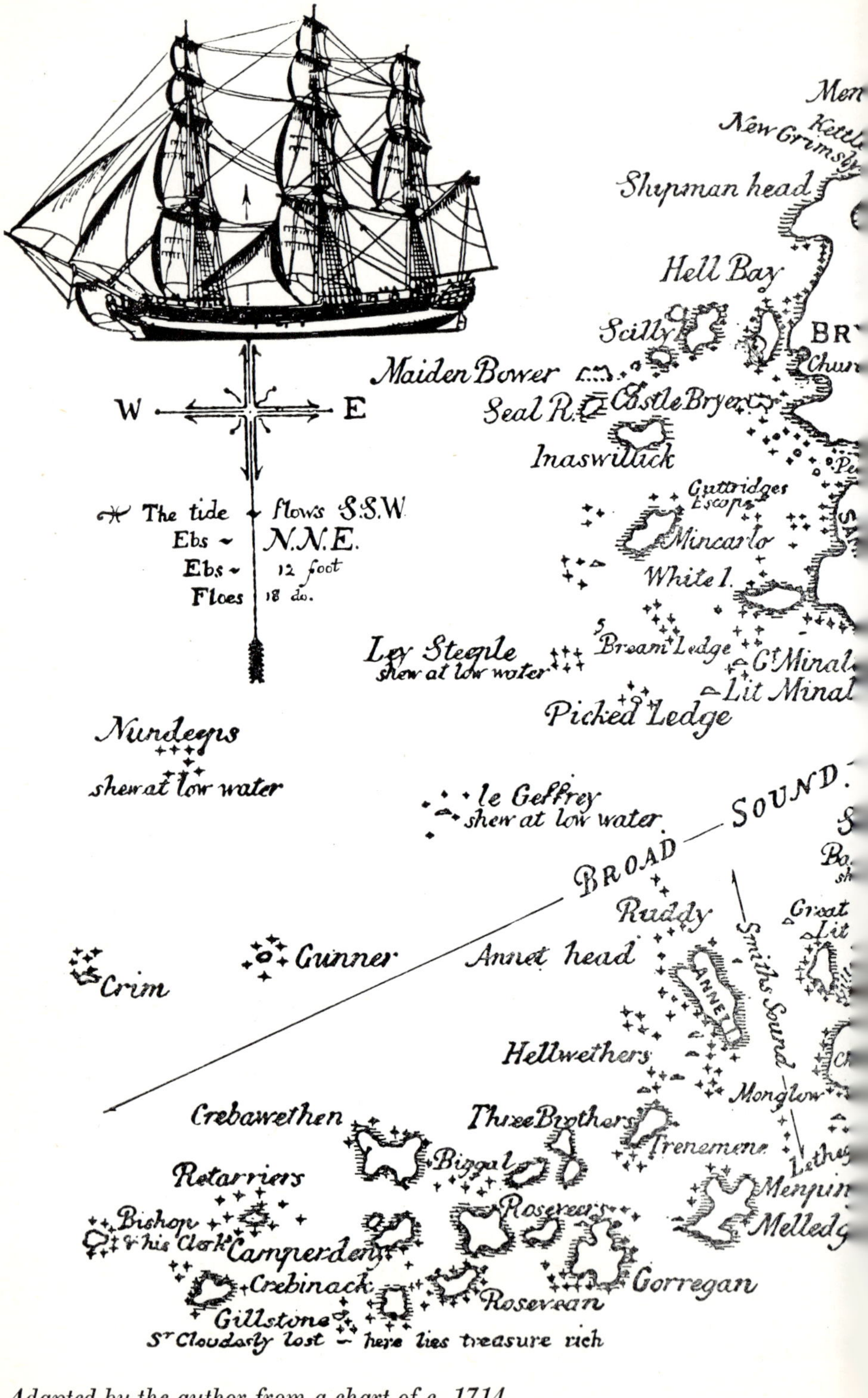

Adapted by the author from a chart of c. 1714

THE

ISLANDS of SCILLY

see its light on the night of the wreck will never be explained. Some say he and his officers 'had sunk caution, and all sense of danger too, in wine'.

After their first twenty minutes down, the divers surfaced with the news that they had located two large bower anchors; these were close to the Gilstone Rock. The divers said they were only too pleased to go below on their second and third dives, conditions down there were a picnic compared with those which Michael and I were undergoing in the plunging storm-boat, they were glad to hop overboard to a more peaceful world—maybe they were telling the truth. From their final dives we gleaned the knowledge that they had swum along a gully of iron cannon; from that day that particular place became known to us as 'Cannon Gully'. We learned that many iron shot were scattered over the site and when the divers came aboard, for the last time that day, they opened their rubber sleeves at the wrists, and let pour forth a deluge of lead musket-balls: our first souvenirs!

Even if the boys of R.N. Air Command had not shown us the way, certainly our old chart would have done so; the area of the rock and its two ledges was abounding with proof that an old time man-o'-war had perished there. The chart swore that it was the *Association*; maybe it was, maybe it was not, should we ever know?

In the Mermaid Inn that evening we held a recap of the day's work. Pencil and paper were borrowed from Heather, the green-eyed bar-girl. Sketches were produced, all depicting plan elevations of the rock and its ledges. It was unanimously decided that the two great anchors from the bow of the stricken vessel must give the vital clue as to how she struck. Pint pots were set up for a practical demonstration, they were the rocks; a model of an R.N. lifeboat heavy with coppers served as the *Association*. How many times that tin model crashed against those pint pots I cannot now say, but it is a wonder

The great anchors lay to the east of the Gilstone. This one was raised by the 'Ros Guill' (in the background) during the later stages of the treasure hunt, and its recovery assisted considerably in identifying the wreck as being the remains of a British Naval vessel. The palms, originally three feet wide, have been reduced by corrosion

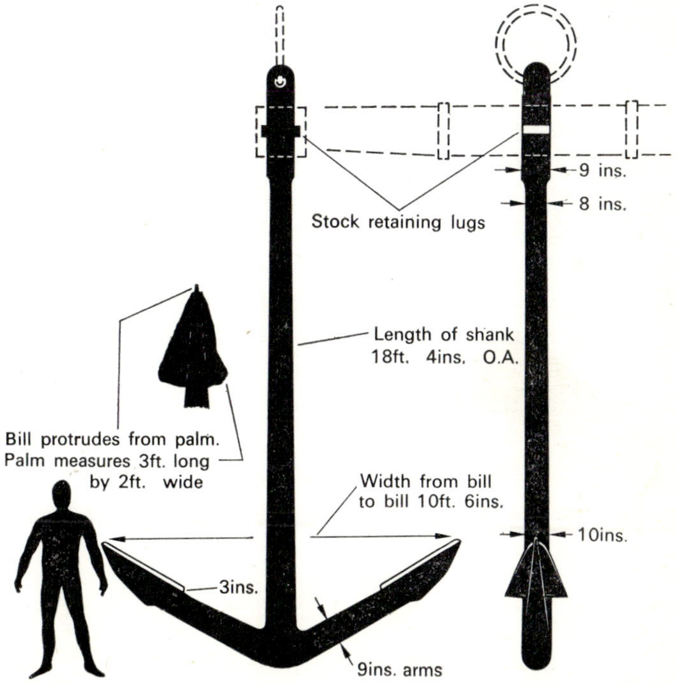

Stock retaining lugs
9 ins.
8 ins.
Length of shank
18ft. 4ins. O.A.
Bill protrudes from palm.
Palm measures 3ft. long
by 2ft. wide
Width from bill
to bill 10ft. 6ins.
10ins.
3ins.
9ins. arms

to me that the coins did not rattle out of that little vessel, as Sir Cloudesley's are presumed to have done!

The great anchors lay to the east of the Gilstone, so it seems almost certain that the vessel must have struck on the deadly Outer Ledge first and then became trapped in the maw of the three rocks. Records state that she sank upright, with but the stump of her mainmast above water to show where she finally settled.

That night, as I lay in bed with the murmur of the sea and the rustle of the nearby dracaena palms coming through my open window, I thought back on the events of the day; my thoughts turned to that dreadful Outer Ledge, and the tongues of water licking from it, and the rough sea—even now my brain was swimming—if it was like that in a four-to-five-force wind what must it have been like in a full gale?

And so my thoughts, turning from one thing to another, just naturally veered back to that autumn month I had so often read about: that time of 260 years ago—the stormy month of October 1707.

At that point of time, and at a point of longitude way down in the Atlantic Ocean, a point that would stand them well clear of the Portuguese Cabo de São Vicente (Cape St. Vincent), twenty-one British warships were beating their way northward. They had left Gibraltar on the 29th September, had passed through the Straits firing their guns and dipping their ensigns in salute to the thirteen vessels they were leaving behind. The Mediterranean Fleet was splitting up, as was the custom at the end of the summer season. The vessels remaining at Gibraltar were under Sir Thomas Dilkes and would be stationed in the Mediterranean for the winter service. The twenty-one ships, including the flagship *Association,* were homeward bound for England; commanding them was the Admiral and Commander-in-Chief of the Mediterranean Fleet himself, none other than Sir Cloudesley Shovell, Rear-Admiral of Great Britain.

4

THE LOSS OF THE TREASURE SHIP

For the twenty-one-ship squadron there now was lying ahead a three-week voyage bedevilled by 'very violent gales' and beset by 'great seas', a voyage which for some of the ships and many hundreds of the men was to end in disaster.

Sir Cloudesley, sailing away from the scene of his summer exploits, must surely have looked back with mixed feelings as to the success or otherwise of his naval operations there. England was engaged in fighting one of her many wars with France. In March 1707 Sir Cloudesley and his fleet were despatched from Lisbon, in Portugal (where he was wont to linger), and ordered to rendezvous off Nice and Antibes. Here he was to consult with the Duke of Savoy as to the best means of using the Navy in the contemplated land attack on the southern French port of Toulon. Meanwhile vast earthworks had been set up by the French around the town, and these defences had been manned in secret by a formidable force, a force far more powerful than had been foreseen by either the Duke of Savoy or Admiral Sir Cloudesley Shovell. During his stormy homeward voyage the Admiral often must have discussed with the company around him the merits or demerits of this last undertaking of his in the Mediterranean, the siege of Toulon. This had been an unfortunate affair, for, although Sir Cloudesley's fleet had bombarded the town and had opened a way for the Allied armies, the attack had not been a success by any manner of means. True, the fleet had succeeded in pillaging and burning eight of the enemy's ships in the harbour, but the land forces had failed miserably in their assault on the stronghold.

Several of Sir Cloudesley's sailing companions, carefully chosen by himself, were either friends or relatives by marriage. On board *Association* were Sir John Narborough, Bart., and his brother Mr. James Narborough, both sons of Lady Shovell by her first husband Admiral Sir John Narborough. Also on board were Henry Trelawney, second son of the Bishop of Winchester, and 'several other gentlemen of good families'. The Captain was Edmund Loades, Lady Shovell's nephew, son of Sir John Narborough's sister. None of these gentlemen was liable to cause embarrassment to the Admiral by not agreeing with him that Toulon had been other than totally destroyed by his bombardment, or for that matter the British forces had carried out anything but a glorious retreat!

So, plunging and rolling like a school of ungainly whales, the Shovell squadron drove its way to more northern latitudes. As they progressed—on some days they were doing runs of a hundred miles or more—so the weather worsened, the winds became even more fractious. Mist and fog prevented them from taking the usual observations, while gales, meeting them from all points of the compass, forced them to tack and tack again. Small wonder, then, that by the time they neared 'the soundings' (the shallower continental shelf) there was not one sailing master amongst them who knew his position to within a hundred or so miles.

By the 21st October the Admiral himself had become seriously concerned as to their whereabouts. On that day he put out a signal to all ships for soundings to be taken and, if possible, observations for latitude to be made. All sailing masters were ordered to muster aboard *Association* at twelve noon, or soon after, to make a report.

I like to belay a while as the Admiral's signal is passed from one ship to another. I like to picture the scene as one by one the ships turn into the wind with much rapping of canvas and flying of spray; one by one they lose way then wallow in the lather of the huge Atlantic troughs. In due course the whole fleet, set over an area of about three miles, is dipping and rolling with sails furled and yards lashed aback

This drawing reconstructs H.M.S. 'Association', flagship of Sir Cloudesley Shovell, on the basis of available information

while the leadsmen endeavour to find bottom and the sailing masters a 'sight'.

There are twenty-one ships in all; as the old records state, '*he bent his course homewards (as hath been already said) with one fhip of the 1st. rate, 2 fhips of the 2nd. rate, 7 fhips of the 3rd. rate, 2 of the 4th, 1 of the 5th. and 2 of the 6th. added to this number are 4 firefhips, 1 sloop and 1 yacht*'.

Up to the middle of the seventeenth century ships of various sizes engaged in naval warfare had fought without any real order of battle. However, in 1653 the British Admiralty ordained that ships must give battle in line, that is to say in single file, so that broadsides would be much more effective. Obviously, as some ships were slower and more weakly armed than others, the vessels had to be graded. Accordingly the ships were divided into rates. A first-rate ship had over ninety guns, a second-rate over eighty guns and a third-rate over fifty. These first three rates were considered powerful enough to fight 'in the line' and so were called 'ships of the line'. A fourth-rate ship had over thirty-eight guns, a fifth over eighteen and finally a sixth-rater would have over six guns. The 'yacht' which was sailing with Sir Cloudesley's squadron had nothing to do with pleasure sailing; the classification 'yacht' in those days stood for 'swift-craft' or 'hunter'.

So there they lay, a valuable and formidable concentration of eighteenth-century naval power: fifteen line-of-battle ships, five of lesser rank and the one yacht. It is early afternoon, but already light is failing, darkness is setting in quickly, the sea is tumultuous, the wind fierce enough to whip the swell tops into a haze. Now the longboats put off from the ships with the sailing masters in the sterns, the crews row in masterly fashion and curse everything and everyone. It is a long haul for the few who are furthest away, but in ones and twos the boats manœuvre alongside the flagship; now, very much on their mettle because of the critically watching eyes, the sailing masters await their chance to get aboard; as each longboat rears to a swell they leap for the entry steps on the steep sloping side of *Association.* The entry port is closed owing to the high seas, this means that the men have to climb the moulded steps, which protrude from the ship's side, right up to and over the upper-deck rail. This is no mean task on a ship which is rising and falling some fifteen feet or more in a gale-racked sea. A ship which tilts and lurches dangerously; a ship which sinks its head into the sea, to raise it again, slowly and ponderously, with water cascading from its beakhead, like some live creature fighting for air. Members of the flagship's crew, securely wedged in the lower shrouds, stand by with handlines in case of need.

Reaching the upper deck, the sailing masters stagger aft and enter through a heavily panelled door into the welcome shelter of the wardroom, aft again of this and they are in the Admiral's state room, or Great Cabin, as it is called. In this cabin they find the Admiral himself, he is sitting with others at a long table which takes up the breadth of the stern; the table is overlaid with charts. Behind the table, and aft of it, the salt-grimed sloping stern windows let in the grey daylight.

I like to imagine the sailing masters as they crowd round the table. They clutch at it for support while the cabin sways and rolls. Perhaps some of them are told to sit, others will stand with hats and papers tucked under their arms. Undoubtedly drinks for each are provided; these are splashed into pewter goblets from large wicker-bound jars. Just as soon as the sailing masters have all assembled, the Admiral calls for silence. Meantime the great cabin rises, sways, drops and rises again without cessation, outside the noise of the gale is a steady clamour.

By all accounts Admiral Sir Cloudesley Shovell, even in his 'day clothes' and wearing his 'third wig', would appear as an imposing enough figure of a man. His face is voluptuously corpulent; it is not his flaccid mouth or his triple chins that draw one's attention, but his eyes—their steady gaze has an even tenor which can put a man at ease or have an immediately opposite effect. Invariably I imagine him in his cabin with his legs planted firmly apart as he sits sideways on his fixed chair; the vents of his faded silk breeches gape unbuttoned over his cheap thread stockings, for he is a man indifferent to his sea-going appearance, yet in other things, such as the weight of ballast his ship is carrying, he is fussy to the point of irritability.

And so there he sits, and I am sure his small Italian greyhound lies between his silver-buckled feet. Near him will be his Second Captain (Samuel Whitaker), for this is a navigational conference, there will be writing to do, reports to take down.

I can see in my mind's eye the Admiral as he holds out a large podgy hand, the forearm of which is enveloped in, and protrudes from, a monstrous silken cuff. When the Admiral speaks his flabby chins and jowls quiver to such a degree that the whole of the lower part of his face shakes like a warm jelly. In what sort of mood would the Admiral have been? It is impossible to say, there is no record which gives the slightest hint of this. Certainly he must have been—anxious, perhaps? Maybe—impatient; let us assume he was the latter. Impatiently, then, he snaps the fingers of that out-thrust hand; someone, probably the Second Captain, passes over a fresh cut quill. The Admiral takes it gracefully enough and examines it at arm's length, slowly rotating the big feather between finger and thumb; two rings show clearly on one of his fingers, they glow dull gold in the dim light of the cabin. A large stone set in the heavier of the rings flashes green and yellow fire; it is an emerald in a setting of diamonds. In less than a score of hours those rings will have been the prime cause of the Admiral forfeiting his life. They will be wrenched from his finger; what little breath his half-drowned body is taking in at the time, will be throttled for ever; and these deeds will have been done by a woman's hand.

But Sir Cloudesley, with no hint of the fate lying in store for him, turns to the waiting sailing masters; he tilts his large head enquiringly, a voice says:

'Found, by the deep, ninety fathom—bottom white sand and hakes' teeth.'

The heads of the Admiral and his Second Captain bend in unison over the charts, and the cabin dips, rolls and dips again.

Overhead, the low-curving beams gleam with oil polish, they reflect warmly all the busy movement of the blending colours below. The ornate cabin, as was the custom in those days, is decorated with splendid carvings and mouldings in cream, blue and gilt, fine enough and fit enough for royalty. The congregated sailing masters eye the magnificent trophies of battle which adorn the sloping panelled walls. They see the great sphere of the world standing on its claw feet, its coloured oceans and continents standing out brightly between its carved and turned legs. They notice the four glossy black cabin guns reclining on their polished carriages, the guns stand two on one side of the cabin and two on the other; they crouch glowering, their squat muzzles within inches of their closed red-painted ports. Their appearance jars grotesquely with the fine brocades and silks of the lavish furnishings. Here, also, are kept the Admiral's personal treasure chests, three of them perhaps, shackled by chains to ring bolts in the floor.

'The *Torbay* at nine o'clock found 135 fathoms fine sand and ooze.'

'The *Somerset* sounded three times finding no bottom at 145 fathoms.'

'The *Lennox* found 88 fathoms with bottom of brown sand.'

'The *Cruizer* found 90 fathoms—coarse sand full of little red shells.'

'The yacht *Isabella* between 50 and 55 fathoms of water, on the tallow—coarse sand intermixed with shells.'

'The *Monmouth* had 92 fathoms and the *La Valeur* 90 fathoms.'

'The *St. George* had 85 fathoms with small black sand. I allowed the Lizard by the depth of water to be 64 leagues distant from me, bearing east nor'east a quarter north.'

And so it goes on, the details are recorded, the charts are consulted and marked; at the turning of a top-empty hour-glass the great discussion is got under way.

Unless any new details come to light—and knowing the Scillies as I do this could very well take place—but, unless they do, then the details of that top-level discussion will never be known. One of the things we do know is that it went on well into the evening. Why did it take so long before the signal for sailing was given? Was there a riotous wine party, as some suggest? My humble guess is—no; what is more probable is the fact that it took some considerable time to get the sailing masters back to their ships in the atrocious weather then prevailing.

Fate and the (save one) unanimous verdict of the hearing has set the scene for one of the most ghastly episodes of shipwreck ever known.

The conclusion that comes from the great cabin conference is that there is no cause for alarm, rather there is cause for rejoicing, for it has been decided that the fleet is in the latitude of Ushant and near the coast of France.

In point of fact, through the very real existence of an Atlantic current, which, unknown to them, has swept them northwards, plus the contributing factors of poor compasses and a low standard of accuracy of navigational practice, the fleet has become hopelessly lost. The truth to tell is that they are nowhere near Ushant as they would like to believe, indeed they are all of a hundred miles from that island. Their position, had they but known it, was to the south-west of the Scillies. They are within two hours' sailing time of those treacherous rocks and isles.

As the consultation breaks up, as the serious-faced sailing masters and others prepare to leave, we can almost hear a voice telling them:

'We are off Ushant, gentlemen, the Channel is open and clear before you, may God go with you and preserve you!'

The vital, but totally inaccurate, conclusion having been arrived at, three vessels are despatched without further preamble: the *Lennox* of seventy guns, the *La Valeur* of twenty-four guns and the small *Phoenix* of eight guns. Now it is the custom for several light craft to precede an important squadron such as that of Sir Cloudesley Shovell's, more especially so if it is suspected that navigational risks lie ahead. But these three ships are not despatched as protective scouts, they are sent post-haste to Falmouth where they are urgently required to take up convoy duties for the protection of east-bound merchantmen; long before the rest of the fleet receive their sailing orders the three ships are hull down bearing away on a north-east by north course, a direction which, if they keep to it, will entangle them in the maze of rocks that lie to the west of the Scillies.

Supremely confident in the declaration that there is open water ahead, and therefore no danger, the Admiral decrees that the flagship herself shall lead the fleet into this storm-racked night.

'Follow me, gentlemen! I will lead the way to Spithead!'

Daylight is dying when the signal for sailing is fired.

If Admiral Sir Cloudesley had stepped into the stern-quarter window, which is high above the storm-tossed sea, if he had peered into the deepening dusk, he would have had the satisfaction of seeing his fleet bearing away astern of him, on the selfsame course as he. He would note also that his lighter craft, always a nuisance, as they tended to show off their paces, are keeping well off from him; this is excellent, for he does not want them fussing about and getting in his way.

The night is dark, it falls even darker as the wind increases to a gale. Rain-squalls lash across the tumbling ships, so much so their great glowing poop lanterns are obscured more often than not by solid sheets of flaying water.

While there is any visibility left the fleet of eighteen ships flounders along the Admiral's chosen course. But as darkness blankets the ship's movements, and incidentally the Admiral's spy-glass, the sailing masters discreetly change their directions; one by one they veer, by but a few points, some go east by north, some go east by south, but one by one they abandon the plotted course of their leader; soon there are but six ships following the flagship; the masters of the other eleven vessels have had second thoughts, they have decided, wisely as will be seen, to work out their own fate.

They double and treble their deck watches, they prudently run before the gale under the restricted canvas of their courses, and as they are wont to do in times of stress they offer up their prayers to Almighty God.

It is five bells—the time is six-thirty o'clock.

The heavy wind-laden vessels rise ponderously to the huge Atlantic swells. Lights from the latticed stern windows glint on the great following seas as they sweep up astern. The ships rise and veer as the seas pass under them from stern to stem, for these seas are running more swiftly than the ships themselves. On the crests a ship will often come close to broaching, but the swell passes and drops the craft sickeningly into the trough that follows; in the smother of foam she has time to right herself and prepare for the next onslaught.

The men who are on watch on the ship's fo'c'sles crouch sheltering from the seas that sweep on board. They hide as best they can from the slammering ferrety wind. They strain their eyes into the driving murk ahead. They tell themselves —but another day, another two days and this voyage, this voyage of violent weather, will be done—thank God!

It must not be thought for one minute that in the great cabin, aboard the flagship, the Admiral is sitting pale of face biting his fingernails with anxiety. If this were the case his ship would hardly be driving headlong into the darkness before a full gale of wind. Rather it can be assumed that Sir Cloudesley is sitting at splendid ease at his polished table, he has eaten well and his beloved wine is before him.

I like to think of him, elbow on table, as—in my mind's eye—he raises his large pregnant goblet to eye-level; he is pleased, he is homeward-bound, so his wide flabby face curls into a smile, he looks through the cut glass and deep into the rich colour of the wine. He is a splendid sailor; he is oblivious of the creak and crack of the timbers overhead, he takes scant notice of the tipping and tilting of the cabin around him, he remains upright and smiles into his wine. Naturally he thinks back to the conference not long closed, the unanimous verdict has delighted him; yes, they are good men, it pays to pick your associates.

Many of the captains were in agreement with him and had backed him up in his difficult decision. There had been one or two who had stuck out with notions of their own, but he, the Admiral, had soon convinced them that the majority verdict must be adhered to. After all, there are some very fine navigators among the ships of this squadron. Who was it that quibbled? He forgets for the moment—ah yes, the chief culprit was the master of the *Lennox*—said we were too far north, something about a current; well, he'd been packed off to Falmouth. Channel convoy work didn't need specialised navigation, he'd be safe enough on that work what with the coastline in view all the time!

The Admiral smiles yet again, he slowly brings the glass of wine to below his nose—the bouquet of it turns his thoughts to Lisbon; he had been in Lisbon River in March he remembers, before that at Alicante Road and in February in Gibraltar Bay. Yes, it must be all of twelve months since he was in the Bay of Oeiras, which was as near to Lisbon as he could get at that time—the Admiral smiles and this time nods his head repeatedly—how he loved that place, its wine, its beautiful women. He pictures in his mind's eye the sun-bronzed face of the Duke of Savoy, a splendid and generous man!

It was in this very cabin at this very table, not four months since, that they had banqueted together, he and the Duke, and their friends, sixty of the most charming people imaginable. What a feast he, the Commander of the Mediterranean Fleet, had put on! How sumptuous it all was! How wonderful this great table looked adorned with his own personal gold plate and Venice glass! How grateful the Duke had been! He had said afterwards:

'If your Excellency had paid me a visit at my palace at Turin I could scarcely have treated you so well.'

The great ship ploughs on with what speed her fore and mains'ils will give her; to carry more would be to court disaster, for she is thrashing through the seas with masts and cordage straining to their limit of endurance.

Following *Association*, veering from side to side in the darkness astern, like a brood of distressed ducklings swimming in the wake of their fleeing mother, come the six aforementioned ships of the fleet. They are the first-raters *Royal Ann* and *St. George*, the second-raters *Monmouth*, *Swiftsure* and *Romney*, and the fireship *Firebrand*.

The night is thick with spume and mist, thick enough to make it difficult for the men aboard the following ships to keep the lights of the flagship in view, but keep them in sight they do, as the records of the ships that survived tell us.

Although this small squadron heads directly for danger, not all its ships will encounter it. Some will bypass it by a hair's breadth, others will meet not only danger but also disaster and death.

It is seven bells—or seven-thirty by the clock.

The remaining ships of the fleet each go their own chosen way; now each has an entity of its own, each relies on itself alone for no help can be expected and no help can be given. They run like vulnerable expendable creatures in a hostile world, where Nature will be satisfied if only a few survive.

So some are lucky and others are not.

Some are destined for destruction—as the old records state: '*What passed on board "Association", "Eagle" and "Romney" can never now be known.*'

Some are lucky and live to tell the tale—'*That which befel the others can best be told in a few words from some of the Log-books which remain.*'

The yacht *Isabella* was lucky; her Captain Finch Reddall states: '*. . . saw ye light of Scilly bearing S.E. by S. distance per judgment about 4 miles. We took it to be one of our Admiral's lights; we steered after it till we perceived it to be a fixed light, it being very thick dark rainey weather, we perceived ye rocks on both sides of us; we being very near to them we immediately wore our yacht and layed our head to ye westward, crowding all ye sail we could to weather ye rocks under our lee; we filled full and full, and by God's mercy we got clear of them all, for which deliverance God's holy name be blest and praised, we caused a great separation in the fleet, for happy was he that could shift for himself, some steering with their heads to ye soward, and others to ye northward . . .*'

The *Monmouth* was lucky; the journal of Captain Baker her commander states: '*in endeavouring to get ye Flagship light ahead of us; we discovered a rock to leeward of us; we immediately wore ship and got clear of it, and in wearing I discovered ye light of Scilly bearing east by northerly, so I made ye signal of Danger and repeated it several times, so it might be taken notice of, and made what sail I could to the westward, which was only with my courses.*'

The *St. George* was lucky: '*we discovered ye breakers off from ye Island of Scilly, we wore ship and stood to ye westward.*'

The *Torbay* was lucky: '*on our weather bow we unexpectedly saw ye breakers on ye Bishop and Clarks: we immediately wore and made the signal of danger, which was very eminent, in which we had infallible demonstrations of Almighty Providence, first our wearing sooner than usual with main and fore courses, secondly when we judged ourselves inevitably on ye rocks, yett preserved from ye mighty danger . . .*'

Of the three Falmouth-bound ships, the *Lennox* and *La Valeur* were lucky; of the *Phoenix* which went with them the crew were lucky, their ship became a total loss but every man was saved.

Talking about these three ships, the records say: '*These ships following a north-easterly course, as had been determined on, soon found themselves amongst the myriad rocks and islets which lie to the S.W. of the Scilly groups, where the "Phoenix" sustained so much damage that her captain and crew only saved the ship and themselves by running her ashore on the sands between Tresco and St. Martin's Island. The "Lennox" and "La Valeur" were fortunately able to beat through the Broad Sound, an anchorage to the west of the principal islands, where they remained until day-break the next morning; they then sailed for Falmouth and arrived there on the 25th. bringing news of wrecks at Scilly, but little knowing or suspecting what vessels were lost.*'

The seventy-gun *Eagle* was unlucky, for she was lost with all hands '*on ye Gunnar or thereabouts*' where she was smashed to matchwood, the wreckage floating over '*to St. Just and other places at ye Lands End and up ye North Channel*'.

The beacon of the lighthouse of St. Agnes Isle in the Scillies burns brightly, the keepers are alive to their responsibilities this night, for many ships of His Majesty's Navy are in the anchorage, many distinguished officers are being entertained ashore.

The ships in Crow Sound include the *Southampton, Arundel* and the *Lizard*, and it is rumoured that the *Salisbury, Antelope, Hampshire* and *Charles*, which have been cruising to the westward, have just put in. So it befits the keepers of the Scilly light to be on their toes. It is well known that they are not always so; it has been said that the light on some occasions has been allowed to die. Tonight it burns as brightly as it has ever burnt, or, come to that, ever will burn. Which fact makes it all the more difficult to understand why those on *Association* do not see it.

She sails towards the light, it must be almost dead ahead, if anything a little on her larboard bow, distance about four

OPPOSITE *The coal-fired lighthouse of St. Agnes, as depicted on his chart by Edmund Gostelo* miles, so why do they not see it? As we know, other men in other ships will bless the Scilly light this night; they will not only see it, they will be warned off by it, they will save themselves from disaster because of it—but not those on *Association*: relentlessly their ship drives on to destruction.

It is eight bells—the time is eight o'clock.

Within a score of minutes they will be amongst the rocks; within those few minutes their great ship will be in her death-throes, for the *Association* is headed straight for the Gilstone Rock and its attendant outriders, the Outer and the Inner Gilstone Ledges. They are headed for one of the most God-forsaken spots in any ocean on this earth, and certainly one of the most treacherous.

The spelling of the admiral's surname has often been disputed: his signature shows that he himself used the form Shovell, with the double 'll'

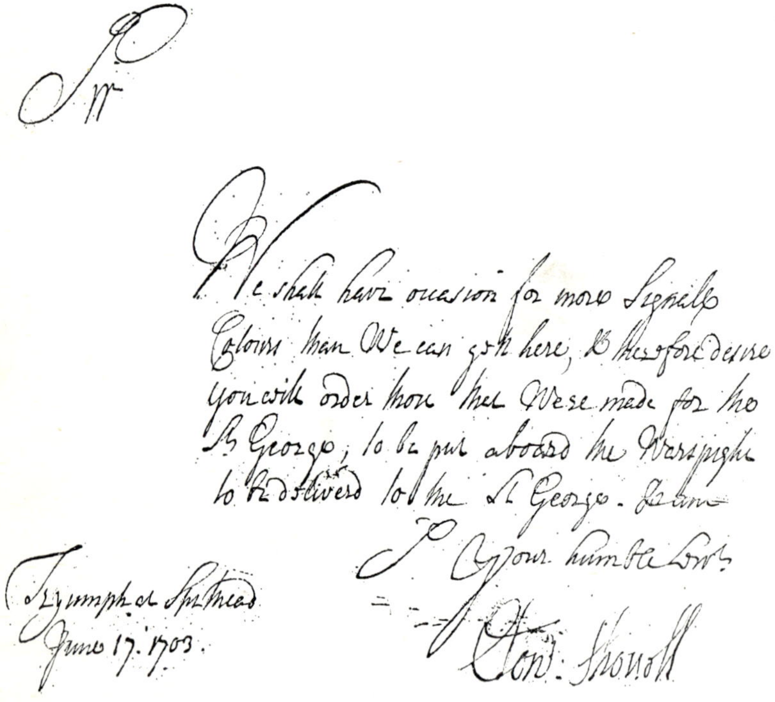
Sir

We shall have occasion for more Signall Colours than We can get here, I therefore desire you will order those that Were made for the St George; to be put aboard the Warspight to be delivered to the St George. I am Sr Your humble Servt

Clow: Shovell

Triumph at Spithead June 17. 1703.

5

BRONZE DOLPHINS COME ASHORE

'If you were to ask me,' said Mike Hicks, 'I'd say you all want your heads examined.'

We were standing on St. Mary's pier in the mid-morning sunlight; below us, nudging the side of the pier, lay the storm-boat, her red carlene mooring lines reflecting in the still water.

'Look at her!' said Mike. 'No buoyancy tanks, no inflatable life-raft, not even a lifebuoy, and you go and take her to the Gilstone. What if you'd ripped the bottom out of her!'

Yes—what indeed; we said not a word, there was nothing we could say. The divers busied themselves with checking their replenished air bottles; I fiddled with my camera.

There was a lengthy silence, then Mike said:

'Well—anyway, how did you get on?'

'Very well,' I said. 'Mind you, there was a big sea running like you said, but the divers did a good job.'

'Did you find the wreck?' asked Mike.

'Gracious yes,' said Geoff, 'you couldn't miss it. it's spread all over the place.'

'What's it like down there?' this from Mike.

'It's like the surface of the moon,' said David, 'with gullies and boulders and ridges—and cannon scattered here, there and everywhere.'

'It's no good, Mike,' said I, 'you'll just have to take the

Sea King down there today, you'll be able to see for yourself how these chaps work.'

Mike rubbed his nose with the back of his hand. 'Well, all right,' he said grudgingly. 'mind—it's still rough out there, but I'm game to have a go. It's slack water there an hour before high tide, and the slack lasts about two hours.'

By 'slack water' Mike meant water with little or no current on the surface, and, for that matter, below; that, of course, is the most advantageous time for diving.

I was more than happy to see our equipment stowed aboard *Sea King*; we had all been in the Islands well over a week now—all we had to show for our time and money was a few lead musket-balls, and a much heavier layer of sun-tan!

Mike, standing at the wheel of his powerful launch, has the loose-limbed stance of one of those Wild West drivers handling a coach-and-eight. He projects his sixty-five-foot craft through the water at nothing less than full throttle; it is always an exhilarating experience. If there be a short cut, maybe a narrow channel of roaring waters, then Mike will take it, and enjoy doing so. On this, our first trip to the Gilstone in *Sea King*, a trip which we were to do many times in all kinds of conditions, we revelled in the ride. With us in the launch was Mike's second-in-command, his younger brother, the full-bearded Alf Hicks, who is a fine boatman, and a splendid 'tender' to the divers.

With the islands of St. Agnes and Annet astern of us we approached the small islet of Rosevean. On this islet can be seen the stark ruins of a small house; this was lived in by the hardy old-timers who built the Bishop Light; if one looks close enough the remains of a landing stage may also be seen. Today the islet, deserted by humans, is the home of thousands of sea birds. As the *Sea King* entered the narrow Rosevear Neck—which is an opening through a great chain of rocks, stretching north and south, from the Codnors right down to Old Bess—hundreds of shags raised their heads to watch our progress. Behind us lay smooth, calm water, but once through the Neck, past the shelter of the great rock barrier, we were met by the full Atlantic swells.

Now the launch was a live thing, great sheets of white water sprang from each of her bows as she slid, airborne for more than half her length, from one swell to drop with a shattering belly-flop on to the next. With the crafty hand of a master mariner Mike brought the bows of his red-painted launch within the white water surrounding the Gilstone. It was our intention to put a buoy on one of the big underwater anchors; and this, our second dive on the site, again was to be one of reconnoitre—we were after bronze guns; were there any more down there? That was the question we wanted to answer.

After the buoy and its wire had been shackled to the anchor, our technique on this occasion was to motor up close to the sea-swept Gilstone Rock, to within a few yards of it. At this point the divers—carefully watching the seas—would wait for a big swell to roll along the side of the launch; as it passed they would drop in behind it, swim two or three strokes to the buoy and descend alongside its cable. Now we would veer away quickly; the backwash from the rock, combined with the big swells coming from the opposite direction, made the handling of the launch extremely tricky.

When divers are down a constant unfaltering watch must be kept over the whole area; usually, even in rough seas, it is possible to locate their air bubbles on the surface; from these it is possible to tell where they are and when they are coming up. At the end of their first twenty-minute dive Geoff and David surfaced well on time; they climbed on board with the aid of two suspended car tyres lashed together in the form of a figure 8; they were well pleased. And so were we when we heard the news—they had located two fine bronze guns! I could scarce believe it, at long last we had met up with guns of bronze! This was something I had cherished and dreamed of during my lifetime; perhaps I felt a twinge of sadness that this moment had not come during my active diving days—but, let's face it, without modern methods of diving this find would have been most improbable. Modern methods have overtaken my type of diving, but have come too late for me—I have, through diving, lost the hearing of one ear—now I work only from the top-sides, for I do not think I would risk becoming totally deaf, even for the sake of a bronze gun.

The moment of rejoicing was mellowed a little when the divers reported that, although one of the guns would be fairly easy to recover, the other was very badly trapped by several decaying iron cannon. This second bronze gun lay in a gully, typical of the many gullies which formed the terrain below, and iron cannon were spreadeagled in a pile above it. Both bronze guns appeared to be identical with the one the Air Arm boys had recovered; the crossed-anchor motif stood out plainly in the dim underwater light. The depth was about eighty feet.

Not long after David had descended on his second dive he bobbed up again, holding something in his hand; we sped alongside him and, with some difficulty because of the rough sea, he handed over his prize. On examining it we found it to be a brass blunderbuss barrel, it had the typical flare at the muzzle. The end of this dive brought news of yet another bronze gun—the third, but this one, different from and slightly larger than the others, lay completely trapped beneath a large rock many tons in weight.

'Yes, I've heard tell there must have been a rock-fall,' said Mike, 'several divers have said so.'

But by the time the third dive had been completed the divers had a full, and startling, report to make. On our homeward trip that late afternoon, with the sun on our port quarter, with the Bishop Light sliding in and out of sight behind the Western Rocks, Geoff and David sprawled on the engine-room top; with the aid of thick pencils and smooth vinyl tiles (our underwater memo pads) they sketched what they had seen below. It was no rock-fall, we decided; as in so many undersea spots in Cornwall, the sea-bed moved in rough weather; it was obvious, guns and rocks lay mixed together in a veritable oceanic salmagundi. The giant boulders were rounded, proving that they rolled about in the gullies. Later in the year we were to establish without any doubt whatever that the *Association* wreck site was at times in a state of flux. For instance: we left the Gilstone in October, when we returned to it in November, after a fierce Atlantic storm, we found our heavy one-and-three-quarter-inch mooring wires trapped under immense rocks which had moved many feet. If gravel from the deep round the Bishop is found on the light's gallery after a storm, it can well be imagined what takes place in the very much shallower region of the Gilstone Ledges. During a typical sou'westerly storm the underwater conduits, troughs, channels, gullies and tunnels of this wreck site would become a complex of hydraulic forces. The giant rocks would squeeze, roll and pound like some crazy sub-aqueous mill running amok. We asked ourselves what chance would the fine antiques, the pewter pots and the firearms, of which the Press and others made so much pother—what chance would these have had over the past 260 years? Now we knew that we could not expect to find whole artefacts in any large quantity. Some, no doubt, would have been flicked away by the currents into safe rocky pockets; but to find these, in the kind of terrain below, could take years of searching.

'Right,' I said, 'no more recce dives, we concentrate on guns until we get them up, we are certain of these, the gold—if there is any—can come later.'

In underwater 'wrecking' it pays to belay a while and imagine your wreck going down. It pays to work out, if possible, how it broke up, then make a guess, helped by all the factual clues available, as to what happened to the pieces.

We know that the *Association* sank upright, with but the broken stump of her mainmast above water to show where she had settled; records state this fact and it is verified by the drawing of the flagship on my old-time chart.

From the heel of her keel to the highest point of her carved stern was a measurement of fifty feet. Therefore she lay with about twenty feet of water covering her highest point. We know that old-time salvors worked on her for a time shortly after her wrecking. The very fact that they did so points to the fact that there was something of considerable worth aboard. It is not thought that these intrepid men, with their brass-bound timber and leather diving engines, had much success. It is highly probable that by the end of her first winter of submergence the hapless vessel would have broken up completely, and her thousand and one artefacts have been scattered to the four corners of the ocean.

Everything points to the fact that *Association* sank slowly. There could have been no sudden going down, for the Admiral's barge is known to have been got safely away. Into this barge went its crew, it would not have been of much use without them; the Admiral was there as we know, soon to make a rendezvous with death at the hands of a lady of the Islands; the Admiral's friends and relations were there, and so was his private chest; also believe it or not, there was time enough and room enough for his pet dog to be ensconced on board.

So from this we can visualise the flagship slowly foundering;

she has slugged the starboard side of her belly against the great sloping rock face of the Outer Reef. This is a mortal blow, for her planking is staved below water, the sea spurts up amongst the boulders that lie packed in the darkness of her bilges, boulders which go to make up the 400 tons of her ballast.

The impetus of her bulk, all 1,460 tons of it, plus the surge of the seas sluicing over the reef, carries her forward and onward. With her stern slewed to larboard she drives crabwise towards the Gilstone Rock. She strikes this with a shattering blow, a blow which the ship takes on the rounding cheek of her larboard bow. The impact snuffs out the lights of her stern lanterns, lights that will never be relit; the doomed vessel lies in the centre of three rocks, she is belaboured by seas in a triangular trap of surging water.

Gnawing and rasping at her larboard bow is the black mass of the Gilstone itself; squat, menacing, with the sea smashing and roaring up and over it with gigantic force.

Slicing at her starboard quarter are the seas that run over the Outer Ledge, cunningly dark and quiet one minute, spouting great heads of sea the next, sea that foams so white it shows luminescent in the darkness.

Off from the vessel's starboard beam, but a few yards, lies the submerged Inner Ledge over which the black unbroken water sluices unseen by human eye.

As she becomes lower in the water, so the giant seas smash at her stern, they tear away the gilded and colourful sternboard which is a magnificent carving of the Royal Arms,

always to be found on the stern of English ships. Later this sternboard, and also a carved lion's head, were to be washed ashore on the Scillies. The lion's head now reposes in the Church at St. Mary's. In a time of near famine, in return for a shipload of potatoes, the sternboard was given by grateful islanders to Penzance. It can be seen there on a wall of the Sessional Court.

As the ship sinks, so tons of water would thunder through the great cabin and its sleeping apartment; this is where the treasure chests are located.

From all this we can only come to the conclusion that the artefacts that were swept from the Gilstone site by the fierce

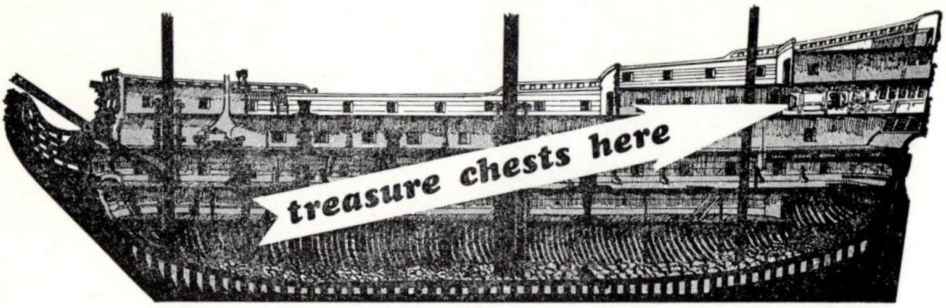

The treasure chests in the 'Association' would be located at the forward bulkhead of the Great Cabin

currents, especially during the period when the vessel was breaking up, might yet be found intact elsewhere. We must not overlook the fact that whole portions of the vessel, some large enough to carry cannon and other weighty articles, could have been taken hundreds of yards from the original wreck. On the other hand, our discovery that the sea-bed at the *Association* wreck site is liable to evolution was an unhappy one, it rather pointed to the fact that any artefacts remaining at the immediate site would be found to be in poor condition. That being so, what of the third bronze gun—the gun beneath the giant rock? How would it have fared under Nature's hydraulic press? We feared the worst.

Certainly a far wider search would have to be made for possible artefacts. Firstly, then, it behoved us to study the Gilstone currents. A good indication of a main stream can be gathered by using floats painted with brilliant day-glow colours, the floats must just have positive buoyancy. They are released from the wreck site sea-bed at half-ebb and half-flood tides. With just a touch of positive buoyancy the float creeps to the surface while being hustled along by the tide. It is surprising how far off these highly coloured buoys can be spotted.

Captain Piercy and some of his men of *Firebrand* were probably the only eyewitnesses of the foundering of *Association*. The Captain and twenty-two of his crew lived to tell the tale although their ship was lost. The *London Gazette* for November 1707 states that the Captain '*reported that at about three quarters past seven at night he heard the Admiral fire a gun and immediately lost sight of his lights. He soon perceived that the Admiral was lost, being then close aboard the rocks called the*

Bishop and Clarks.' The Captain's report, made some time after the event, was inaccurate as to time, as were the officers' journals of other ships; it seems also that he was a little adrift as to location, and this is understandable; the Bishop and Clarks are, on the old charts, the first obvious obstruction to be met with if one is coming up from the sou'west. In the thick weather of that night no-one could have pin-pointed a solitary rock, or cluster of rocks, as being the fatal spot.

As to what happened to the men on board—a favourite talking point of ours—that must be left to the imagination. While the Admiral was on board his ship, discipline reigned supreme, for he held sway of life or death over all who were beneath him. The *Association* was forty-five feet wide and had an overall length of 165 feet. On board were 640 men, but the vessel carried boats for but eighty of this vast crew. What *did* happen on that sinking vessel after the Admiral's barge had disappeared in the night? There were no *survivors.*

The morning following the night of wrecks dawns fine and sunny. What little wind there is comes from the nor'east.

The Islands of Scilly present a fresh, well-washed appearance after the heavy rains and violent storms of the previous days. Scilly's many long and curving beaches, groomed by the giant Atlantic breakers, show up white and crisp in the sunlight; even the long drifts of weed and wreckage lie stacked neatly along the surf's edge, the wreckage as clean and scoured as a carrot fresh scraped.

The calm, light blue waters of the North Channel are dappled with the slow-moving shadows of white billowing clouds. The sea, in Broad Sound and St. Mary's Road, shimmers into splendour as the light wind wafts its glittering meandering way across the surface of the water. The air is crystal clear and cold, but the sun strikes hot in the le'ward of the wind.

Many vessels of all types are anchored in the roads. Most of these are coastal ships, but several men-o'-war stand out prominently; their sails hang like limp banners, drooping and drying in the sun. There is a score and more of small craft crossing and re-crossing the anchorage. The warship's pinnaces are busy plying backwards and forwards; they make an eye-catching display with their oars flashing in unison in the sunlight. These boats search the area haphazardly, like buckets

in a well, for there is much wreckage floating in, and many bodies of drowned seamen.

It must be said that these bodies are treated with scant respect; they are hauled inboard with boathooks, their clothing is removed, the pockets are run through for anything of value. They are buried in any waste plot of land which is above high-water mark. No indication is left to mark the place of burial.

Shipwrecked sailors, it seems, are not allowed to be buried in churchyards; the notion is that men who might not be Christians should not therefore have a Christian burial. It is to take 101 years exactly to remedy this sorry state of affairs.

The bodies, then, are a nuisance to everyone and cause a deal of trouble and hard work, but the wreckage that accompanies the drowned and battered sailors is a heaven-sent bonus.

Timber galore is floating in on the tides and currents. Great spars and planks, giant blocks and ornate carvings, boxes and cases of every size and shape—containing who knows what—drift in through the rocks and islets. In come bottles and jars, casks and kegs, all of which bob and curtsy enticingly in the gentle tide-rips. In float skittish tubs of oil or tallow which roll and ride high in the water. There are ponderous pipes of wine which float secretly below the surface, with just the rounds of their bellies on show. Every article, great or small, that floats from a wreck converges eventually to the coves or beaches, for the unquiet tides of Scilly flow round the islands like a great wheel, they allow very little of what they have harvested to get away.

Overnight, the beaches have become garnished with the all-too-familiar trappings of broken ships; the familiar scrubbed and bleached timbers, timbers cleansed and smoothed unbelievably by the short time ravage of the waves. The familiar rope of shipwreck, rope swollen and tousled with seaweed, rope with its ends combed into long blond tresses, which entwine and tangle with everything. Familiar shipwreck canvas from wind-slashed sails, canvas deposited on the storm-smoothed sands in bulky grotesquely shaped bundles roped and secured with knots tied by Davy Jones's own particular cunningness and which no human hand can unravel.

There is timber for winter fires, timber for building and timber for sale. There are tables and chairs, cupboards and wooden buckets, doors and hatches and boat's gear of every description, there is food and clothing—a veritable assemblage of flotsam and jetsam, and it is yours if you can get it away without the Authorities knowing.

No matter if the drowned sailor's shoes are too big for the youngster, a stitch through the toe-cap will bring them down

to size. A soaking jacket from a bruised and bloated corpse can go straight on a young man's back; better that than the Navy men—who have just hove in sight—should claim it.

The underwater wrecks, as they slowly break up and give of their contents, will provide goods and materials for months to come. From now on no islander can afford to take both eyes off the sea at any one time. Not that a Scillonian, down through the years, has ever done such a thing.

The narrow streets of Hugh Town, in St. Mary's Island, are thronged with seamen on this bright sunny morning.

The thatched-roofed inn is busy, the doors are wide open, several of the customers are drinking in the sun on the rough granite platt outside.

There had been a moment of excitement earlier-on when the report of a gun came from the direction of Broad Sound.

On running up the nearby knoll the men had seen that two ships of the line were leaving the anchorage. These were the Falmouth-bound *Lennox* and *La Valeur*. It was later learned that these two vessels, in company with the *Phoenix*, had miraculously but quite unintentionally sailed up through Broad Sound in the darkness and storm of the previous night. The first two vessels were unharmed, they rode out the storm at their anchors. The *Phoenix*, however, '*became engaged with the rocks*': she was so badly damaged that she had to be beached, half full of water, in a rocky sound near New Grimsby. She became a total wreck.

This is the topic of conversation of these men, these bearded islanders who stand in the sun outside their inn, a topic of which they never tire—shipwreck. Conjecture is rife as to how many ships have been lost, for it has been a night of alarums and excursions, the sound of many warning guns being fired has kept people from their beds, most have stayed awake in a ferment of speculation.

And now news is spreading as only news on an island can—like wildfire.

The *Association* and the *Romney* have both been lost in the region of the Gilstone Ledges. Some say it was the Bishop and Clarks, but this is not now thought to be true. Of the many hundreds of men on board these two ships one only has been saved; he is George Lawrence, quarter-master of the *Romney*, who has been taken from a rock badly bruised. He is now being questioned by several captains and lieutenants of the Admiral's squadron with regard to the wreck from which he so providentially escaped with his life.

The *Eagle*, endeavouring to run through Broad Sound, has come to grief on the Gunners, a series of ledges just to the north of the Sound. She has been lost with every man aboard.

It is said that the fireship *Firebrand*, sailing in close company with the flagship, struck the same set of ledges as she. Providentially the *Firebrand* cleared from the rocks but was so badly holed that whilst heading for the Scilly light—and thus St. Agnes Island, on which the light stands—she foundered. Her Captain and seventeen men have saved themselves with the aid of the ship's boat. Later it is told that five other men have managed to gain the shore on pieces of wreckage.

So five ships have been lost, five ships out of the squadron of twenty-one; the loss of life is between 1,800 and 2,000 men.

So it is no great matter for surprise that the men standing in the sun outside the inn at Hugh Town, on this 23rd day of October in the year 1707, should have more than a deal to say about shipwreck.

It must be borne in mind that the islanders are desperately poor. It may be a startling statement to make, but truth to tell they depend on the proceeds from shipwreck, not only to boost their meagre earnings, but virtually to keep them and their children from near starvation.

Fish, and shipwreck—the sea can be a good provider in these lean times, for although fish may often be scarce ships are driven ashore in welcome regularity; one wreck in a night? —yes, often times; two wrecks in a night?—sometimes, if your luck is with you; but five ships torn apart in one night is an act of grace almost too great to contemplate, like putting butter upon bacon.

The men talk also of the finding of Admiral Sir Cloudesley Shovell's body at Porth Hellick, which is a small cove on the south'ard side of St. Mary's Island. It seems that the Admiral, Captain Loades, Sir John and Mr. James Narborough, along with the Bishop of Winchester's son, were all cast ashore in the same cove. The '*naked, small greyhound*', as well as the stern of Sir Cloudesley's barge, were found close to the bodies. When discovered by a Mr. Harry Pennick the Admiral's body had been stripped by two women of its clothes ('*his name was at ye gusset at his waist*'). It was noticed that his two rings were missing, though their impression on his finger was still plainly visible. An interesting item that crops up in all the chronicles is that '*his chest, which was by him, was taken up floating*'.

Like all the other bodies found that day, the Admiral's was taken a few yards up the beach and there buried. Very soon after, however, when news of his burial had reached a friend, the body was taken up and despatched to London; it was embalmed on route, at Plymouth.

Although Lady Shovell raised a rumpus about the missing rings, nothing was heard of them until years after; then a Scillonian woman, on her deathbed, confessed to stealing them; with her dying breath she confessed to having throttled the life out of the half-drowned Admiral for the sake of the rings.

The story of the finding of the Admiral has always interested me, particularly of the '*chest which was taken up floating*' and which was obviously empty at the time. This must have been a personal chest, of the kind in which personages like Sir Cloudesley would have kept their private papers, and possibly a great deal of personal wealth. As regard his papers, there is a mention that '*his Commiffion was brought on fhoar*' by a person unnamed, these having been found in the water.

Across the mouth of the cove in which the Admiral and his companions were found there runs a reef. I have for long been of the opinion that the Admiral's barge, in a fruitless attempt to enter the cove, ran aground on this reef. The craft would capsize, the occupants and the private chest would be thrown out. The barge would be smashed to pieces. the men would either be drowned, or partially drowned, before their bodies would wash up on the sands.

As a salvor, and now more particularly a marine archaeologist, I have thought of the possible contents of that private chest. Surely a man like the Admiral, leaving behind a vast fortune, and with time enough to spare to put a frightened animal on board his barge, surely he would have taken along with him treasure to the value of several thousands of golden guineas? I simply cannot see him coming away from his flagship with just a few scrolls of parchment. So let us presume that his private chest contained specie. If there is this possibility, then would it not be wise to mount a thorough search of the Porth Hellick reef? I was of the opinion that this would be well worth while. I say 'was', as now I am not so certain;

the search would be lengthy and difficult, I know, but it is not that which worries me; it is island hearsay that has me troubled.

During our spells of bad sea conditions, when no diving was possible, I would take myself off on various enquiries, some of them concerning offshoots of the main treasure hunt. One of these enquiries had to do with rumours that had come to my ears from time to time, rumours regarding the Admiral's barge. So I visited the locality on St. Mary's Island known as Watermill Bay:

'Oh yes, 'tis a well known thing that she' (the barge) 'came in here first, oh yes, that's a fact that is!' said one of the locals.

'But what happened then?' I asked. 'How was it that the bodies were found at Porth Hellick?'

'What happened? Well, she was towed out—you see; that's what happened, she was taken out to sea.'

'But what for? Who would tow her out—what would her crew be doing meanwhile?' said I, puzzled.

'Ah, I can't tell about that, all I knows is that the Admiral's barge came here first, we all knows it, always have!'

And then I met a charming lady. She told me a story of a seaman who is supposed to have come ashore on wreckage from the *Firebrand*; this vessel sank off St. Agnes which is about half the distance from where the *Association* sank. I relate the story in a very much foreshortened form, as the seaman himself might have told it:

'Well, after I was thrown ashore—an' that was early this morning, mind—I was making headway over the rocks as best I could, for I was feeling like death itself, when I saw a boat just off, it was headed into the cove in which I had just landed. The boat, to me, seemed to have the sweep of an Admiral's barge. Well, the people aboard were in a sorry state, I can tell you. As far as I could see there were only two oars going and they only in fits and starts. The others seemed to be fallen forrard and was just piled up in heaps. There were two people aft hunched together, but 'oo they was I couldn't say. Anyway, they was making progress towards the beach, but before they reached it a boat put off from the shore with six or seven men in it. They came up to the barge and without as much as a word they began belabouring the men in it with their oars. The two men in the starn weren't touched, as they looked as if they were done for anyway.'

'Who were the attackers—what were they like?' the man was asked.

'Oh, I could in no wise tell, it was light enough to see what was going on but not daylight enough to see their faces; but the one 'oo was doing the most devilment was a hunchback, 'e was standing up and going for it like as if 'e was mad!'

'And then what occurred?'

'Well then, two of these swabs went aboard the barge and passed over a chest, this was upended in their boat and thrown back empty into the barge again. Then they took and towed the barge out to sea; while they did this I thought I'd better make myself scarce; so with what speed and silence I could muster I made my way out of the cove. I walked up the lane and fell in with a boy leading a cow; he said the place was called Watermill Bay.'

Now that is hearsay, and hearsay coming from a tight-knit community such as that of an island should—I think—be taken heed of. Shall we organise a search of the Porth Hellick reef? Yes, perhaps we will; it would be foolish not to do so.

6

OUR FIRST GOLD COIN

We had met over coffee at the café overlooking the harbour; there we had discussed the plans for the day; now we were sitting on the sea-wall near the end of St. Mary's pier. The rough wall was warm to the touch, here it was sunny and breezy; we awaited the arrival of the motor vessel *Scillonian* from the mainland, from her we expected nylon rope and other stores. In the summer the arrival of this vessel is a daily event; the remark, 'Let's go down and see the *Scillonian* come in', gives a pleasant promise of whiling away the time, it is a congenial way of meeting others and of spending half an hour. First-hand knowledge can be gained of who is arriving at the Islands, and first-hand knowledge of any happening on the Islands is essential. It is pleasing to see the luggage and the cars unloaded, to see the hearty and the pale-faced passengers file up the gangway. But the *Scillonian* does not arrive until midday, now it was but midmorning, we had plenty of time to spare; we were not due at the Gilstone until early that afternoon, so we could relax.

Doug Rowe and Terry Parr were with us this day, they had completed their scrap-metal diving and were now free to assist us in our guns-and-gold enterprise. Doug was pale of face, blue of eye and bewhiskered of chin; Terry was sun-tanned, lean and lanky, clean-shaven and bespectacled; these two

H.M.S. 'Association' drawn to the same scale as R.M.V. 'Scillonian'—the passenger-freight carrying vessel which plies between the Islands of Scilly and the mainland:

SCILLONIAN
Length overall 208 ft 6 in
Tonnage 921
Crew 14
Ballast (water) 76 tons
Accommodation for 500 passengers

ASSOCIATION
Length overall 165 ft
Tonnage 1459 tons 12 cwt
Crew 640
She carried also:
Round shot (cast and hammered) 30 tons 12 cwt
Gunpowder 9 tons 15 cwt

lived in the conversion the *Girl Sharon*, which was anchored 'off' in the harbour. Doug had converted a ship's lifeboat into a very comfortable, roomy and seaworthy craft. She was a home and a workboat, both snug and efficient.

While talking over the problem of salving the bronzes, Doug told me that he had a small supply of explosives on board. I suggested that we take some along with us that afternoon, it was probable that we should need it. One of the bronze guns was trapped by iron cannon; Geoff and David were of the opinion that one, maybe two, of these guns could be levered out of the way. Two iron guns, however, were crossed over the bronze in the shape of an X; these were solidly cemented together and, also, were jammed into the rocks at each side. I proposed that we cut the iron guns in two with explosives; very small charges would be required as the guns were soft after two and a half centuries in salt water. This decision of mine to use explosives was to raise a storm of protest from all manner of people, and was to have repercussions in all manner of ways. Personally, I did not think twice about it; as I have said before, explosives can be harnessed to undertake whatever task you want of them, they can be controlled to exert the tap of a toffee hammer or the whack of a steam hammer. Here the prize was a bronze gun, a thing of beauty, a work of art. The iron guns were expendable; there were some eighty to ninety of these rotting artefacts lying among the debris of the sea-bed. To lose two or three of these for the sake of a piece of history was to me of no consequence. And for why? For the simple reason that iron guns which have been underwater for anything over 200 years are best left where they are; bring them to the surface, into the atmosphere, and they will crumple and disintegrate, as I very well know. I have managed to preserve several iron guns, but these had been submerged for less than 160 years.

I was taught the art of blasting, for it is an art, from an old Cornish miner, one Sam Reynolds who hailed from the village of Ludgvan. To show his everlasting regard for the Navy, with which he served in the First World War, Sam named his one and only daughter after the ship he was in, she was H.M.S. *Arethusa*. Sam taught me all the many tricks which are to be known about explosives. In the last war, when the need for cast iron became urgent, Sam and I toured sou'west Cornwall on behalf of the Government. We blasted down all the many tin-stamps that were to be found in the countryside in those days. Very often cottages and larger dwellings surrounded these monstrous machines; mostly they were driven by enormous cast-iron water-wheels. They were all blasted down in perfect safety; as Sam would say, 'Everything's all right, as long as you know how!' Sam became famous in 'dowsing' (water divining) and well-sinking circles by successfully sinking over eighty wells, all in sou'west

Cornwall. He would sink his wells, of course, by explosives; there he would be, down the half-completed well, with a 'tender'—usually an old man—keeping watch on top. Round the periphery of his well Sam would have five separate charges ready for firing, all with very short fuses. He would light the first fuse with two matches held together, at the same time shouting 'Fire!' at the top of his voice. Then, with the first fuse spouting sparks and smoke, he would use this to light the remaining fuses. At the next shout of 'Up! up!' the old man at the top of the well would leisurely wind Sam to the surface with the aid of a wooden-barrelled winch. It seemed that no sooner would Sam step out of harm's way than with a whoosh! and a scattering of rocks and stones the blasts would go off.

'Why don't you use longer fuses and give yourself more time to get away?' I once asked him.

'What!' said Sam. 'With fuse at nearly a penny a foot?'

At one time Sam was sinking a well slap in the middle of a farmyard. He was in despair. Although he had located water with his dowsing twig, at eighty feet down the well was 'as dry as an old boot'. It looked as if it was a failure, the farmer was furious, it had cost a lot of money. Sam was down in the depths contemplating his bad luck; idly, with a mason's hammer, he was trimming the rocks that protruded from the side of the well; he gave one rock a blow and to his utter amazement the whole side of the well fell away. He was looking dumbfounded into the black void when, from far, far below, he heard the splash and crash of debris falling into deep water. Sam had been sinking his well parallel with an old, long-forgotten tin-mine shaft; he had been within inches of it for all of the eighty feet down. There was water there, all right, but it was 400 feet below!

I can give an example of the gentle application of 'high' explosive, as it is called. Some years ago, under an order by the Penzance Council, I was given the task of dismantling a timber vessel which had been found derelict in Mount's Bay. She was the schooner *Hetty*, and a fine stout vessel she had been. Oak, teak, pine and cedar all went to make up her hull, while her two stout masts were of pitch-pine. She had been condemned as having a broken back, though, sadly—because it was then too late—I found that this was not so. She lay in Penzance harbour, and there she had to be broken up.

In spite of the fact that she lay alongside the quay wall, with people and cars within yards of her, despite the fact that other boats were near to her, she was taken apart by the use of explosives, without damage or inconvenience to anyone. She was held together by thousands of split-timber peg fastenings, and by hundreds of copper bolts. With the aid of a very large number of very small charges of explosive I dismantled her hull plank by plank and rib by rib. The greater part of her timbers was used again, certainly much of her material was used in the Admiral Benbow.

It had been announced in the local paper that the *Hetty* was to be broken up by explosives. On the day I was due to start operations I was surprised to see a vast concourse of cars and people on the other side of the harbour. On enquiring the reason for this unusual gathering I was told they had come to see the 'blowing up of the schooner *Hetty*'. In their understandable ignorance of the use of explosives those people fully expected to see one enormous and spectacular eruption of water, with the ship going sky-high in a thousand pieces. Like many others, they had no idea as to the gentle application of 'high' explosive. To be able to use explosives one must 'know a hawk from a handsaw'; handle them with adroitness and explosives can be a lusty yet gentle servant, a friendly, all-powerful genie. Without the aid of this servant, this genie, two very fine bronze guns would still be hidden from sight in the regurgitation and murk of the Gilstone depths.

As we talked together on the warm and sunny sea-wall, suddenly someone said:

'Look! What on earth's this coming in!'

We all looked up to see, coming round from St. Mary's Sound, a strange black-and-white-painted vessel. From her tall stack there issued a high plume of blue diesel smoke, the light following wind carried this along with her like a pall. Slowly she came on. She was a strange-looking craft, her bow reared high out of the water, her superstructure towered up like a river boat, and yet, when she turned bow on, her beam seemed peculiarly inadequate, for all this top-hamper.

My mind went back to the phone call I had had from the *Telegraph* man:

'Well, what do you know,' said I, 'here comes competition, suction gear, powerful winches, underwater cameras—the lot!'

'But they'll never get her out to the Gilstone,' said someone, 'she's miles too big.'

Anyone with half an eye could see that this was true; without any doubt this vessel was the last thing one would have chosen for working the *Association* wreck. Still puffing out diesel fumes, looking strangely out of place, the ship came slowly towards the harbour.

'If she carries on as she's going,' came the remark, 'she'll go aground on Bacon Ledge.'

We all held our breath. The vessel chugged innocently onwards, with her crew lolling nonchalantly about her decks, serenely unconscious that her keel was within inches of rock; the only tense figure was the barely distinguishable outline of the man on the bridge, without a doubt he was better acquainted with the draught of his vessel than were we. The name *Regency* stood out clearly on her bow. Going over to the Sandy Bank side of St. Mary's Pool the vessel stopped undecided. Then, as if making up her mind, she snorted rapidly from her funnel and again went ahead, this time she aimed for the quayside. As she approached we could make out more of her details; it was a certainty that at one time she had been a well-found, if peculiarly shaped, vessel. But now her paintwork was peeling, her anchors and cables were rusting, she had seen better days.

Within minutes of her crunching against her car tyre fenders alongside the pier, we had learned that she was the 150-ton 'survey vessel' from Yarmouth. She was skippered by Mr. Bill Sutton, had been chartered by a London syndicate, and had a crew of nine, including four experienced divers. As the *Scillonian Magazine* of the time said: 'The treasure race is hotting up.'

But now the *Scillonian* was coming in. From a distance she appeared black with passengers, and she had a pronounced list to starboard, this was caused solely by all the passengers concentrating on that side, most of them were getting their first glimpse of St. Mary's.

Amid the hustle and bustle of the embarkation of the holidaymakers, most of them over for just the one day, our stores were thrown on the quay. These included coils of nylon rope, rope half the size of a man's wrist. Shining, beautiful off-white rope; very strong and very expensive. This rope had come to me by way of the wreck of the French trawler *Jeanne*

Gougy. This unfortunate vessel had gone ashore at Land's End in November 1962. Having struck the rocks at the foot of the high cliffs, the vessel was turned over on her port side by the enormous seas which were running—it was high water. It looked as if everyone had been drowned, huge seas continued to wash over the hull of the vessel which was completely hidden by broken water for several minutes at a time. But, as the tide dropped, a miracle was unfolded before the eyes of the watching rocket apparatus crew. Men who had survived in the submerged wreck in a 'bubble' of air were seen to be clambering up and out of the sea-racked hulk. These were rescued by the gallant efforts of helicopter and rocket apparatus crews.

That ultra-modern rope, coming from a modern sea tragedy, was to be used in an age-old wreck, and used successfully, in the recovery of cannon some three centuries old.

Having stowed our equipment on board *Sea King*, and visited the *Girl Sharon* for Doug's and Terry's gear and explosive, we set off. From the quayhead we headed out into St. Mary's Sound, passing the Newman Rock close to. Out between the Bristolmans we surged; past the Little Smith, on our port side; now we went inside the Quoins (pronounced Coins) and so made for Hellweather's (Hellwallis) Neck; through this; and then across the Neck of Muncoy, passing Luitreth (Louis-treath) on the way. Now through Rosevear Neck, past Rosevear Ledges and so down to the tumbling water of the Gilstone Rock.

This day we put down a big mooring wire and a large orange-coloured 'buff' buoy. While two of the divers busied themselves with this, Doug and Terry had a look at the cannon that were trapping the bronze gun. After hot soup for the divers, and coffee and sandwiches for the boat's crew, we sat around in the bucking, wallowing launch and discussed tactics. It was decided to lever two iron cannon from those covering the bronze, not in order to save the iron guns, but because we thought if we blasted them the falling segments might wedge the bronze even more securely in the gully in which it lay.

Consequently, Doug and Terry got on with making up several small charges, while the others went below to manhandle the iron guns. This is a dangerous task and I did not like it at all. We could use no form of air-lift, as the weather on

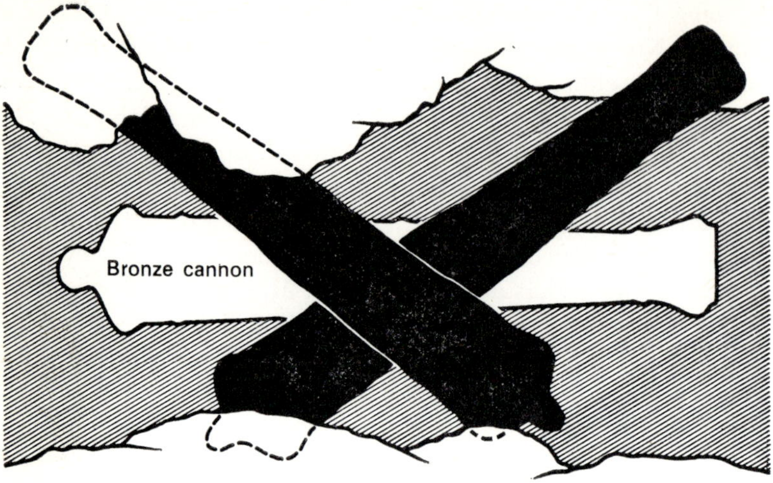

The Number One bronze cannon trapped by corroded iron guns straddling across

the top was too severe for this; manhandling air containers needs calm sea conditions; this we had not had since we had been in the Islands. However, by a great deal of skill and brawn, and a fair sprinkling of luck, these movable guns were disentangled out of the way. This left the two immovable iron guns to be blasted; this was to be done electrically. Down went Doug and Terry with the small square packets of explosive, these had the size and appearance of dog biscuits; trailing down behind them went the white plastic-covered electric cable. Down in the depths the explosive was wired flat against the iron guns, the positioning had to be judged so that the guns would fracture and roll out of the way; no possible damage must come to the bronze gun.

Up came the divers, spluttering and gasping in the rough water as they took out their demand valves and slipped off their face-masks; air bottles were slung on board, the divers climbed over the side of the launch. As the charges were small there was no need to move the launch away. Doug placed one of the blasting wires to one terminal of a battery; he paused for a moment, then he brought the other wire to the second terminal. There was a small, deep-seated 'crack', as if Davy Jones had broken a broom handle down below. Several minutes later a few fish—wrasse and pollock—floated slowly to the surface.

'We'll wait a few minutes for the water to clear,' said Doug, 'then I'll do a recce to see what's happened.'

While Doug and Terry had been laying the charges, Geoff and David had investigated the second bronze gun; they said that very little work would be required to make it ready for lifting. This set me furiously to thinking what we should use if the sea conditions remained poor. Air-lifts were out. I now started planning in terms of lifting the guns by boat—a boat with a powerful winch, I decided—in other words, a trawler. I thought I knew the very thing; if she was available.

Doug made himself ready for the final dive of the evening. A full set of twin air bottles was harnessed to his back, his air was turned on for him, he 'blew' his valve to make sure it was working correctly:

'Give me a wire strop,' he said, 'if the bronze is clear I'll strop her ready for lifting, besides anyone coming along can see that we've been working on her, and leave her alone—we hope!'

This was the first mention of others coming to dive on 'our' site. We viewed the probability with a queasy feeling of unease. Would they have a go at our bronze cannon as the Air Arm boys had done with the iron guns of the *Anson*? Time alone would tell.

Now Doug was sitting on the side of *Sea King* with his back to the rough sea; he held the wire strop in his hand—a wire strop is a short length of wire rope, an eye splice at each end. Positioning the mouth-piece of his demand valve to his liking, Doug pulled the face-mask down over his eyes and, still keeping his hand on this, he threw himself backwards and overboard. There was a mighty splash, with globules of water spattering into the launch.

The other divers were changing; Mike's brother Alf was starting up the twin Lister Blackstone 54 h.p. engines—a whir-whir-whir of the self-starters and they were running sweetly. As soon as Doug was aboard again we would be off.

We had not long to wait, someone warned that he was coming up, and as we were ready for 'off' we lined the side of the launch to watch him surface. He came up with an arm stretched high above his head, in the upraised hand there glistened a golden disc—it was a golden coin! Doug's blue eyes twinkled behind his glass mask, he jerked his outstretched hand as if to say 'Take it!' I reached down and held

Our first gold coin—a Portuguese 'reis' dated 1706. The date was a vital clue as to the identity of the wreck, for the 'Association' was lost in 1707 and no coin subsequently found —except one gold reis dated 1707—bore a later date

his wrist with one hand, and with the other I very carefully extracted the gold coin from his clutching fingers—I was not taking any chances. Everyone crowded round to have a look; it was a coin in brilliant mint condition. It was dated 1706. What did it say? We all peered hard; on the date side were the words: -IN-HOC-SIGNO-VINCES- on the reverse side was a shield surmounted by a crown and the words: PETRVS-II-D-G-PORT-ET-ALG-REX, and alongside the shield the figures 4,000. Reverently it was passed from hand to hand; it was an exciting occasion. Was it Spanish? No, we thought not; Portuguese then? Yes, that was more like it, yes, a Portuguese 4,000-reis gold coin!

There came a shout from outboard:

'Hi! what about me?'

It was Doug, we had forgotten all about him.

We were all in high spirits as the launch headed back to St. Mary's. A golden coin—a piece of gold from the seafaring days of the past; a link with wooden-walled battleships—why, Admiral Sir Cloudesley himself could have handled this piece of gold! We felt we were hot on the trail of treasure.

'It's like shaking hands with history,' said Mike Hicks.

'What's it worth, I wonder?' asked someone.

'Who wants its worth?' I replied. 'Just give me the coin!'

'I found it just by chance,' said Doug, shivering a little as he towelled himself down. 'I was putting the strop round

A round shot recovered from the interior of an iron gun and bearing the British Naval mark of a Broad Arrow. So perfect is its condition that the casting ridge shows plainly

the gun—she's all clear, by the way—when I saw something shining just below it. I reached down and picked up the coin, just like that. I put it on the gun while I finished stropping her up, and there you are!'

Later that evening we trooped triumphantly into the Mermaid Inn. I went up to Len, the bearded barkeep, and ordered drinks all round. I tossed the coin on the bar, where it spun and tinkled expensively. Len eyed the gleaming disc as he set up the drinks.

'Sorry, Guv,' he said, his eyes still on the coin, 'it's not legal . . . ' He stopped, a drink half completed. 'No!' he exclaimed, he grabbed the coin, looked at it closely, 'Congratulations!' he said.

As we sat and drank our drinks, Mike Hicks handed me a small heavy parcel. It was done up in hessian. I unrolled it on the table in front of me. It was a cannon-ball, perfect even to the ridged casting mark that ran round its centre. Cast deep into its surface was the shape of a broad arrow.

'But where did this come from?' I asked.

'I had it with me when I came up with the coin,' said Doug, 'I almost let it drop, I was holding on to it while you lot were busy looking at the coin.'

'It's in perfect condition,' said I.

'It's come out of one of the iron guns we blasted,' said Doug, 'the gun must have been loaded.'

Many divers who find old-time cannon with cannon-balls

inside think that the gun was left loaded, but, in fact, this is not the case. It was the custom in those days to keep the bore of iron guns in good condition by putting about half a gallon of oil into the gun, then a round shot; at the muzzle end there was a rope ball attached to the tampion, or oaken plug, which was driven hard into the bore. With the gun aligned almost level in its carriage the movement of the ship, at sea, would set the round shot rolling (in its oil) to and fro in the barrel; at the breech end it would squish against the oil, at the muzzle end it would roll softly against the rope ball and thus would not displace the tampion. In this manner the bore would be kept oiled and free from rust. In our case the cannon-ball, or, to use the correct description, the round shot, was itself, naturally, in perfect condition; the same condition as when 260 years ago it had been rolled into the gun by a gunner's mate, whose earnings, swept into his hat from the pay table at the end of the month, would not have amounted to more than ten shillings. A man who, more likely than not, had been 'pressed' into the Navy against his will.

The Broad Arrow on the round shot was interesting; it proved beyond all doubt that the shot, and therefore the gun, were British. The Broad Arrow, used as the mark of Government stores, was the distinguishing device of Lord de L'Isle, who was the First Commissioner of Ordnance in the reign of Queen Elizabeth. Pepys did not take kindly to it; in his Naval Minutes he writes: '*One would have thought that our Princes valued themselves so much in all ages upon their sea doings and sea power, they would have taken this publick brand, especially that which was to serve them in sea matters, from something really relating to that element rather than to an arrow-head, a consideration that would easily have inclined one from the common figure of it to have drawn it to the signifying* (*tho' rudely*), *an anchor rather than an arrow-head.*' Later we recovered other artefacts which bore the sign of the Broad Arrow.

Later still that night I phoned the owner of the trawler *Ros Guill;* I knew this vessel was at that moment lying seaworthy, and with a skipper on board, at Newlyn harbour. Was she available? I wanted to know; yes, she was available, either for charter or for sale. How much for charter? I asked; the answer was expensive:

'Three hundred pounds a week, with a minimum of three weeks.'

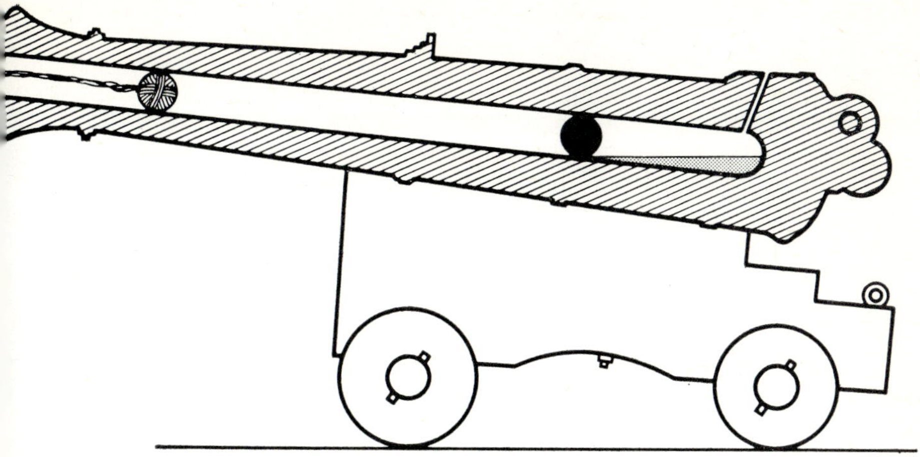

ABOVE *To keep the bore of an iron gun rustfree, the muzzle and touch-hole were plugged after a cannon ball and half a gallon of oil had been inserted, and the motion of the ship kept the ball gently moving from breech to muzzle, so keeping a film of oil over all.* BELOW *An oaken tampion (plug) and a hempen ball—to cushion the blow of the cannon ball at the muzzle end —from a forty-two-pounder gun*

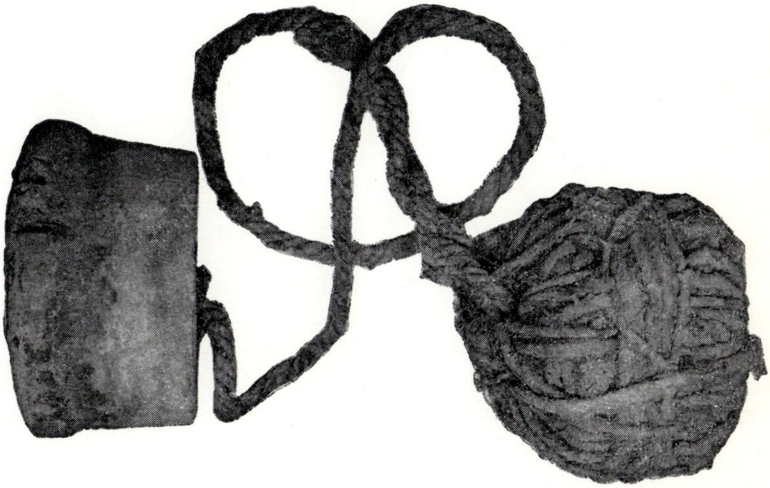

Expensive or not, I took the vessel on; she would be coming over as soon as the weather permitted.

Now I, and I think all of us, could breathe more freely; the bronze guns—two of them at least—were as good as ours. But

preparations had to be made for the safe working of the trawler. Heavier moorings had to be put down at the wreck site; she would have to be moored both fore and aft in order to obtain the best 'lift' out of her.

On our next visit to the Gilstone the weather was atrocious; the sea conditions could not have been worse. Big Atlantic swells were coming in, with white caps sizzling along their tops. Heavy showers of rain kept everyone in their oilskins and sou'westers. The launch did everything but topple over on her beam ends. The Gilstone Rock was a smother of giant combers, so big were they that the spillage of hundreds of tons of foaming water appeared as if in slow motion. That sink of iniquity, the Outer Ledge, was up to its heinous tricks as usual; fierce and sinister cross seas rebounded from its raven-ing convulsions. With the divers down, with everyone busy handling the sinuous mooring wires with one hand and holding on for dear life with the other, someone warned:

'Look out, Big Brother's watching us!'

We glanced up to see, about a mile off, the ungainly shape of the 'survey vessel' *Regency*. She came slowly and cautiously towards us, rolling and pitching in the rough water; at a point about a quarter of a mile off she stopped, and stayed for some while; we could feel the binoculars and spy-glasses upon us. We wondered what her people thought of the Gilstone. Certainly it must have been only too plain to them that they would never use their powerful winches, or suction gear, in the vicinity of the *Association* wreck. And they never did; I think this was the only occasion when the *Regency* went near the rock and its ledges. She steamed off after a while, but having travelled some two miles or so, she hesitated, as if she could not quite believe what she had seen. So she turned and came back for another look; finally, after wallowing about in the rough seas for twenty minutes, she departed, and left us to our rain-soaked, topsy-turvy misery.

As Mike Hicks said at the time: 'Rain or no, rough sea or no, we've got our moorings down.'

And very satisfactory that was; on top of that the divers had made another discovery: they had located a small bronze breech-loading cannon; this was found jammed between two rocks. We promised ourselves that we would recover this on a finer, sunnier, more pleasant day.

We went back to our evening meal tired, wet to the skin, but content that all had gone well.

7

THE MYSTERY OF THE SILVER PLATE

It is not for me to enter into the vexed and complicated subject of amateur divers versus professional. There will always be differences of opinion between these two factions. As in car racing, or for that matter any other pastime with an element of danger in its make-up, skill in diving can only be judged by the behaviour of the participant in a time of dire emergency. And in professional diving emergencies are bound to crop up. Just as ordinary run-of-the-mill, but nevertheless very good, car drivers cannot enter car racing without passing stringent eliminating trials, so the same thing should apply to divers. I talk, of course, of aqualung divers. A copper-top diver works as one of a team and very rarely does he operate without intensive training. In other words, I believe that a diver should prove his worth before risking his neck and, what is of more importance, the necks of others.

It is not for us to warn amateur divers that the Gilstone is a dangerous place, they would assuredly place the wrong implications on our advice. If one man can dive in treacherous currents and savage undertows, and get away with it, so, they think, can they. They have enough confidence in themselves to think that they are as proficient as the next man. Probably they are—until the emergency arises; that is the crucial test, and, as we well know, very often they fail to pass it.

Whilst awaiting the arrival of the trawler we went out, one boisterous afternoon, to try to recover the bronze breech-loader. As rocks firmly held this small artefact in their grasp, a small explosive charge was to be used to free it.

I had been told by a boatman that he was taking out two divers, these had come down from 'up country' expressly for this purpose. They were intending to dive at the Gilstone Ledges.

I should have saved my breath, of course, but on the way to our launch, as I passed the older of the two divers, I told him that we would be putting down one small charge, it would take a matter of minutes only and should not delay anyone unduly. The young man's words were caustic:

'You can't frighten me with your threats of explosives!' he said.

At the Gilstone we arrived first, and duly moored up to our buoy. As Mike Hicks would say, 'the sea had quite a lop on it', and this made it tricky for the divers coming aboard. Moreover, the launch was snatching badly at her mooring, so we put in a length of nylon rope to give her more 'spring'. Work was slowed down considerably owing to the erratic and violent movement of the launch. Geoff and David went down to do further work on clearing bronze guns one and two. Doug and Terry concentrated on the muzzle-loader. There was no sign of the two 'up country' divers, perhaps they had given up the attempt. But no, their launch appeared just as Doug and Terry went down with the made-up charge. We hoisted a slip of red bunting as a warning, but we might just as well have flown the hammer and sickle for all the notice they took of us. Through the monocular glass from my camera I watched the divers in close-up. They were kitted up and ready to dive, though the younger lad seemed in a distressed condition, he seemed to be weaving about in the boat. Presently, as the two divers sat on the side of the boat, preparatory to launching themselves outboard, the younger one actually fell inboard by mistake. We heard afterwards, from their boatman, that this younger lad had been 'very boat-sick'—or, in mainland language, seasick. Now to be taken with seasickness, then to go diving, is about the most crazy thing anyone can do.

By the time Doug and Terry had surfaced, the 'up country' divers had gone down. Doug held out his twin blasting wires, and looked at the battery expectantly:

Typical rough, wet, dreary weather in which we first went treasure hunting

'What do we do now, then?' he asked.

'Well, we certainly can't fire the charges while they're down.' said I. So in the toppling, weaving launch we waited and we watched. First one diver would surface for a few minutes, then he would go down; then the other would come up, and go down again; but never once did they both come up together. Had they done so we could have fired our charge, recovered the small gun and finished work for the day. Meanwhile, our divers were whistling and waving, but no notice was taken of us. We might as well have been on the other side of the Atlantic;

I wonder if our presence would have been noticed had one of their divers met with a crisis?

Now the tide was running strongly, the launch, in spite of the nylon spring, was snatching dangerously at her mooring; we still had the blasting wires connected to the explosive charge below. Now the light was failing and still these two unthinking people kept us waiting, two divers who had never even heard of diving etiquette, two people entirely taken up with their own pursuits.

Just as we were losing all patience, there was a 'bang' and our mooring wire parted, and no wonder, it had withstood an hour or more of hectic buffeting. With the mooring wire gone we started to drift so that our blasting wire went also.

'Let's push off,' I said, 'we've lost the tide.'

I remember saying other things too, but they were suitable only for the open sea. As we headed for Old Bess we turned and watched the amateurs who had spoiled our day's work for us. One had surfaced at one point, he was waving his arms for a pick-up; a considerable distance further east, almost indistinguishable in the evening light, the other diver had surfaced also, he too was waving his arms. The boatman had seen only one of them, as we had spotted the other we drew the boatman's attention to him; after all, the boatman would have got into trouble had he lost one of his charges.

On our return trip we went along inside Old Bess, then south about Pednathise and Shoal Neck. Passing the Biggal of Gorregan, we headed in for Hellweathers Neck and so home to St. Mary's. It was dark when we got in; we drew alongside the quay. Wearily we unloaded our air cylinders, these would have to be recharged ready for the morning. Tomorrow, early, we must go out and see to our moorings, and—most important of all—we must fire that charge.

It has long been a maxim of mine that not only must one celebrate one's successes, equally one must celebrate one's failures. It is true it was not our fault, but nevertheless the day had been a failure; it had cost some seventy pounds and all we had done was to sit around and watch the inane gambols of two divers who obviously had no set plan or motive.

So we celebrated; we sat comfortably and drank rum and shrub, it makes a change from iced coke; we reminisced as divers and others are wont to do. I remembered in the last war we were breaking up coastal wrecks at Lowland Point, near the Manacles. One morning we arrived at the site to find great gaping craters in the beach, near which we were working. It appeared that during the previous night a German 'E'-boat squadron had made a torpedo attack, from out at sea, on one of our convoys that had been creeping along in the shelter of the coast. Several torpedoes had missed and had exploded on the beach. But one of these giant weapons had not gone off, it lay trapped between two big rocks with its warhead crumpled but with the remainder of it perfect and intact.

There is one thing about salvage that never ceases to please: one day is never the same as another. This day was to be vastly different; I donned my wading suit, the kind that comes up to one's neck; after fabricating a specially long box spanner I was able to separate the head of that torpedo from its long gleaming body. This latter containing the big compressed-air chamber and aft of that the motor compartment with its complicated mechanisms, and its fins and propellers. We rigged an overhead Blondin so that we could sling the torpedo over the rocks. It took us all of one morning, and the best part of the afternoon, before that hefty tin fish was lying securely in our van. To get it in the vehicle we had to take out the front passenger seat, in this fashion the torpedo was lashed in position up against the steel dashboard, even then its tail projected from the rear of the van by many feet. While the others prepared to leave work I saw to the final lashing down of our big load. I noticed that near the tail-end of the torpedo there was an intriguing inspection cover retained by two set-screws. I could not resist unscrewing these and removing the cover; inside was a maze of miniature machinery; I recognised the small gyro wheel with its wind vanes machined into its outer edge, like a bijou water-wheel, though in this case, of course, it was driven by compressed air. I was fascinated, but as I was replacing the inspection cover my fascination turned to apprehension. The torpedo was ticking! I placed my ear to its cold clammy exterior—sure enough, from inside came a steady ominous ticking noise. My blood ran cold; I walked backwards from the great steel bulk of it, now it had taken on a portentous, pregnant look. Could it be some form of fearful booby-trap? I wondered. Still keeping a safe distance from the van, so as to allow the chill to leave my spine, I carefully thought the matter over—

it just did not make sense. The deadly portion of the torpedo was down on the rocks, the remainder of it was composed merely of machinery and a big compressed-air tank.

Let me see, I thought, after a while, the only thing that should be ticking in that van is the clock in the dashboard. In fear and trembling I tiptoed across the rough grass; plucking up my courage I reached behind the dashboard, I unscrewed the two knurled nuts from behind the big clock and removed it with my stomach turning. Cautiously I placed my ear to the tail-end of the torpedo—there was a comforting silence, the ticking had gone. Having gone through a nerve-racking ten minutes I could now show fight once more; with a devil-may-care abandon I started up the ticking in the torpedo again by replacing the clock. The ticking, of course, was being transmitted to the torpedo via the steel dashboard. Having badly shaken the nerves of the men as they came up to the van in ones and twos, I had the best joke yet to come.

At the top of the cliff where we worked was a coast-watchers' hut; most of the men engaged on this work were very fine chaps, but one in particular was a nasty piece of work, the authority vested in him had gone to his head. Luckily, this day he was on duty.

As we ground up the steep cliff road with its 'S' bends we saw him standing waiting for us. He had been to the farm close by; he held a small jug of milk in one hand, from his other hand there hung a large basket of brown hen's eggs.

He had been watching us all day, he said; what right, he wanted to know, had we to go tampering with this piece of mechanism?—he indicated the tail of the torpedo protruding from the back of the van. Who told us to do it, since when had we the authority to salvage this, that and everything?

I let him rant on, switched off the van's engine and got down from the driver's seat. I told him he was quite right, we should not have touched the darned thing, we were acutely worried about it, it was ticking.

'Ticking?' he asked, the expression on his face changing instantly from one of agression to one of anxiety.

'Yes, come and listen!' said I.

Hesitatingly he placed his basket of eggs and the bottle of milk on the tailboard of the van. He bent his tall frame and gingerly put his big ear to the body of the torpedo.

Quick as thought he straightened up, sprang for the nearby hedge, and was amongst the scrubby trees that lined its top before one could say 'Knife!' For a split second he turned: 'You fools!' he cried. 'Don't you realise that thing is about to go off!'

He disappeared from view, but as we climbed back into the van we could see his head bobbing across the field. At the far hedge he was gone. It was a pity to waste the milk, so someone drank it. The same thing applied to those big brown hen's eggs, they were hard to come by, so we shared them among us.

The Flag Officer in Charge (Navy), stationed at Pendennis Castle, Falmouth, directed me to take the torpedo to Newlyn.

'By jove,' he said, 'the backroom boys will be glad to get their hands on this! And, my goodness, you've done yourself a bit of good, I must say!'

We delivered the torpedo to the Navy depot at Newlyn; in spite of the numerous black eagles and red swastikas stamped on the body of the thing, not to mention stencilled words indicating VERSENKUNG, SICHERSVENTIL and the like, the officer gave me a receipt cagily stating: 'Received one Torpedo *—believed to be of German origin.*' We unloaded it via the Trinity House crane at Penzance. A fortnight later the Flag Officer at Falmouth rang me up to say:

'You know, the backroom boys are delighted with your torpedo. Yes, it's the first three-cylinder motor they've seen. So, jolly good for you! You'll be hearing more about this—definitely!' As a matter of fact we never heard another word, but it had been a lot of fun.

And so we celebrated our lost day; we drank our rum and shrub, or iced coke whatever it might be, and we reminisced. At the far end of the long bar the *Regency* crew were congregated.

The next day one of the London papers had this to say:

'A team aboard the survey ship *Regency*, a converted American minesweeper equipped with radar, echo-sounders and recovery equipment, is ready to dive alongside Mr. Morris's expedition. Her skipper is 36-year-old Bill Sutton, aviator, diver and sea survey expert, whose firm, Diving Systems, has been hired by a consortium of London businessmen. The nine crew has agreed to carry out the academic survey for

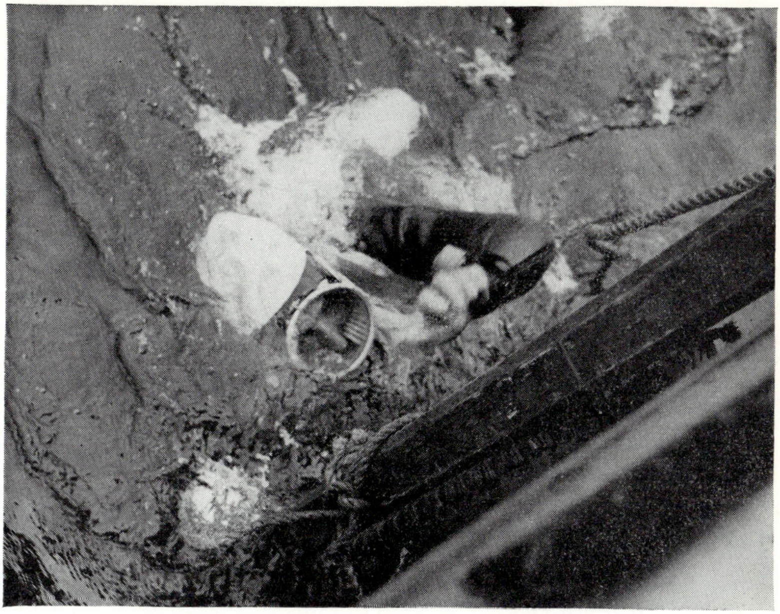

Geoff Upton fights for the ladder in a rough sea

twenty-five pounds a week, half pay, plus an interest in any treasure recovered. But the crew members insisted:

' "The treasure is only secondary. If we raise a bronze cannon we intend to present it to the people of the Scillies."

'In port at St. Mary's the two teams moor their boats alongside the same quay. But they drink in separate bars at the harbourside Mermaid pub, and dress differently—the *Regency* crew in smart casuals, the Penzance crew in salty fishermen's sweaters.'

And it was the next day, during the afternoon, that the *Regency* crew went out to the Gilstone, this time in their small inflatable dinghies. They brought back a round shot that had come from the second of the iron guns that we had blasted. This round shot, like ours, had a Broad Arrow mark on it.

The reason we did not meet up with the *Regency* crew was that we went out early in the morning, so early the gulls were just setting out for their fishing grounds. As we passed Rosevean the beat of *Sea King*'s engines set the gulls winging skywards in their thousands; they went away in a sou'westerly direction, out into the Atlantic. But not so the strange assemblages of those solemn sea birds the shags; nothing seems to frighten these parsonic-looking creatures.

The Bishop Light was still showing its stab of brilliance, every fifteen seconds as is its custom, when we arrived at the Western Rocks. Away in the diametrically opposite direction, away behind the islands to the east, the sun rose into a pale golden sky; but the forecast for the morrow was poor, 'high winds', the Met man had said, and high winds meant high seas. So what we had to do we had better do right away.

Everything had been carefully prepared. The broken mooring had to be recovered and a new one installed; the moorings, at the sea-bed end, were attached to the most conveniently situated of the iron guns. Geoff and David, the two divers working on the moorings—a most exhausting job—were told that as soon as they had finished this they could go exploring. Doug and Terry, as usual, were the shot-firing merchants; they had to lay a second charge alongside that which we had been unable to fire the previous evening.

The small bronze breech-loading gun brought up by Doug and Terry is here supported by (left to right) David, Geoff, Mike Hicks of the 'Sea King' and Doug

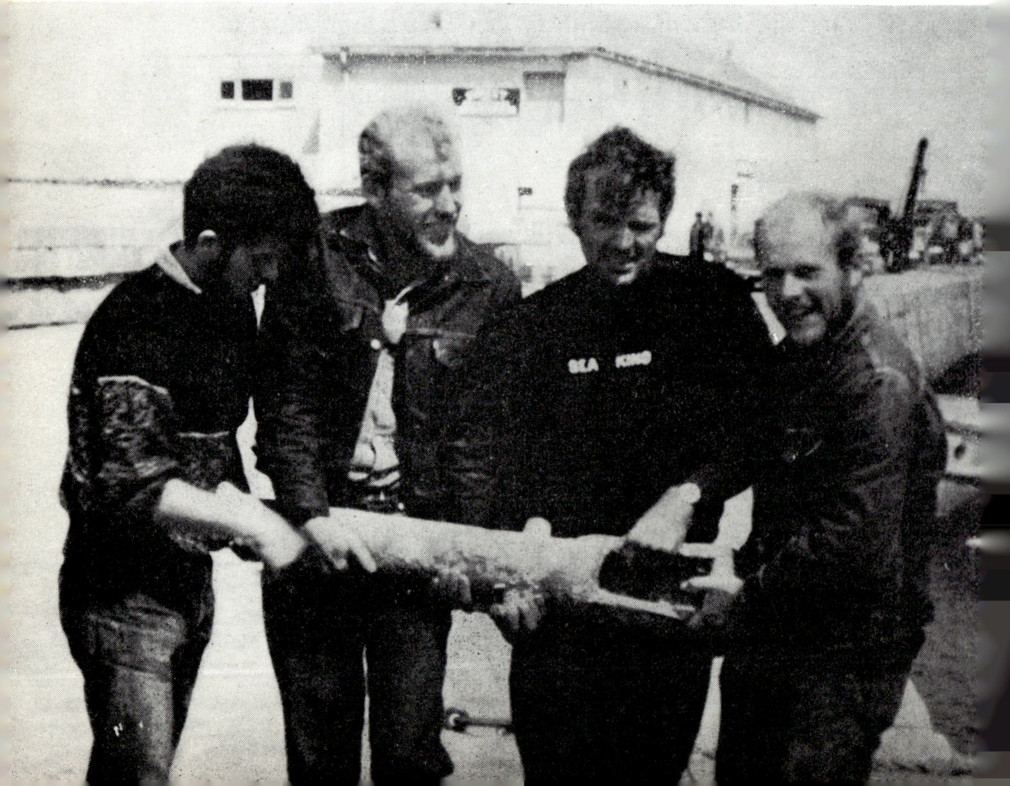

After the twenty-minute spell below all four divers rendezvoused on board the launch. They were diving at between seventy and eighty feet so should have taken some seven minutes to ascend. Doug sorted out his blasting wires, he held these in his hand as he looked slowly and carefully about him at the barren seascape:

'Good heavens,' he said, in mock surprise, 'we've got the place to ourselves. Where is everyone?'

Someone fetched the battery, Doug pressed the wires to its terminals and down in the depths a chunk of granite became dislodged by remote control. There was speculation aboard *Sea King* as Mike Reynolds, Mike and Alf Hicks and I saw the four divers go down once more; especially so as Geoff came up requesting an air-bag. These bags are of canvas and are about the size of a sailor's kit-bag; they are used when the diver has found something beyond his capabilities to lift. He attaches the air-bag to the object, takes his demand valve from his mouth (underwater) and with this fills the bag with air. Doug and Terry had taken a bag with them as they fully expected to bring up the small bronze breech-loading gun. They, and we, were not disappointed, for within a matter of minutes they had surfaced with the bloated-looking bag bobbing up between them. They held up their thumbs as a gesture of success; we threw them a rope and hauled the bag, gun and all, into the launch. It was a splendid little object, it was in good condition and had, under its sea growth, signs of a crest surmounted by a crown. It was about three-and-a-half feet long and weighty enough for a man to have difficulty in lifting waist-high.

Within minutes—once again—the other bag plopped to the surface; this time Geoff and David had brought up a big bronze sheave—or pulley wheel—such as we had seen in the Customs shed. It was stamped on its centre boss with the mark of the Broad Arrow. This was indeed satisfactory, proof was building up that the remains of the ship we were working on was British, and the more proof we had of this kind, the better. The remainder of the diving time was spent in further clearance of the big bronze guns. Then we hied for home. We reached St. Mary's at 10 a.m. and by the time we had landed our air bottles, and our prizes, the holidaymakers were thronging the pier for their launches. After the launches had gone their respective ways there came walking along the quay a

Bronze pulley wheel, or rigging block sheave, showing British Naval mark of the Broad Arrow: sea growth was cleaned from the marks with acid

figure in open-necked shirt, slacks and open sandals; he carried a haversack and smoked a pipe; as befits a man who holidays in Scilly, he was healthily sun-bronzed. I went over to him:

'Excuse me, Mr. Prime Minister, sir, would you care to have a look at our finds?'

'Gladly!' said Mr. Harold Wilson, for he it was. 'Ah, you have a breech-loader, I see. Yes, they had a lot of trouble with those; you know, I believe they were only in use for a few years.'

Mr. Wilson spoke knowledgeably of old-time cannon; he wished us every success in our venture.

That afternoon I visited the Island Museum. There, displayed in the marine section, is a silver spoon. It is reputed to have come from Sir Cloudesley Shovell's personal plate. In the Islands there are several such items of silver, some of these bear Sir Cloudesley's crest; because they think the Receiver may take possession of these articles the owners refuse to bring them to light. The story of the silver plate is interesting; my search took me to several localities. I met several charming people, but I was allowed to photograph only one of the silver items I saw.

My investigations led me back to the year 1875 and the loss, in May of that year, of the German mail steamship *Schiller*. This great vessel—of steam and sail—which was on her way from New York to Plymouth, struck the Retarrier Reef which is close to, but inside of, the Bishop Light. It was a fog-bound night, the vessel sank almost immediately; only forty-five of the 354 persons on board were saved.

Some years later, hard-top salvage divers worked at the scene of the *Schiller* wreck. During their investigations of the reef they came across a small cache of silver plate some of which bore the crest and name of Sir Cloudesley Shovell. A quantity of the silverware was disposed of to interested Scillonians.

Now, the Retarrier Ledges are nor'west by nor' of the Gilstone; they lie a little over halfway between the Gilstone and the Bishop Light. The question is: if Sir Cloudesley's flagship was lost at the Gilstone how did the silver plate come to be found on the Retarrier? Records show that one of the Admiral's squadron, the *Romney*, was to the nor'ard of the *Association* at the time of shipwreck. My invaluable old-time chart gives the wreck of the *Romney* to be on the 'Creebennack', which is shown as just to the south of the 'Bishop and Clarks'—the Bishop Light of today. So the records and the chart agree; let us assume, then, that the *Romney* indeed foundered on the Crebinicks, as it is now spelt. This vessel could possibly have been carrying some portion of Sir Cloudesley's treasure; it is feasible indeed that the Admiral had prudently divided his personal wealth between this vessel and his own; this was very often done on sea voyages. In the course of breaking up, the *Romney* could very well have spilled out her crates, or chests, of silver plate; with the prevailing west and sou'west winds these would drive towards the Retarrier Ledges, which are due east of the Crebinicks. Even if some of these crates survived the Retarrier they would have carried on in a straight line, due east, and finally landed up at *Silver*

Carn; for the Crebinicks, the Retarrier and Silver Carn indeed stretch in a straight line—east and west. These three intriguing spots are just crying out to be explored by treasure-seeking divers, and when we have the time we shall certainly have a go.

Many years ago I met an old man on the Island of Bryher. He sold me a washbasin that had been cast up from the *Schiller* wreck, it is old-fashioned and encased with teak—'tick-wood' the old man said—and in the glaze of the basin insignia can be seen depicting an eagle with wings outspread; in a circle round the bird are the words 'DEUTSCHE TRANS-ATLANTISCHE DAMPFSCHIFFAHRTS GESELLSCHAFT'. The old man told me a story of the many bodies that had come from it at that time of the disaster:

'I mind,' he said, 'we ran through the pockets of the drowned—you know—just like you would, and we come upon some interesting articles. A friend of mine was walking around for ever so many months with a little gold tube fixed to his watch chain. It had two little knobs on it and no-one could get to know what it was for. He would not let anyone see or touch it—no, nor go near it. Until one day he got so drunk he showed it to us. Seems it were a little machine for putting holes in cigars; you pressed the two little knobs and out poked a silver knife. He got it off some gent that was washed ashore somewhere to the back of the island.'

As rough seas and high sou'westerly winds kept us from diving at the Western Rocks, we decided to go 'wrecking' in the shelter and calm waters of the Eastern Isles. Doug had a diving job to do on a wreck just east of St. Martin's, so we followed the *Girl Sharon* out into St. Mary's Sound in the storm-boat. Out through Crow sound we went with Geoff and David kitting up *en route*. Soon the great rock of Hanjague (pronounced on St. Martin's as Ann Jigg) came into view, our venue was just to the north of this. Here in 1856, on the Hard Lewis rocks, the sailing vessel *Chieftain* was lost; this is probably the only surviving timber wreck to be found at the Scillies. I wanted some pieces of her worm-riddled timbers for the Admiral Benbow. The divers excelled themselves; not only did they recover splendid chunks of timber, sea-worn and driven through with solid copper bolts, they found a great bronze rudder pintle to boot. The figure-head of this fine vessel, a bust of a Highland chieftain, can be seen in the

Valhalla at Tresco Island. Here also are some of the finest figureheads in the world; Valhalla is a building specially constructed and prepared for the preservation of these beautiful ornamental carvings by Augustus Smith, in about 1860, and what finer task could a man have set himself than this? An autocrat, but a benevolent one, Augustus Smith was the first of the emperor lessees of the Islands. He found the islanders a half-starved race of smugglers and kelp-burners, but by the time of his death in 1872 they were a prosperous, thriving community.

On the way back to St. Martin's, with time to spare, we went in search of the wreck of the *Little Western.* This small Scillonian vessel of steam and sail went ashore many years ago on the Southern Wells. In this same region the *Collossus* had foundered in 1798—some of the great guns of this latter vessel today serve as bollards on St. Mary's quay. Diving to the south of the Island of Samson, amid the thick kelp that flourishes there, Geoff and David quickly came upon the weed-encrusted boiler of the *Little Western.* With very little effort and a lot of luck they managed to recover a bronze valve part as a souvenir. But by now the weather had deteriorated, the sun had gone, the wind had increased, the rain came down in sheets.

Fine weather was in the offing, however; we knew that the Fleet Air Arm Sub Aqua Club members were due to arrive in two or three days; the Scillonian boatmen swore that these divers were blessed with fine weather, so maybe they would bring a spell of calm seas with them—and as luck would have it they did.

Three days before the Air Arm boys arrived the trawler *Ros Guill* hove over the horizon. She was a welcome sight; now we could get down to some really serious salvage work, after the frustration, and bad weather, of the past two weeks.

8

THE LORD HIGH ADMIRAL'S CANNON

The trawler *Ros Guill* was reputed to be a lucky boat. It is said that she once sailed into the fishing port of Mevagissey with the largest catch of sprats ever.

'Another couple o' sprats, boy, and she would 'ave gone undar!'

If she was a lucky fishing boat, then the luck stayed with her in fishing for treasure. So lucky was she, and such a good worker, that at the end of her charter period I could not let her go; I bought her—lock, stock and fish barrels.

It was not the trawler's fault that she missed out on the first task we gave her; we had one or two temporary people helping us, they would have been better off tailoring rather than salvaging.

Our immediate and urgent task was to recover those two fine bronze guns that lay, ready and waiting to be lifted, at twelve fathoms down. So obscure are the laws of salvage in this country that, although we had prepared those guns for recovery, had spent time and money on them, in our absence anyone could go along and lift them provided they had fine weather and the right equipment. The *Regency* people I was not worried too much about, but I knew the Air Arm divers had expensive buoyancy bags capable of lifting fairly hefty weights. For instance, if they had a buoyancy bag measuring fifteen feet by four feet this would be capable of a lift of just over five tons. So it behoved us to recover at least one gun before the Navy arrived.

As is usual with this class of vessel, the trawler was fitted with a powerful winch driven from the main engine. But a winch is only as capable as its flexible steel-wire rope. So new wire ropes were purchased to be on the safe side; not everyone knows how to handle wire rope; never must a coil of wire be laid on the ground and the end drawn away from it, kinks will result and the rope will be completely spoiled. One of the correct ways to uncoil a wire is to roll the coil along the ground, allowing the wire to lead off in a straight non-kinking length.

We set off on our maiden trip in the *Ros Guill* with everyone on board in high spirits, but my spirits would have been considerably depressed had I known that our new winch wire was full of hidden twists and turns. It was my fault, I should have been on hand when it had been installed.

It was great to feel the trawler wallowing along beneath our feet; what we on the top-sides had lacked so far was action. We had been well equipped with lifting bags and gadgets of all kinds, but the rough seas, to date, had deprived us of the use of these. Just imagine trying to sink a forty-five-gallon drum in a rough sea; it flings itself about like a mad thing and when it is half full of water it can crack the side of a boat like an egg. I have lifted anything from small boats to giant engine crankshafts with the aid of massed drums—one drum will lift about four hundredweight—but one has to have the right sea conditions in which to operate.

The *Ros Guill* was small enough to get right over the *Association* wreck, her powerful winch would thus be able to take a direct lift over the three-ton cannon. Even with this method there were snags; the trawler would have to be handled expertly by one competent enough to put her in the middle of the rock and its two ledges; with the tides running as they do there this would be tricky—a job for Mike Hicks, of course. Lifting by wire, with a sea running, can be dangerous; with a boat rising and falling several feet it can be imagined there may well be the danger of a terrible 'snatch' or jerk.

Everything went well to start with; the trawler was brought up to her moorings in masterly fashion, with Mike bulging out of the small wheelhouse window, issuing orders to all and sundry as befits a pilot and skipper. The trawler's charter skipper was Dave Hooper, he was to be winchman, and a very good hand at this he proved to be. Our engineer, with us for a while on a working holiday, was Brian Pellow.

Although our Number One bronze gun was clear of iron cannon, it was still 'stuck' to the rocks by sea growth; it would need all the lift we could give it. Consequently we decided to use a double purchase on the lifting wire. The wire rope from the winch was rove through the hawse pipe (well greased), down through a snatch block attached to the submerged gun, and up to the stem of the trawler. The sea, as usual, was rough, but by expert handling of the winch a strain was put on the wire; the winch started to haul in slowly and steadily. Geoff and David were below, watching for snags, and all too soon they appeared. Just as when a receiver is replaced on a telephone and the loop of twisted wire curls up on itself like a snake, so our bight of wire looping down into the sea was doing the same. The more strain that was put on it by the winch, the more it twisted round itself; this was entirely due to the mishandling of the new wire when it was first uncoiled. With the gun halfway to the surface, the strain on the wire became intolerable, it began to smoke at the hawse; with this, and the snatch caused by the considerable swell running at the time, the wire parted with a resounding crack.

The gear was overhauled, and a second attempt was made, but with the same result, the wire could not withstand the strain. The breaking strain of that Extra Flexible one-and-three-quarter-inch Steel Wire was ten tons. There was nothing else for it, we would have to reeve a new wire, we were lucky to have a spare one aboard. But fitting a new wire was not all that simple. Many things had happened at one time; the old wire was jammed in the submerged snatch block and could not be freed; the block could not be taken off the gun because the shackle pin had also jammed. So a new block, a new strop and so on had to be rigged. This all took time, and the divers' energy. Meanwhile, we on deck were uncoiling the second new wire, this time in the approved fashion. At long last everything was ready for another lift.

It seemed that the winch had been turning for but a few

seconds when I noticed a whiff of smoke coming from the wire where it rounded at the hawse:

'Woah!' I shouted. 'Keep her there!'

Dave, at the winch, belayed his wire; the divers came up to say the gun was lying horizontal, about twelve to fifteen feet below the surface.

'Then that's where she stays!' said I; it would have been foolish to have risked a further lift. Nylon safety strops were attached to the gun, in case the wire parted, and also to prevent it swinging on the journey back.

We could just make it out down there in the depths—a green dull shape, deformed and contorted by the movement of the sea. It writhed sinuously in the grasp of the wire rope like some tethered monster of the deep.

Wearily we looked at each other with half-smiles on our faces. What a task it had been! There is nothing more exhausting than working with wire and equipment on a boat that is leaping about in a savage sea. On top of that, just about everything had gone wrong; no one spoke, we just stood at the bow of the trawler and looked down at the shape in the water. Weary or not, what a wonderful warm sense of achievement it gave just to know that after a hard tussle we had captured that shadowy blob down there. The divers were jubilant—they were better aquainted with the prize than we. I do not smoke, but this is the time when one wishes one did; everyone lit a cigarette (with the exception of Doug and Mike Hicks, who also do not indulge) and their cigarettes seemed to add so much to their appreciation of the moment.

We were all brought back to our senses by a shout from the wheelhouse:

'Am I all clear to come ahead?'

It was Mike. He had a particularly trying navigational problem ahead of him. Taking the draught of the gun into consideration he would want eighteen feet of water wherever he went, and that depth of water in the Scillies is a lot. On the consequently slow journey back to St. Mary's we brewed coffee, or was it tea? For now we boasted a galley; I raised my chipped mug:

'Here's to the next one!' said I

'Here's to the next two!' Doug said, enthusiastically.

And, at that remark, I had a fleeting moment of doubt—should I carry on? I had realised a life's ambition, to recover from the sea a gold coin and a magnificent bronze gun, why not stop at that? I looked about me, undecided, as the trawler chuffed her steady, winding way through the rocks and islets. I looked at the deck cluttered with an entanglement of ropes, and all the hotchpotch of salvage equipment. I looked at the sea flowing past the side of the vessel—like green syrup, and astern, at the wide bubbling wake the beamy vessel had ploughed for herself. I looked at Annet as we swam past in the now sheltered water, an island aglow with sea-pinks. The sun, coming down over Samson, was paving the way for its usual evening spectacular. My thoughts swung back to the shape under our bow, it seemed unbelievable that we were in the process of returning that gun to the world of man, to the light of day. The sea had taken so much in the past, it was incredibly satisfying to be instrumental in wrenching something back from its clutches.

I reached for the enormous, chipped, brown enamel teapot, I poured myself another mug of piping hot liquid:

'All right! Here's to the next two!' I said—to myself, actually—for everyone was busy, preparing to enter harbour.

The quay was agog with people. From where we were, down below, the pier seemed to be lined by an elongated monster with a multi-coloured body supported on hundreds of bare brown legs. As we came alongside we could see that we were the centre of the crowd's interest; word had got around that we were expecting to recover a gun. We should have looked pretty foolish if we had returned empty-handed! Now I am sure we all put on an air of knowing a thing or two—of being up to snuff, not to be caught with chaff—sort of thing. We had an audience, so we went about the task of unloading that gun with just the right touch of sang-froid that seemed applicable. This was the first time in our lives that a bronze gun had come our way, we must not appear bowled over by the event. We would have loved to have shouted and to have waved flags, but that would never have done; we mastered our feelings—we went about our work with a staidness and a sobriety that would have done justice to any old-time Quaker. Our audience was quietly expectant, so were we—outwardly, but inwardly we were exultant.

In silence we tied up alongside the quay in way of the ancient crane that was to be such a good servant to us. With his rounding cheeks flushed, the immortal half-inch of cigarette

between his podgy lips, Dave stood solemnly at the winch. Several of the crew scrambled up on the quay to man the crane, which was provided with a hand windlass. Doug had stayed kitted up in his diving outfit, he it was who went overside to attend to the underwater work. I went aboard the storm-boat so as to be able to take close-up shots of the dramatic surfacing of the gun. After the nylon strops had been cast off, Dave lowered the gun to the harbour bed. Here Doug replaced the winch wire with the swivel hook of the crane. Now came two orders in quick succession:

'Take up the slack!' And then, 'Haul away!'

The layshaft of the crane's windlass was slid into low gear, two men flayed their arms round in exhausting circles as they wound at the cranked handles; the exposed sprockets and gear-wheels gnashed their sticky black-oily teeth; as it felt the strain the ancient crane nodded its black jib, as if offering up some incantation of its own, and no wonder, it was lifting over three tons.

The first object to break surface was Doug's head. He was standing upright on the gun, holding on to the taut wire of the crane. Steadily, slowly, ever so slowly, in complete silence except for the 'clack'-'clack' of the windlass pawl, Doug rose out of the water. Then a few feet away from him there appeared the gun's muzzle. It sparkled gold and green with spots of red in the light coating of sea-growth. Now the rising gun was showing more and more of its length, presently Doug's blue flippers came into view, then the bulging breech of the gun. At that the spell of silence was broken, for those on the very edge of the quay began to laugh; the partly up-ended gun was full of water, from its ornamental touch-hole there came spilling out a curved stream. In all honesty I must say it brought to mind that little boy in Brussels!

Higher and higher went the gun, high enough to be swung round on to the quay; then, at the request of many photographers in the watching crowd, even higher again. As it swung there over the people's heads, as we looked at it admiringly, someone started to clap; this was taken up by the whole crowd.

The *Cornishman* had this to say of our day's work:

'Although Mr. Morris was sure his team and the Fleet Air Arm divers, expected soon at the Isles of Scilly, could both work at the Western Rocks without conflict, he was anxious to recover at least one of the cannon before the large Services expedition arrived. They succeeded with one day to spare in spite of sea conditions which Mr. Morris described as frightful and not really fit for diving.

'The trawler's skipper Mr. D. Hooper, said that there was a 15 ft. swell close to the Gilstone Ledges and it was so difficult standing on deck that the divers found it hard to get into their frogmen's suits. For most of the time Scillonian Mr. Michael Hicks was at the wheel. Twice the cannon was winched to the surface and on each occasion the hawser broke and it sank to the bottom again. The third time the cannon was only raised to within 18 ft. of the surface and it was towed to St. Mary's—an extremely tricky operation. Shortly after 7.0 p.m. the cannon was winched out of the water and on to St. Mary's quay.

'The cannon weighing two tons, 18 cwt., was seen to be

OPPOSITE ABOVE *Higher and higher went the gun* BELOW *High enough to be swung round on to the quay*

ROS GUILL
ROS GUILL
FY428

ROS GUILL

We must not appear to be bowled over: (from left to right) Geoff and Doug, divers; Dave, the winchman; Urst Burkhard, a friend; myself in striped shirt; Mike the boatman; Mike Hicks, pilot; and Terry, diver

very similar to the one raised by the Fleet Air Arm divers six weeks ago. It had the same embossed decorations of fleurs-de-lis, a crest, crossed anchors and a crown, and dolphin lifting handles. A feature which was not noticed on the first cannon was a lizard close to the muzzle. Instead of the name, "Le Duc de Beaufort" the second cannon is embossed "Le Comte de Vermandois".'

For once we had arrived back in good time for an evening meal—it is a lucky person who can obtain a meal after 9 p.m. at the Scillies. So, after a quick wash and change, we were all sitting down to a champagne dinner. In a bantering, good-humoured way, everyone blamed everyone else for the mishaps of the day. But our troubles were over, I said, what we wanted was a good snatch block below and a very good block at the bow of the trawler (running a wire through the hawse is suicidal for the wire) and I knew where I could get the very things—they were hanging up as part of the décor at the Admiral Benbow. The bronze gun was a gem, it being in perfect condition. The two lifting eyes, formed by two gam-

After cleaning in the Benbow workshops, Gun Number One, as it would appear when mounted on its carriage. The wide-angle lens used gives some distortion

bolling dolphins, were superb. The gun was nine feet six inches long, fleurs-de-lis decorated its chase and the same motif was used where the barrel swells at the first and second reinforce. These guns were cast in honour of well-known personages, this one bearing the name of Le Comte de Vermandois. The Count was born in 1667 as Louis de Bourbon, and was an illegitimate son of Louise de la Vallière, one of Louis XIV's earlier mistresses. At the age of two the baby was created Lord High Admiral, this was in 1669. It was common practice for Louis XIV to give high appointments to his illegitimate children. The boy Count had a short life, he died when he was sixteen, unmarried and with no successor; it does not seem that the title was given to any other member of the Royal Family at a later date.

It is almost certain that the gun was forged in Le Havre. Cast in the swell of the muzzle is the figure of a lizard, the raised diamond-shaped head of which actually forms a 'sight' for the gunlayer. The 'lizard' could well be a salamander, for Le Havre's coat of arms includes this little animal that is supposed to live in fire. Le Havre and its harbour was named and created by Francis I, whose badge was a salamander.

From where could these French culverines have come? How came they to be aboard the *Association*? At the moment it can only be a matter for speculation; further research, however, may bring fresh information to light, clues are probably abounding if only one had the time to search them

OPPOSITE ABOVE *The dolphin lifting eyes: when raised by these the gun hangs perfectly horizontally. Resting on its trunnions, of course, the cannon would be heavier at the breech end.*
BELOW *Gun Number One bore the name of Le Comte de Vermandois, the little illegitimate son of Louise de la Vallière, mistress of Louis XIV. The raised portion of the fleur-de-lis, surmounting the crown, served as a back-sight for the gun-layer.*
ABOVE *Polishing and burnishing reveal the hand-tooling marks made by the old-time ordnance workers*

The salamander sight on the muzzle

out. For instance, this is what I found in Vol. 1 of *The Byng Papers*—it is a letter from Sir Cloudesley Shovell and is dated aboard the *Association*, Lisbon River, March 28th, 1707: '. . . *and whereas there was brought out of England with Sir Thomas Dilkes on the ships in the margin a considerable quantity of Tin in cask, each cask containing four hundredweights, shipped by directions of the Lord High Treasurer for Her Majesty's account in order to be carried for Italy, which Tin you were directed to cause to be taken on board the ships of the Squadron going with you, and to send to Italy in the ships you are to send thither, all,*

The ornate decoration of the breech

The crowned monogram among the fleurs-de-lis on the barrel

or so much of it, as you should think proper. You are to order about 40 tons of it to Genoa to be delivered to Messrs. Boissiers & Partners, and the rest to Leghorn to be delivered to Messrs. Arundell & Bates and receipts to be taken as you have been before directed.

'And whereas Her Majesty has commanded that what guns the Duke of Savoy should think proper for executing the design and project should be furnished from the Fleet. I have written to Mr. Stanhope to borrow, if possible, 20 brass 24pdr. guns with the carriages from His Catholic Majesty, you are to inform yourself wither the said guns can be had, and where, and give such proper directions as you shall think fit for taking them on board the ships of your Squadron, or the transports of the Fleet . . .'

In *The Royal Navy*, a history by Laird Clowes, Vol. 2, 1603–1714, can be found an account of the action in Vigo Bay in which Sir Cloudesley took an active part:

'In 1702 an English and Dutch combined fleet totally destroyed a French-Spanish Fleet of 21 ships and captured or destroyed 17 Galleons. The date was October 12th. Of the 17 Galleons 4 were captured by the English, 5 by the Dutch, 2 went ashore and 6 were burnt. The treasure and booty were of enormous value, the flotilla of Galleons having been the richest ever to have reached Europe from the West Indies. Some of the lading had been removed, but it was estimated that Gold, Silver and Cargo to the value of 13,000,000 pieces of eight fell into the hands of the victors or were destroyed. Most of the French Officers and men got ashore but 400 people fell into the hands of the victors including—The Marquis de la Galissioniere, the Spanish Admiral Don Jose Checon, the Captain of the 'Assuré' and the Captain of the 'Voluntaire'.

'On October 19th 1702 Rooke sailed for England leaving Sir Cloudesley Shovell to refit the prizes and save as much treasure and as many guns as possible. He sailed on October 26th, having completed the destruction of such vessels as could not be moved. At the same time he effected an exchange of prisoners. The passage home was a stormy one, and the fleet was dispersed, yet the whole of it, except a prize galleon and a French vessel which had been taken at sea by the 'Nassau', ultimately reached port in safety.'

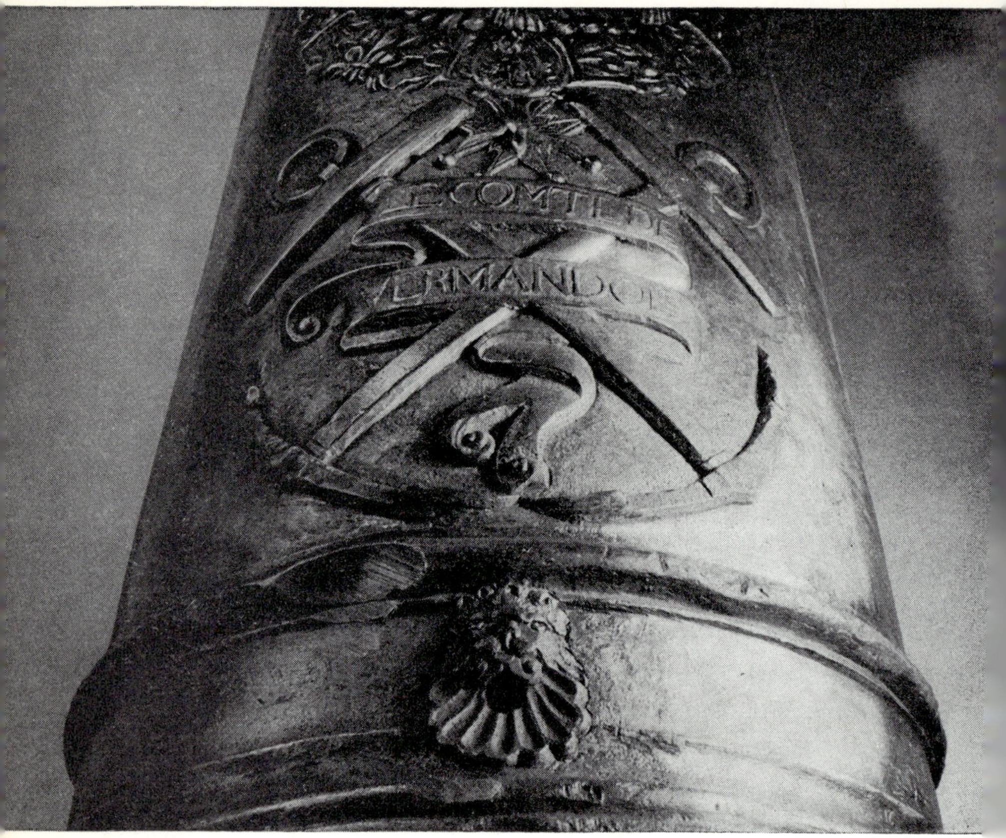

The scar to the left of the vent, or touch-hole, could very well have been made by a round shot during battle. The coppery colour of the metal at the breech end of the gun is a sign of extensive use

It is interesting to note the names of the casualties of the Franco-Spanish squadron. Who knows? one of these names may appear on a gun recovered at the Gilstone or elsewhere in the Scillies. The following ships were captured by the English and brought home: *Prompt* (76 guns), *Assuré* (66), *Ferme* (72), *Modéré* (56) and *Triton* (42). Those taken, looted of their armaments, and destroyed included: *Espérance* (70), *Sirène* (60), *Superbe* (70), *Volontaire* (46), *Jesus Maria José* (70), *Bufona* (54) and *Capitana de Assogeo*. Many ships were completely burnt or cast ashore and it is doubtful if anything in the way of guns, or the like, would have been taken from them. These were: *Forte* (70), *Solide* (50), *Prudent* (60), *Oriflamme* (64), *Dauphin* (40), *Entreprenant* (22), *Choquant* (8) and *Favori* (fireship).

It was common practice for the French to impress on the outer face of their gun's trunnions the weight of the gun, together with the names of the various ships on which the gun had been mounted. Unfortunately, in shipwreck, the outer face of the trunnion is the most vulnerable place for abrasions.

The day following the raising of our bronze gun Number One the members of the Sub Aqua Clubs of the Fleet Air Arm arrived in force. They brought with them two Naval craft, the XSVs *Odiham* and *Shipham*. The presence of these two smart vessels, with their continuously running generators, added to that of the lurking shape of the *Regency*, made our little trawler look very gimcrack and insignificant. But we were in no wise depressed or overawed by the vast amount of equipment and the numbers of divers these vessels boasted. None of these craft was so admirably suited for the job in hand as the small, beamy, canoe-sterned *Ros Guill*.

On that day, also, there arrived by helicopter our two vital pulley blocks, two powerful brass-sheaved blocks that had been cast ashore in the 1963 wreck of the *Juan Ferrer*; these had been on view as souvenirs in the Admiral Benbow ever since. One of these blocks was lashed to the bow of the trawler; here it was utilised as a bow roller and very satisfactorily, too, for in the next few days it was going to withstand a direct lift of nearly five tons.

But prior to that we tackled the bronze gun Number Two. The recovery of that gun went like a dream; not only did everything go swimmingly for the divers, it was a picnic on top-sides for us; we had time to catch our lunch, clean it (much to the delight of the kittiwakes), fry it and eat it—to tell truth we were eating our mackerel within twenty minutes of its being taken from the sea—and if that does not give a man 'heart' to carry on I do not know what does.

The winch turned over without effort, the wire rolled in like silk. The divers reported the gun suspended about halfway to the surface—'a fantastic sight', they said. Having hooked our quarry so easily, it was a pity to press our luck while we were over deep water. Consequently we made for the shallows and sandy bottom just east of Rosevean—

between that small islet and the Rags. Here, out of the wind, in the clear tranquil waters of Broad Neck, with the gulls swooping and protesting, we lowered the gun to the bottom. While it was resting there on the sand Doug took some underwater flash photographs; with the sun filtering down through the green water plus the reflection from the white sand there was ten times more light there than at the Gilstone; the photos came out well, for underwater colour photography needs plenty of light.

With an extra strop on it for safety, the gun was again lifted, this time in ideal conditions, it came up just awash. Lashing it so that it would not damage the boat was a matter of minutes. We came back in grand style.

Our landing of the first gun could have been a dress rehearsal for the handling of the second. For there were the same milling crowds, the same crash of camera shutters as the gun left the water. For the holidaymakers we had performed a belated encore. Instead of one gun lying on St. Mary's pier now there were twins, and they were identical, though I fancy gun Number One was the better-looking. The raising of our second gun called for yet another champagne supper. By the time the last drops were shaken from the last magnum we were cock-a-hoop, I remember walking out under a triumphal arch of empties. Had we known that our third cannon was to be up high and dry within a matter of three short days, we should probably have gone out and roasted an ox!

A quote from the *Cornishman*, our local paper, said:

'The *Ros Guill* sailed into St. Mary's with yet another 9½ ft. cannon. Mr. Morris described the conditions as the most favourable they had experienced in their five weeks at Scilly. The cannon was towed to a sheltered place close to Rosevean island, raised to the surface and lashed to the trawler's bows. Decomposing iron cannon had to be carefully blasted away in order to free the cannon. Because of this, the iron cannon is not in such good condition as the other two. A fourth cannon is buried under about 25 tons of rock.

'The original cannon raised by the Service divers, which has been insured for £30,000 and about which 800 Scillonians and their visitors signed a petition to keep in the islands, is now on show to the public at the Tower of London. It is still officially in the custody of the Receiver of Wreck at

St. Mary's presumably being on loan according to instructions from the Board of Trade.'

This gun, which the newspaper article mentions, was the one we had seen in the Customs shed on our arrival at Scilly. It was insured by a television company for the enormous sum of £30,000, surely as a gesture only; it was then the only one of its kind in the world, its value could have been 'beyond price'.

I was amused to overhear two Scillonians discussing this very point:

'How'd they come to price that cannon at thirty thousand pounds? Doesn't make sense to me!'

'Well, I don't know—I'd reckon that's about what it cost the Navy to get her outa the water!'

9

CAPTURED—ONE BRONZE PROPELLER

Not long after we had arrived at the Scillies there occurred an event which sent the Island's inhabitants agog with excitement; this was the long-awaited Royal Visit of H.M. the Queen and H.R.H. Prince Philip, accompanied by Prince Charles and Princess Anne. It was the first time in sixty-five years that the reigning monarch had visited the Islands, the last occasion being the visit of King Edward VII in 1902. Prince Charles, being Duke of Cornwall, is of course landlord of the Islands. The Royal Family travelled to Scilly in the yacht *Britannia,* which anchored in St. Mary's roadstead. In the brilliant sunshine this vessel made a proud show, the strong westerly winds ironing out her masthead flags as flat as flukes; at her mainmast the Royal Standard, at her foremast the Lord High Admiral's flag—a golden anchor on a red background—at her mizzen the Union Flag. During the Royal Party's inspection of the figureheads at Valhalla, the Duke of Edinburgh was heard to say:

'It just shows how efficient they were at wrecking in those days.'

Many of the Press reporters, sent to the Islands to cover the Royal Visit, stayed on to follow the treasure hunt. Things were a little slow for them during the period of rough seas, but now that the Navy had arrived they fully expected dissension among the diving teams. But we had no crow to pluck, we wanted no feud or faction, we were the 'local boys', we were in our own territory. On 14th August 1967 *The Times* said:

'There are treasure hunters eager to impress Mr. Wilson with their skill and ingenuity; a rumour that only the most qualified team will be allowed to continue diving on the supposed wreck of the man-o'-war *Association*, has made impressing everyone imperative.'

In the same article the writer goes on to say:

'Four groups of hunters are involved: Naval Air Command divers who found the wreck about six weeks ago, two teams of professional divers and a sub-aqua club from Birmingham, who flit in and out of the scene like a group of rubber-clad black and yellow Pimpernels. The most successful team, it would seem, is one led by Mr. Roland Morris, a wiry, tanned gentleman who owns one of Penzance's most famous restaurants, the Admiral Benbow, bought from his earnings as a professional diver around the Cornish Coasts.'

One ever-hopeful London 'daily' representative stated:

'On shore, animosity between teams is confined to different drinking venues, and the occasional remark about the others trespassing.'

Captain Sutton of the *Regency* is alleged to have said, according to one news item: ' "The first finders of an archaeological wreck had to show that they were not going to destroy its historic value. If they could not prove that, it was up to somebody else to show that it could be done." ' My reaction to this remark was that it must have been made before that fully experienced diver, Cap'n Bill Sutton, had seen the seabed at the Gilstone.

Cap'n Sutton is alleged to have said also—according to another quote—' "Of course we are in it for the profit, but we intend to do it archaeologically—in a way that makes sense—and not by grabbing things up; I am absolutely against the use of explosive charges. The bullion added a spice to the thing. Everyone dreams of buried treasure and that sort of jazz." '

One newspaper article quoted Mr. George Naish, deputy keeper of the National Maritime Museum, as being concerned about the activities of 'treasure-seeking divers', some of them prepared to use explosives. ' "They will cause irreparable damage to wrecks of great historical interest," he said. "In the Mediterranean", he went on to explain, "old wrecks are fully protected but in British waters only ordinary salvage laws apply." '

To compare Cornish underwater conditions to those of the Med is typical of the illusionary pictures of diving conjured up by many people.

'Have you broken into her after-cabin yet?'

I was asked this question by a holidaymaker in the main street of Hugh Town on St. Mary's Island. The gentleman, who was from the Midlands, listened gravely as I attempted to explain that there was no shape of a wreck, no semblance of a ship; in fact, I said, an amateur diver could swim over the site and not be aware that a ship had foundered there.

'It's like searching through the debris after a house has been burnt down,' I said.

'Under the sea?' asked the gentleman. He put on his spectacles and peered at me closely.

'Yes, well, sort of—only in this case it's not a fire but the sea that's done the damage; the currents you know.'

The gentleman replaced his spectacles in their case: 'You must all be bloomin' mad!' he said, as he walked away.

As far as the Press coverage of the treasure hunt was concerned the situation was now becoming farcical. The reporters, kept on at the Islands by their editors, just had to turn out an article at regular intervals. The story of the Shovell Squadron and the mess its officers made of the navigation of their ships on the simple voyage from the Med to the Western Approaches was splashed far and wide. The life and doings of Sir Cloudesley were there for all to read, but the readers were getting a little tired of this.

Subtly, then, the correspondents started reporting not what they themselves thought of the situation, but what others were saying about us—what the Scillonians, for instance, thought about our 'carryings on'. One fisherman—who on earth could it have been?—is quoted as saying:

'Well, up to now they've been diving first come first served sort of thing, but what'll happen when they all gets out there at one time is something more than I dare venture to say!' Shades of ramming on the high seas! Of underwater fisticuffs! Of cut pipelines and of divers surreptitiously hacking holes in their rivals' rubber dinghies!

But, sure enough, as the weather improved, as the times of the tides became more favourable, there did come the day when the Navy, the *Regency* men and we were all at the Gilstone together. It was a hazy, misty day; all that morning the television men had been loading up their launches with equipment. They need not have bothered with some of the most complicated of this, they said it failed at the crucial moment. Photographers by the score, pressmen by the dozen. One good feature came out of it, the Scillonian boatmen reaped a bonanza.

We had operation 'Bronze Gun Number Three' on our hands; this was a complicated salvage job which needed all our attention. The gun was trapped by one enormous rock and several smaller ones. This day we concentrated on the lesser rocks. We were placing strops round them and then winching them clear; once lifted we would steam off a short distance and then lower them. I hope we did not upset anyone's survey plans! We carried out these tricky little manœuvres in a lively sea and to the accompaniment of a hubbub which I can only compare to that of a power-boat race on the Seine. Boats loaded with set-faced men in tweed coats and odd-shaped hats zoomed past us. They were all looking at us through some kind of expensive equipment or other. We looked at them sorrowfully. Why could they not go away and leave us to our work? They in their turn looked sorrowfully back at us; what a scoop they would have got had we been seen wrangling and bawling with each other! We must have appeared quite the most docile treasure hunters they had ever seen. Come to that, as no treasure has yet been brought up on an English coast, this must have been their first experience of a treasure dive. No wonder, then, they did not know how to handle the situation. Why could they not have reported the truth—the rough seas, the deadly nature of the place, the bravery and skill of the divers? Why did they have to give the public the impression that we were rampaging through an underwater vessel of priceless antiquity, blasting out the most valuable articles in a quick, money-making, plundering raid? Would anyone in his right senses do such a thing? According to one or two of our newspapers, he would.

We were not dealing with a wreck like that of Sweden's *Vasa*, which remained very nearly intact for 330 years at the bottom of Stockholm harbour. The thick mud had held and

Pottery fragments from the 'Association' in all colours and glazes

preserved her until May 1961, when she was raised and towed into dry dock. But at the *Association* 'wreck' site we have the last pitiful remains of a fine ship scattered over the very worst kind of sea-bed—of moving, pounding rock. Most of the timber, glass, pottery and leather we were to find had been diced into smaller pieces than the top of a tea-cup. What artefacts we were to recover were damaged in nine cases out of ten. The sea-bed at the Gilstone has been raked over a thousand times by giant seas, it can bear no resemblance to the sea-bed of the time of the wreck. In my opinion to talk of making a survey of this is like talking of making a survey of the bottom of Niagara Falls.

The cost of salvage was the next titbit to occupy the minds of the voracious reporters. One article had a headline saying: ' "We are not in it for the cash", say treasure hunters'; the article went on: 'Two rival expeditions have begun a treasure hunt—costing £1,000 a week each. But no one will admit wanting to make money out of it.' I cannot speak for others but, with my hand on my heart, I can honestly say I did not enter the *Association* project with the intention of making money; if I do make a profit it will be the first venture of its kind, to my knowledge, to pay off.

I took on the *Anson* wreck knowing full well that it would cost money; there was a very remote chance indeed of finding a bronze gun. We worked solely on—what the Press calls 'despised'—iron guns, we raised seven three-ton iron guns and a smaller iron carronade. If one 'despised' these things one would hardly expend hard work and money on them over a period of four years, as I did.

How marvellous it would be if one could carry out this work on old-time wrecks—and make ends meet. In other words, to carry it out at no cost; if one were lucky enough to be able to work it this way, and one would need all the luck in the world, then it would mean that the work could continue. For there are plenty more wrecks in this part of the world to explore.

To salve means to save, salvage from the sea means rescuing things from the depths, surely a worthy undertaking. From an early age salvage had me in its grasp. Where many of my friends of the time had an urge to become engine-drivers (steam, of course) my desire was to be a diver; the impressive title used in those days was—Deep Sea Diver.

My enthusiasm was unbounded. When I was a youth I begged a group of salvage men to give me a lesson for the price of a pint. Luckily Cap'n Phil Nicholls, of the salvage vessel *Greencastle*, was on hand, or I do not know what would have happened. Cap'n Phil was a character indeed. He was a shoemaker by trade, but was available at a moment's notice to skipper the '*Greeny*' if he was so required. He had an intimate knowledge of the whereabouts of any wreck round these coasts; the chart which Phil and I at one time drew up, of the local wrecks and their marks, is one of my most prized possessions.

'Come on, Rowley!' Cap'n Phil would say. 'When are we going to have a go at Sir Cloudesley's gold?'

And I would say: 'I don't know, it'll cost a fortune waiting for the right sea.'

'Get on!' this from Phil, 'you can drop down there at any-time! We'll give you lots of extra weights to keep you down, besides'—he'd give me a dig with his elbow—'it won't be any hardship in waiting, the pubs are open all day over there!'

And so they were, in those days; those sensible, pleasant days, when the islanders were free from income tax.

My diving lesson, my very first, was given to me from the deck of the *Greencastle*. She was moored alongside Penzance quay, and the tide was at flood with a depth of but eighteen feet. Cap'n Phil had agreed to superintend the operation; the other men helped me to put on my two sets of rather scruffy woollens, my red diver's cap—inside-out, so that the 'tossle' did not foul my valve—and my voluminous suit. My corselet and boots came next and then my chest and back weights. I got overside and stood on the iron ladder (I hope someone put a round turn on the ladder with my lifeline, in case I slipped). I was ready for my helmet, but before this was installed I was briefed as to what I had to do. It seemed simple enough; in the centre of the harbour was a large black buoy, under the buoy was its chain-cable-mooring and sinker. The task allotted to me was to walk out to the chain and signal that I had reached it by pulling the buoy up and down in the water. Now my helmet was screwed into position by a quarter-turn, the safety stop was snapped down and, with my knife and belt being buckled on, the air was started up. With some final instructions shouted into my helmet my front glass was securely screwed into position. Air was coming to me via a Siebe Gorman twin-cylinder pump, driven, believe it or not, by steam, the only one of its kind I have seen, and very good indeed it was.

I heard someone smack the top of my helmet, so I clumped down the ladder in my lead-soled boots and, with my fingers crossed, I dropped down the short distance to the bottom of the harbour. Through my glass I could look up and see the weed-coated bottom of the *Greencastle*. The water was clear, very clear.

Turning, back to front, I started to walk towards the centre of the harbour. I found that I had to press forward as a man would when walking against a strong wind. Every now and then I would pause to enable me to pull up some slack on my pipe and life-line. There could have been several other reasons for the water leaking into my suit on this, my first, day of diving, but certain it was that the 'spitcock' on my helmet was open, when, of course, it should have been closed. The 'spitcock' is a tap enabling one to suck in a mouthful of water; with this water one washes down the inner side of one's face-

The 'Greencastle' in a corner of the floating dock at Penzance. On deck, diver 'Long Tom' is having his corselet and boots removed, and another diver is clumping up the ladder, while in the background the steam-driven pump 'turns over' slowly and effortlessly. The five men in attendance, plus an engineer below, emphasise the difference between the old method and the 'free range' skin diving of today

glass should it become clouded with condensation. I had not been told of this tap, so I had no more knowledge of it than I had of the water seeping into my suit. It must have entered so insidiously that it gave no feeling of discomfort; besides, I had too many other things to worry about.

For a while I made good progress, but long before the weed-coated chain of that buoy hove in sight I was exhausted. I had been told that I could make myself as light as a feather by closing my air-valve. I kept that valve shut until I was in imminent danger of blowing up like a balloon, but to no avail. I felt as if I was carrying a millstone, my feet and legs were a burden to me, I struggled forward like some groggy, floundering robot. Reaching the buoy, I feebly pulled at the chain cable and promptly started on my return journey. I thought I would never make it. I became so hot with my struggles that my front glass completely frosted over, I could see only by licking strips of visibility in it with my tongue. I was guided back to the salvage boat by the pull on my life-line and pipe. Arriving back under the ladder, I found to my relief that I could grasp the lower rung, but I was totally unable to heave myself up, I was too heavy. It was only then that I realised that there was something amiss, but I could not even guess what it could be.

In the diver's code of signals four pulls on the life-line means 'I am coming up'. I gave this signal, pressed the centre spindle of my outlet valve, and the noise of escaping air ceased immediately. The incoming air started to build up in my suit—but it gave me no increased buoyancy; hastily I had to release this excess air or my arms would have been flung apart like a scarecrow's. On the top-sides the men were puzzled by my non-appearance, they watched my air bubbles in perplexity—he was at the bottom, under the ladder, why did he not come up? Now, in desperation, I gave four pulls—this time on my airpipe; this meant 'Haul me up'. At this the men on top strained on my pipe and life-line, but I was too heavy for them. The next thing I knew I heard something clanging against my helmet; it was a hook attached to a wire rope. I got the message immediately, I draped the wire around my waist and hooked it on to itself. Again I gave the signal to haul up; on board the *Greencastle* the winch coughed and spluttered, the wire leading down from the outswung derrick into the water tautened. Presently, to the howls of laughter from the men on deck and many interested watchers on the quayside, a bloated figure appeared from out of the harbour water—it was I. They swung me over the deck on to which I was lowered, looking for all the world like that figure out of a famous tyre advertisement. My front glass was removed, as were my helmet, leads and boots. The water in my suit was well above my waist, so, ignominiously, I was hauled up by the winch again, this time by my feet. As I hung suspended there like some prize shark, the water gushed out, over my head, from the neck of the suit. My lesson in deep-sea-diving was over. The men told me laughingly that had I stumbled and fallen underwater, I could have drowned inside my own suit. I was scared enough as it was without being told that! Although this first try-out gave me plenty to think about, I carried on with my 'lessons'; later I was able to go through a professional course.

The thrill of salvage is well worth all the snags, the worries, and the hard work entailed. One thing I delight in is the diversity of the work. No two days are alike, or should not be, for if there is a risk of their becoming so, then it pays to arrange things otherwise. I thought we would be discreet and leave the Gilstone for a day to the R.N. Air Arm boys, for the divers of the Sub Aqua Clubs were massed for the attack. No bones were made about the fact that through their efforts in research among old records and maps, they had discovered the wreck in the first instance. They had come across a chart with a rock called the 'Shovel' and it was this that led them to assume that the outer Gilstone was indeed the site.

Having a day to spare, then, and the day in question being one of the most beautiful one could imagine, we set off in the trawler on a spot of modern salvage.

Unlike this particular sunny day, the 21st of January way back in 1955 had been a day of dense fog. On that day, coming in from the Atlantic, while on passage from Hampton Roads to Rotterdam with a cargo of coal, was the Panamanian steamer *Mando* of 7,176 tons. Soon the hapless vessel found herself entangled amongst the more northerly of the outer rocks of the Scillies. Between the Kettle and Golden Ball—sounding her foghorn continuously—she struck the western ledge of Golden Ball Bar. To the nor'east of this lies the giant bulk of Man-a-Vaur; this is pronounced 'Men-o-War' and, indeed, the rock has the appearance for all the world like that of an old-time warship with all sails set and drawing. The one favourable aspect of the *Mando* disaster was that no lives were lost.

With the sun beating down on us from astern, we headed north to make contact with the remains of this twelve-year-old wreck, now a pile of flattened steel plates and jumbled girders. Doug Rowe had been working on her for several months: I understood he had bought the 'rights' to do so from the owners. With him, as mate and co-diver, had been Terry Parr.

It being low water, we went round about by the rock that gives its name to the islands as a whole, the Scilly Rock. From here we rounded Shipman Head with the sun now on our starboard side; and so by Doug's marks we came into the calm waters over the grave of the *Mando*; she lay in 120 feet of clear water. Our task was to lift the major part of a bronze propeller on which Doug and Terry had been working. It weighed four tons three hundredweights, as we were to discover later; at the moment it was entangled with several pieces of iron. With the trawler swinging to a wire mooring the divers went down in ideal conditions. Away to the nor'-east, behind Men-a-vaur, lay Round Island with the white tower of its lighthouse stuck on top, like a candle on a pudding. High overhead a jet, on its transatlantic way to America, drew a straight, white, expanding wake across the vivid blue of the sky. There was silence, except for the lap of water against our planking, there was not a living soul to be seen outside the gunnels of our boat. We could have been 10,000 miles from civilisation; who would want to go abroad—we asked ourselves—when you had weather like this, and locations like this, on your very doorstep?

Down below, at a depth of twenty fathoms, Doug and Terry swam and worked in a different world; a world of clear dense water, a world of unseen pressure—at fifty-three pounds per square inch. Presently the divers surfaced, the effect of their encounter with pressure showing on their faces; they lay on the deck to rest. They announced that the prop was ready and waiting to be raised. I do not know how the *Ros Guill* behaved that time she bore the record catch of sprats, but I do know that on this day, when she 'caught' the propeller from her bow, she resembled a feeding duck with its head beneath the surface. Her bow was down and, consequently, her canoe-shaped stern was high out of the water. With the state of the tide, and the depth at which the prop was suspended, we knew that we should not have enough clearance to reach St. Mary's. We would go as far as we could—until the propeller grounded—drop it there and come back for it another day.

We made for St. Mary's via the channel of New Grimsby; this is the passage between the islands of Bryher and Tresco. Entering the channel we noticed over on our port side, under Kettle Point, the dark cavern of Piper's Hole; this runs a long way in and has a stygian lake in its midst. Ahead of us lay the calm placid waters and anchorage of New Grimsby harbour. The shores here are thickly grown to the water's edge with gay, vivid-coloured mesembryanthemum, an alien plant, the star-shaped flowers of which reach their peak of opening around midday.

Slowly we steamed through the channel between the islands, Mike Hicks, as usual, taking up the 'most' of the wheelhouse. Mike had to navigate cautiously, the channel shoaled quickly from fifteen fathoms to nine fathoms and then, almost as quickly again, to three fathoms. At this point, just under the ruins of 'Cromwell's Castle', our salvaged propeller touched the ground. We slacked off the wire and allowed the prop to settle on the bottom. While the divers were down unshackling the wire we had plenty of time to view the castle on our port bow, and, away on our starboard bow, the small Hangman Isle.

Up on the side of the rounding walls of the castle there protrudes a finger of granite. This grim stone beam bears

Not winkle-picking, but sorting lead shot from the 'Association' site

the mark of the hangman's chains. Several feet below, and a little to one side, there projects the platform on which the poor wretches stood before being pushed off into eternity. Vague legend has it that the bodies of those hung at the castle were thrown on Hangman Isle, and there left to rot. On a sunny day, such as the one we were enjoying, it seemed macabre to dwell upon such dismal things.

Somewhere along this channel there lies the site of the wreck of the *Phoenix*. This was the vessel of Sir Cloudesley's squadron that was so badly damaged, while going through Broad Sound, that she had to be beached; there could not be much of her left, the old-time salvors would have been able to have got down to the greater part of her.

Just as soon as the divers were up we set off for St. Mary's, leaving a yellow marker buoy bobbing in our wake; it was pleasant to be back on an even keel once again, now that the load had gone from the trawler's bow. Way down through the channel, and across the Roads, we could see St. Mary's Island with the node of Star Castle high on its profile.

As we came into the Roads, Doug, who was still kitted up in his diving gear, suggested that we do one further job of work before we went in. He wanted us to lift the condenser from the wreck of the *Brinkburn*, a steamer that had foundered among the nor'ard rocks in 1898. A condenser is a large chamber filled with tubes of non-ferrous metal, its end plates are of very thick bronze; the whole item is looked upon as a 'plum' in marine salvage.

So we headed west and then turned north. We came up to, and 'made fast of', Doug's marker buoy; and away went the divers into the deep-green water. The sun was sinking in a veritable blaze of colour; the long, low smoky clouds that lined the western horizon were on fire. The reflection on the sea reached out to us in a wide restless iridescence of hot burnished copper. As the sun sank out of sight, the winch rattled, the wire over the bow tautened and creaked, and there—awash under our stem—lay what looked like a giant bundle of gigantic drinking straws; they were the condenser tubes. It was not long before we had two such bundles lashed to our bow; and before we had finished we had all slipped on our shirts and guernseys, for now there was a chill in the air. The colour had gone from the Islands and from the sea, a grey wash was creeping over all. The cold blue of the western sky held pale colour shades of russet and gold, of aquamarine and sapphire, and of lemon and topaz. To the west of us now, the rocks stood in dark silhouette, the gulls flew silently overhead; in the half-light we turned and made our way back to harbour.

10

PIECES OF EIGHT

At the time the divers located the bronze guns—and these had been found in a total diving time of one-and-a-quarter hours—it was decided to forgo any exploratory work until all three of these beautiful works of art had been recovered. First things first, we said. We knew the guns were there, why waste weeks in looking for that which might never be found? So 'guns before gold' was the maxim. But no diver goes about with his eyes closed, hence it came about that as they carried out their work on the third bronze gun the divers began to come up with silver coins—in ones and twos. These coins were in poor condition, being mere discs of silver, with no recognisable marks on them; but, poor condition or not, every coin brought up caused great excitement and gave a chance for others to shower congratulations on the beaming finder.

On our second day of work on the third gun we had gone alongside the *Girl Sharon*, as usual with the trawler, to pick up Doug and Terry. While passing across their equipment Doug said:

'I dreamt last night that I found another gold coin.'

And, sure enough, find another he did. We had not been at the Gilstone Ledges for longer than the first dive when up Doug came; after handing up his air bottles he climbed aboard in silence; he fumbled at the wrist-band of his rubber suit:

'There!' he said, holding out his hand, in the wet palm of which lay a glittering disc. 'That's my dream out!'

We all crowded round for a glimpse of the golden coin; it was in fine mint condition, exactly the same as our first, but this one was dated 1703. From that moment Doug was to be known as 'Goldfinger'.

With the finding of the coins pressure was put on me to allow more prolonged exploratory work to be undertaken. But after talking it over the divers agreed that it would be wise first to make sure of recovering the gun. This third gun lay completely trapped under a huge rock. On top of this large rock was a smaller one the size of a Mini car. A wire strop was placed round this smaller rock, and with the expenditure of considerable exertion from her winch the tubby *Ros Guill* lifted this from its bed. The growl of the winch, travelling down the taut wire to the rock seventy feet below the surface, could plainly be heard by the divers. They watched as the rock was lifted clear and deposited in another place.

The big rock posed a formidable problem; to start with, a great many measurements had to be made and underwater sketches drawn. These measurements and sketches were undertaken with the aid of nine-inch-square white vinyl tiles; to these are attached, by a short cord, thick carpenter's pencils. Measurements are made in multiples of nine inches—the width of the tile—the details are written, or drawn, on the smooth surface of the vinyl.

In the sketch (page 144) it will be seen that rock B almost completely covered the gun. Geoff had discovered it by the merest chance; he had noticed the small portion of its breech showing, down in the depths of a small crevasse. We had grave fears for the condition of the cannon, as it was found that the full weight of rock B was pressing on it. Moreover, there was every indication that the rock had been on the move.

How to set about recovering the gun without damaging it further? It was quite impossible to lift rock B; our estimates of its weight ranged from twenty-five tons to thirty-five tons. Blasting the rock was out of the question, this would seriously endanger the bronze gun; besides, the falling debris would clutter up the passages in the rocks round about, and thus would hamper further exploration of the region.

The weather was sunny and the breeze was warm, the sky was cloudless and blue; we who were not diving worked with

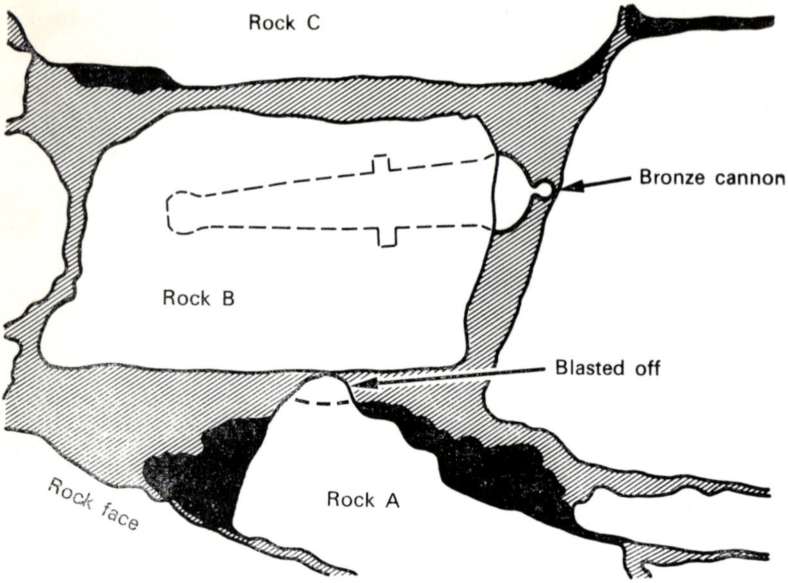

Gun Number Three was rescued by blasting the 'nose' from rock A, which enabled us to tilt rock B sufficiently to lift the gun between rocks B and C

our clothes thrown off from the waist up, we were burnt the colour of wet teak. But although the sun beat down with an intensity that made the deck seams bubble, the sea—as ever—'had a lop on it' and this 'lop' kept the trawler continuously rolling, and pitching, and corkscrewing; never for one moment was she still.

To enable us to have our lunch in peace and quiet we took the trawler into our hidey-hole behind Rosevean. Here, in the region between Old Bess and Trenemene—round about Black Rock, the Daisy, the Vink and Dry Splat—the men fished for their midday meal. By the simple expedient of lowering into the sea a line with a dozen hooks on it, by raising and lowering this line with a steady motion, many fish were caught in a matter of minutes, these included pollock and mackerel. In next to no time at all the fish were cleaned and split, the fry-pan was sizzling with butter; drooling at the mouth we queued with our plates at the ready. It was as well that we had a good meal, it was to be late that night before we fed again. The divers were the unlucky ones, a heavy meal was not for them; they took sparingly of hot soup from

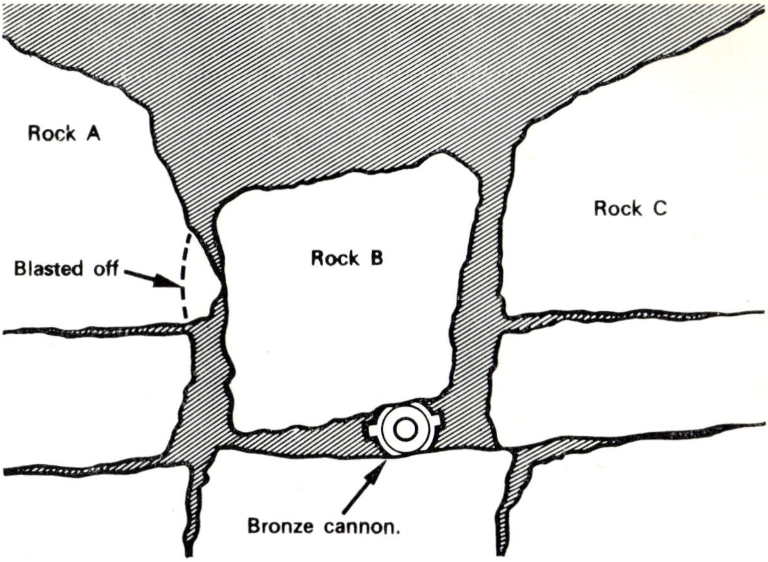

It lay completely trapped under the huge rock

thermos flasks, flasks set up every day for us by the kind and thoughtful manageress of Tregarthen's Hotel. It was at this point that we discovered, to our dismay, that we had run out of fresh water. This was a tragedy indeed, we could not make our usual pot of tea! To finish off our meal without a cup of tea to wash it down was unthinkable, the more we dwelt on the prospect, the more parched our throats became, desperately we looked about us for some means of succour.

Away north of us, to the east of Jacky's Rock, on the permanent mooring that had been laid, was the black-and-white shape of the *Regency*. Would they—we wondered—let us have some fresh water? Why not? said Geoff, it was but a few days since he had repaired an outboard motor for them—at no charge—so one good turn deserved another.

As we had the storm-boat with us, the divers loaded what equipment they required aboard it; they went back to the Gilstone.

With Mike Hicks at the wheel, we approached the *Regency* at our best speed; she was lying broadside on to our bow as we swept up to her in fine style. Cap'n 'Bill' Sutton appeared from out her bridge, several members of her crew were sun-bathing along various parts of her ample superstructure. Among the sun-bathers I recognised two newspaper photographers, who, as usual when they saw us, levelled their cameras at us. Whether our speed was a mite too great, whether the trawler took longer to pull up—with her prop racing full astern—than usual, I am not sure. But personally I thought we were going to slice right through the ungainly wooden vessel and come out on her far side. We came up in such a grand manner, and at such a speed, that everyone—including the Captain and crew of the *Regency*—froze in their tracks, even the trigger fingers of the cameramen were chilled into frigid immobility. Noticing that everyone on the trawler had spreadeagled themselves on the deck, as would marines under a hail of fire, I ducked down behind the wheelhouse, a vision of the pale worried face of my insurance agent floating before me. Suddenly, quick as thought, Mike spun the wheel to port, our starboard side swept towards the other vessel in a great wash of water. I had a momentary glimpse of the rubber inflatable between the two vessels, it was buckling-up in two as a youngster would fold a thick slice of bread and butter. The next minute, without as much as a bump or a bash, we were stationary and Mike was shouting, from behind a cupped hand:

'Can you spare us a kettleful of fresh water?'

Like all of us (except Mike) no one on the other craft was capable of saying anything for a full half-minute. Then Cap'n Sutton said—a trifle unsteadily, I thought:

'Jolly good seamanship! But please don't make a habit of using our inflatable as a fender!'

Cap'n Sutton was a good sport, as I was to prove much later, when he and I spent a pleasant evening together at the Benbow.

We were given the water as required, but while we were waiting for this the photographers were busy. Several weeks after this a coloured picture, taken from the deck of the *Regency*, was to appear in the Press, depicting my team and me alongside in the *Ros Guill*; a more desperate band of pirates I have yet to see! The caption under the illustration stated, simply and succinctly:

'Competing expeditions meet on the high seas. Mr. Roland Morris, in the centre...' and there I was, bare of chest and bare of back, looking for all the world like Cap'n William Kidd himself, and with an expression on my face as of one well on his way to Execution Dock! The caption went on to explain that I was a Penzance restaurateur who had raised three French cannon: 'that he estimates to be worth £15,000 or more. He chats with divers on the *Regency* to discuss timings for blasting underwater obstructions.'

Once again the dirty word of 'blasting' had been dragged into the open, and for no reason. We had gone to the *Regency* wholly and solely for fresh water; nothing was further from our thoughts than a discussion of our plans with others, especially relating to blasting.

Well fed, regaled with hot tea, we sauntered back to the helter-skelter of the Gilstone Ledges. By now we had sorted out all the underwater sketches. After examining these it was obvious that there was only one thing for it—I looked cautiously up and down the deck, I peered searchingly at the rocks as they slid past; heaven knows; who can tell? But there seemed to be no reporters about:

'That "nose" on rock A,' said I, softly, 'that will have to be . . . ' I lowered my voice still further. 'It will have to be—blasted off!' I whispered.

'Blasted?' asked Terry, loudly.

'Sh-h-h-h!' we hissed, looking agitatedly round the skyline with a finger to our lips.

As we came down from Rosevear Neck, with the Rosevear Ledges on our starboard beam, we could make out the storm-boat as she danced to her moorings at the Gilstone. She looked very tiny amid the rolling swells, disappearing altogether for seconds at a time as one swell dipped and another rose.

Mike Reynolds, who was acting as tender on board the storm-boat, reported that the divers were below clearing away all debris and silt from around the gun. We took over the moorings from the storm-boat so that she could range free. By now the sun, with a wide halo round it, was a pale disc in a vaporous sky; up north and round about the Bishop Light there was the merest sign of fog.

When the divers surfaced, one by one, after what had been a short dive, they came on board the trawler for a parley. Surprisingly they were disconsolate; they told me glumly that we had probably taken on more than we could chew. Their great trouble on this particular recovery job was lack of space in which to manœuvre; the rocks were very close together, it would be almost impossible to get the gun out, in fact someone said: 'You'll never do it!'

To which I replied: 'We can but try.'

We got down to a discussion and decided to blast off that projection on rock A. This would allow rock B to roll back sufficiently to give us room to lift the gun up between rock B and rock C: this was our only chance.

Accordingly two small charges of polar ammon gelignite were made up; these were linked with a short length of Cordex detonating fuse, an electric detonator and the shot-firing cable completed the requirements for the blast. I detailed Doug to undertake this job, as he was fully experienced in shot-laying. While the other divers rested, the point of granite was cracked off without a hitch.

The more the sun clouded over, the lower became the morale of the divers. All the buoyancy and enthusiasm that Mike Hicks and I could bring ourselves to bestir turned out to be of no avail. What was it I wanted done? the divers asked. Put a strop round the muzzle end of the gun, if they could get to it, I explained, as tactfully as I could. I wanted to get the winch wire on the gun with a two-fold purchase, as we had done on the previous two. In order to do this one of the big Benbow blocks had to be dragged, with its wire bight, down below and shackled on to the gun's strop. This was exhausting and frustrating work; underwater a wire will catch on every obstruction that it is possible for it to snag on. Time and time again a diver will have to return over the same ground to free the wire, and each time the diver will get more angry and more weary. I understood only too well what was going on; I understood better than most how the divers were feeling; as a diver I had invariably lost my temper under prolonged pressure, a temper that fled as soon as I had decompressed.

The atmosphere this late afternoon was tense in more ways than one; the sun was a ball of gold up there behind the high swirling fog, the sea had calmed surprisingly; the wind had 'dropped away to nothing'. At last the divers had done the seeming impossible, they had 'hitched' the double purchase 'fast' the gun. Now it was up to us, top-sides, to free the gun by a series of surging lifts, using the winch and the weight of the trawler simultaneously.

The divers came on board and lay about the deck with expressions on their faces denoting: 'You can try if you like, but you won't succeed.' Dave took up the slack on the winch wire, while Mike Hicks, at the wheel and engine controls, sent the trawler surging ahead and astern. To free the gun we had calculated that we should have to 'surge' ahead in a nor'-westerly direction. But every time we rebounded astern from those trials of strength the trawler came perilously close to the Outer Ledge. Indeed, after one particularly violent thrust forward, the *Ros Guill* came back with such force that we found ourselves over the ledge and on top of a swell; as the swell passed it allowed the heavy boat to come down with a 'thud' on the rock which we could dimly see below us. But luck was with us on this our nearest escape so far, it was our keel that had struck the ledge, had it been our planking we should have lost the trawler. As the Cornish salvors say—when the ominous thud of timber, or steel, on rock is heard—we had 'tapped'. Were we concerned? of course we were; we may have allowed our eyes to rest reassuringly on our B.O.T. life-raft for a second or so, but we suffered no great pang of dismay. We were not struck all of a heap—like ducks in thunder, nor did we 'sit upon thorns' as might have been supposed; in fact we chanced it—and tried again. After several further attempts to tilt that rock, and thus shake the gun free, we parted the wire—luckily as we were going ahead and, so, away from the Outer Ledge.

Terry went down to reconnoitre; he came back with the news that we had smashed a wooden cheek from the Benbow block, but what was more encouraging, the muzzle of the gun was showing down between rocks B and C. The gun, said Terry, was different from the others we had raised, it was very much larger; as far as he could make out, it was undamaged.

It had been a difficult time. I went round thanking everyone for a job well tackled. 'Forget about it now,' I said, 'we will continue where we left off—tomorrow.' Thinking that I would be able to 'catch' an evening meal at my hotel if I travelled back in the more speedy storm-boat, I scrambled down into her. But, as it was to turn out, not one of us was to get an evening meal that night. No sooner had we scampered through Rosevear Neck than the threatening fog dropped down around us like a blanket. Geoff pulled the throttle lever back and the revs of the outboard died away to a tick-over.

Suddenly visibility was twenty-five yards or less; the sea, now that we were through the Neck, was like a sheet of opaque glass. The sun appeared through the fog like a large round shot, red-hot and smoking, but none of its heat reached us; the mist was wet, clammy and cold. We waited for the trawler to catch up with us.

'Go on ahead,' shouted Mike from the wheelhouse, 'but mind! keep us in sight!'

Cautiously we went ahead; the mist and the sea were of the same pearly colour; they blended one with the other, it was as if we were floating in space. The trawler followed us like a wraith, her engines and the voices of her crew sounding strangely clear and loud. She chuffed along with her white steamy exhaust belching out from her port side, the vapour wreathed and writhed and merged into the mist. From where we were—away off from her starboard side—with the smoky sun dropping low behind her, the beamy vessel made an unforgettable picture as she slid through the mist and over that glassy sea. Her bow wave curled her dusky reflection, and that of the molten image of the sun, into weaving, waving, spectral distortions. Someone aboard us shouted:

'Rocks ahead—and to starboard!'

Across our course stretched an obscure line of grey shadowy rocks; one of them towered up like a mysterious ill-defined cathedral; in its misty embrasures stood gigantic birds, quiet and still as statues. We had lost all sense of proportion, of course; although we came to realise the birds were but seagulls, the rocks unbelievably befooled us. The mist shrouded and disguised them—even Mike Hicks was puzzled.

'Turn up north!' he called. His voice sounded strangely near at hand, oddly it had an echo to it. He went on:

'Keep a watch-out for the Old Lady's House!' and 'House-House' came the mimic from out of the mist.

Old Lady's House was a rock we all knew well—that is, with the sun and shadows on it. North we went, with Geoff opening and closing the throttle as rocks disappeared or reappeared; we seemed to have a barrier of rocks about us. We looked back to make sure the trawler was following, but she was no longer in sight, somehow we had become separated. We came to a stop and listened; we heard voices—faintly, they were receding from us; we shouted and listened. Except for the far-off five-minute gun of the Bishop and the slap of water at our sides there was utter silence.

There is no doubt about it, we were perturbed; we were cold and wet. All our warmth, food and shelter were contained within the trawler; the sun had set, it would soon be dark, very dark; we did not relish the prospect of spending the night at sea in the storm-boat. With the aid of our compass we continued in a northerly direction—until we came up with further rocks. We were poring over our soggy chart, debating whether to go round these rocks, or through them, when we heard the faint wail of a foghorn. It was the trawler; she was sounding at every half-minute; we shouted in return.

The fog was now so dense it had closed about us like wet muslin; Mike told us afterwards that from the trawler's wheel-house he could not see the men at her bow.

I will not go into lengthy details of our wanderings that night over the 'vasty deep', of our dodgings and turnings and doublings back in our efforts to trail that wailing siren. I will not bore with tales of our doings in that muffled, silent world in which, so suddenly, we had been plunged. A bitter, dank and dewy world, a freezing, soaking swashy world. An icy world of moisture: in our hair, our eyes, down our backs, in our boots; sticking in frigid beads to our eyelashes and eyebrows; hanging in clay-cold droplets from our chins and noses.

Sufficient to say that with a large slice of luck, and the exercise of a great deal of skill on the part of our pilot Mike Hicks, we finally rounded St. Mary's quay-head long after the Islands had gone to sleep. Newspaper reporters and a few anxious friends were there to meet us. We were shuddering with the cold; perhaps I was warmed by the fact that we had two silver coins to show for our day's work, and that which was burning a hole in my pocket—the 1703 golden coin.

As so often happens in Cornwall, the following day was a torrid, tropical one; all sign of the previous night's fog had been driven out by the rising sun. During the morning the divers rested, the previous day they had put in eighty minutes of diving at a depth of sixty-five feet, this called for rest and relaxation. They drank cokes and coffees in the shade of the bars and cafes, and they talked of diving, and so did I.

I told of the time when a copper-top diver called 'Long Tom' was diving on the wreck of the *Tay Craig* in Mount's Bay. Tom was sending up great sheets of ship's steel plate to the salvage vessel which wallowed in the sea above. The many rivet holes in the steel plates were a great convenience; in these Tom placed the hook of the derrick lifting wire. But as one great plate of steel was being lifted to the surface, the vessel dipped to a swell, the hook slipped out. The plate swooped down to the bottom again like a monstrous falling leaf. It knocked poor Tom flat, and settled over his spread-eagled body, completely covering him. The salvage crew were greatly concerned; they were attached to Tom, he was a great drinking companion. What best to do? They were not quite sure, but keep the pump going they certainly must. Some of them went overside in the ship's boat; using a 'sea-glass'—a box with a glass bottom—they looked down through the water; by great good luck they saw one of Tom's hands protruding from under the steel plate. By even greater luck they managed to dangle the lifting hook into that grasping hand. It was the work of but a few seconds for Tom to insert the hook into a rivet hole—and up came the plate. Tom followed, looking very much the worse for wear; he vowed that never more would he use a hook for that kind of work, henceforth he would use a shackle. A very wise decision and one which, had he thought of it sooner, would have saved him the most stomach-turning half-hour of his life.

That beautifully fine afternoon, at the Gilstone Ledges, we had company. The Fleet Air Arm men were busy in their inflatables, just to the north of us. Standing well to the west was one of their naval vessels. What could they be working on? —we wondered. They seemed to be engrossed by something of import; our interest was heightened when a naval helicopter hovered over the inflatables then flew out to the vessel that was standing off.

Meanwhile we got on with the intricate and time-consuming task of lifting gun Number Three. We had to re-rig our lifting wire and its blocks. On the last attempted lift we had parted the wire and damaged the submerged block. Luckily we found we could still use this block. Work of this nature takes time and accounts for an enormous expenditure of energy by the divers. At long last, however, the lifting gear was ready for a trial. Two divers stayed down to watch results, the others came on deck as stand-by. The rock that was trapping the gun was very large, but it must be remembered that the weight of a substance submerged in water is a great deal less than its actual calculated weight in air. For instance—a simple case in point—a forty-five gallon drum of water submerged in water is but the weight of the drum!

We knew we had every chance of—not lifting the rock—but of tilting it sufficiently to free the gun. The pull on the wire had to come from the right direction, the trouble was it had to be just right. The divers could give us a compass bearing of the approximate direction, after that it would have to be hit or miss.

As we cast off our bow moorings and prepared the *Ros Guill* for her trial of strength we were intrigued by the further activities of the Air Arm divers. Still north of us, and going north away from us, they were obviously towing something which they had raised by air-lift. At the same time the Navy vessel to our west was going astern, indeed she went astern the unconscionable distance of half a mile. Stern first, where her winches are, she met the inflatables. We learnt afterwards that they had raised one of the huge nineteen-foot bower anchors from the *Association* site. This must have weighed all of four tons; it was a good piece of salvage work, for there is nothing more awkward to handle than an anchor of this size—above or below the sea. Later the anchor was lowered into Broad Sound, pending arrangements for it to be landed and preserved.*

The fight to raise our third gun took two solid hours of hectic activity. At one point Geoff came up from down below to tell us:

'It's fantastic! It's standing straight up and down in the water! It's caught between the rocks by its breech!' As the strain on the big rock began to tell, as it began to move, so the divers would insert rock wedges in the widening gap to prevent its closing. By raising and lowering the gun on the winch, by taking the trawler first one way and then another, we plucked the gun out from these inclasping rocks. Suddenly it came clear; the divers surfaced, Geoff with his thumbs up, Doug, always the most demonstrative, splashing the water with the flat of his hands. With us this day, giving invaluable help to the divers, were Donald Bates and Urst Burkhard.

With everyone back on board we slowly turned south and then east; in deference to our precious, low-slung load, we took the deeper water for our return journey; it would be late before we got in. As usual, Mike was at the wheel; Alf Hicks, Mike Reynolds and one Mark Horobin helped the divers to peel off their 'skins'. We were a big crew, everyone had done a grand job.

Doug came up to me and flipped a silver coin on the engine-house roof.

'Got that from the rubble under the gun,' he said. 'We ought to be out first thing in the morning to search the rest of it, before anyone else gets there.'

'That's not possible, unfortunately,' said I. 'We can't off-load the gun tonight, there's not enough water under the crane, unloading the gun is a job for first thing tomorrow.'

'That's a pity,' said Doug. 'I'm sure there are more coins where the gun was lying.'

We used our bronze gun Number Three as an anchor that night. We arrived at St. Mary's harbour after dark; choosing

*** Many months later we salved the second bower anchor, its shank measured 18 ft 4 ins in length.**

a clear spot just off the quay-head, we lowered the gun on to the sandy bottom, the *Ros Guill* rode to it all night.

In the morning we landed the gun on the quay; now we had three cannon in a row. The photographers and chemists of Hugh Town said that never before had their sales of roll film reached such peaks; those must have been the most photographed bronze triplets ever.

The third gun was longer by six inches than the others. Its decorations were just as ornate, although there were quite a few differences; for instance the embossed name 'Le Comte de

ABOVE *The triplets in close-up showing the differences in decoration. From left to right, Number Three (3 tons 2 cwt), Number One and Number Two (both 2 tons 18 cwt).*
BELOW *The only damage Gun Number Three had suffered by its imprisonment under the rock was to the embossed crown, as seen here in the plaster cast we made*

Vermandois' was placed forward of the dolphin lifting eyes. The only damage this gun had sustained by its imprisonment under the rock was to the embossed crown over the main crest; the high spots—the fleurs-de-lis—were crushed, as is indicated in the illustration.

With time to spare that morning, we all set to and partly, but carefully, cleansed two of the differing guns. Then, with a hundredweight of dental plaster of Paris, we made a plaster mould from each of the embossed crests.

I had promised the St. Mary's museum authorities a plaster cast of each of the gun's crests. Whether they received this news with enthusiasm or not it was hard to tell, what they really wanted, of course, was a real bronze gun; I rather think they will get one in time. Besides the museum at St. Mary's I had also in mind, when I made the moulds, the museum at the Admiral Benbow; and here, most certainly, samples of the plaster casts, suitably bronzed, will have a special place of honour.

For me the afternoon of the day in which we landed the third bronze gun was far and away the most exciting of my life. The divers came up with ten blackened silver pieces of eight. I recognised them immediately; these fabulous, chunky coins had always intrigued me. At the age of eight I had read in Robert Louis Stevenson's *Treasure Island* of Cap'n Flint the parrot; with starry eyes I had learnt why this bird would persistently say, with great rapidity, 'Pieces of eight! Pieces of eight! Pieces of eight!' Explaining to Jim Hawkins—and in my mind's eye I could see myself as Jim—was Long John Silver:

' "Now that bird," he would say, "is, maybe, two hundred years old, Hawkins—they lives for ever mostly; and if anybody's seen more wickedness, it must be the devil himself. She's sailed with England, the great Cap'n England, the pirate. She's been at Madagascar, and at Malabar, and Surinam, and Providence, and Portobello. She was at the fishing up of the wrecked Plate ships. It's there she learned 'Pieces of eight', and little wonder; three hundred and fifty thousand of 'em, Hawkins!" '

I had read in recent years the fascinating articles by Kip Wagner of the treasure trove he has recovered, and is still recovering, off the Florida coast. I had seen the photographs of some of the pieces of eight that had been brought up; the details of those coins had become impressed upon my mind,

almost as indelibly as the old-time assayers had stamped their marks on those chunks of silver. The photographs showed pieces of eight from the vast treasure, in silver and gold, that Mr. Wagner had recovered from the rotted remnants of Spanish plate—or silver—fleet ships lost in 1715. I had read how the intrepid Robert Marx had dived on the muddy bottom of Kingston, Jamaica; and how from the submerged ruins of Port Royal, that wealthy, wicked city that vanished beneath a tidal wave nearly 300 years ago, he had brought up many artefacts, and many mint-fresh pieces of eight. I had read and I had marvelled. I had studied the illustrations of the finders as they handled the recovered coins. Often times I had wondered what it must have felt like to hold cobs of silver in one's hand; pieces of silver that had sailed in the treasure chests of Spanish plate galleons; knubs of silver that had come from any one of the Spanish mints of Lima, Potosi or Mexico City. Now that I actually held such coins in my hands, now that I could hear them clink one against another, I had a feeling, firstly, of considerable surprise. Never had I for one moment even dreamed of becoming involved in recovering such coins; I did not think it was possible, for, with the exception of the Spanish galleon at Tobermory, I did not think there was a wreck this side of the Atlantic which could produce these chunky pieces of silver; not even the *Association*. But now here they were; they must be the first pieces of eight to be brought up in British home waters. After my surprise I was overcome by a feeling which can best be described as 'being out of this world'. I could not really believe that I was 'shaking hands with history' in this fashion.

Naturally I can only speak for myself; the others, I am sure, had their own personal feelings of exuberance, I cannot hope to describe what they felt. Personally there was no thought of the monetary value of these things, any more than one would think of the cash value of someone saving one's life. It was a happening in which values, as regards money, just had no meaning. These ten little pieces of silver could have been ten little pieces of clay, just as long as they had those 300 years of history behind them. For history of this kind is the fascination of my life.

'Where did you find them?' I asked the divers.

'Why, where the third gun had been lying; these must have been underneath. There must have been many more, we should have been out here sooner, someone's beaten us to it!'

Oh, well—as one of the 'other teams' is quoted in the Press as having said: 'They say all is fair in "diving for money, love and war".'

11

THE TREASURE HUNT

The daily papers were now working up to full pressure on the treasure-hunt theme, and they had some interesting items to report. One had the news that as a result of approaches made to the Defence Department by the Prime Minister himself it was thought that the R.N. Air Arm divers would be given further facilities to carry on with their survey work. These divers are quoted as saying that it would be 'necessary to lift dozens of decomposing cast-iron cannons and huge granite boulders', presumably to see what lay beneath. The quote goes on to say that 'The Navy Air Command divers intend to use only buoyancy methods, which inevitably takes a lot of manpower and time. Commercial divers are bound to use short-cuts like explosives.'

It was also reported that during the last few days the Service divers, using the Auxiliary Service Vessel *Shipham*, found nine gold coins and ninety two silver coins. But what was, I think, the most important find of all was a plain gold ring, on the inside of which were engraved these words: 'God above increase our love'.

This was a magnificent discovery, one which certainly went a long way to help fathom the enigma of the sunken wreck's nationality, if not its identity.

The gold coins recovered, say the Press, were five English

sovereigns, or guineas, also four Portuguese four-thousand-reis coins similar to those already found at the site. The earliest date on the English coins was 1669 and the latest 1701. The Portuguese coins were dated from 1689 to 1706.

Also recovered by the Air Arm Sub Aqua Club divers was a silver spoon; this has a hammered design on the underside of the handle of a mailed fist rising out of a rope-like sea, the hand holding a short dagger.

Not content with this magnificent 'bag', the Service boys brought in another bronze gun—their second. A more than interesting point about this gun was that the dolphin lifting eyes had been worn away, or certainly they had every appearance of this, as if some giant had filed into them with a huge half-round rasp. I imagined all sorts of reasons for the absence of half of the dolphins; could this gun, like ours, have lain at some time under a rock, or, what is more likely, a pile of rocks? Very probably, I thought.

The papers also reported that the *Regency* divers, who were now preparing to leave the Islands, had, during the week, found nearly a hundred silver pieces and coins, also an English gold half-guinea.

But all this exciting news of treasure trove was shadowed a little by the allegation that 'great disturbance had been done to the site by commercial divers having used explosives'. One diver is quoted as having said that the 'underwater scene' (at the Gilstone), which at one time 'had been indescribably beautiful', was now 'unrecognisable', it being 'littered with bits of shattered iron cannon'. 'About half a dozen of the fifty of so iron cannon have been broken up by explosives', he is reported to have said. My retort, in the Press, was to the effect that 'such talk about damage done by small charges after two and a half centuries of gale and sea damage was a lot of nonsense'. And such it was—a lot of bilge. Let it not be forgotten that the *Association* wreck site is far larger than any football pitch. Cannot this area of sea-bed be indescribably beautiful even if it has one spot where shattered cannon lie? Can it not be beautiful even if every cannon in sight is shattered? Is the sea-bed less beautiful because all the cannon, at present lying at the site, are corroded into shapeless lengths of decomposing metal? This diver who had made such an allegation against me, an allegation which the Press took up with such avidity, this man, most probably, held the view

situated. We know also that these chests would be chained, or roped, to the floor of the cabin. It is more than likely that the heavy seas, with tons of force behind them, could do one, or both, of two things to these chests. They could smash one open where it lay, high up in the wreck, thus allowing the contents to scatter over the whole area like confetti on a blustery day. On the other hand, the seas could wrench a chest free from its fastenings, so that with the ship breaking apart the chest would be deposited intact upon the sea-bed. Here it would rot and allow its contents to spill out over a fairly limited area.

The fact that coins and 'pieces of silver'—that is coins so badly worn as to be unidentifiable—were being found in chance numbers, here, there and everywhere, suggests at once that the first of our surmises was right: a chest had 'exploded' in the heavy seas, allowing the coins in their hundreds to shower down, to be wafted into every cleft and crevice, every nook, every cranny. The fact that most of the coins so found are worn indicates that they have been mobile at one time or another, only those that have lodged in crevices, or under rocks or guns, only those which have lain in a state of quiescence, survive with their designs, legends and dates intact. Doug found his second gold coin at the lower end of a long vertical tapering crack in a rock-face, its very position proved that it had fallen from above.

Now that we had completed our heavy work on the site we had a reshuffle among the team. David had gone back to his crayfish diving, Terry also had pressing work to complete; we were left with the two senior divers, Geoff Upton and Doug Rowe. One or two diving friends, who had been pressing us to allow them to dive when the sea was favourable, now took the opportunity to come out with us. One of these, a Scillonian gentleman, was to cause us the only anxiety we were to experience at the Gilstone. It was not his fault, it was entirely the fault of his equipment; a new valve, which he had received by post that day, let him down. At a depth of seventy feet this demand valve 'packed in', water leaked in and the diver's supply of air was suddenly cut off. We vetted our diver friends before they came with us, only the most experienced were allowed to dive; it was his experience that saved this man's life; he knew what to do in such an emergency. Naturally he leapt for the surface as quickly as he could, but

The Gilstone and its Ledges—the rocks and tunnels, gullies and caverns, of the 'Association' site, seen as though looking down through a completely clear sea from high above the surface

site. They said, 'Will do,' and at the end of a day of deep thought, of much squeezing and mashing of plasticinc, of much argument, they produced what must be the only model of its kind. It was complete with every gun and detail they could call to mind. The positions were indicated from where the bronze guns, and also the coins, had been recovered. In subsequent dives the model was added to, or alterations made, where it was found necessary to do so. This model, which covers a large-size drawing-board, has proved invaluable in our quest for treasure.

It may be remembered that when we drew on our imagination, when we visualised the *Association* foundering, we thought of her sinking slowly, with the seas pounding at her stern. As she sank, so tons of water would thunder through the sloping stern windows of the Great Cabin and its sleeping apartment. It is here, we know, the treasure chests would be situated. We know also that these chests would be chained, or roped, to the floor of the cabin. It is more than likely that the heavy seas, with tons of force behind them, could do one, or both, of two things to these chests. They could smash one open where it lay, high up in the wreck, thus allowing the contents to scatter over the whole area like confetti on a blustery day. On the other hand, the seas could wrench a chest free from its fastenings, so that with the ship breaking apart the chest would be deposited intact upon the sea-bed. Here it would rot and allow its contents to spill out over a fairly limited area.

The fact that coins and 'pieces of silver'—that is coins so badly worn as to be unidentifiable—were being found in chance numbers, here, there and everywhere, suggests at once that the first of our surmises was right: a chest had 'exploded' in the heavy seas, allowing the coins in their hundreds to shower down, to be wafted into every cleft and crevice, every nook, every cranny. The fact that most of the coins so found are worn indicates that they have been mobile at one time or another, only those that have lodged in crevices, or under rocks or guns, only those which have lain in a state of quiescence, survive with their designs, legends and dates intact. Doug found his second gold coin at the lower end of a long vertical tapering crack in a rock-face, its very position proved that it had fallen from above.

Now that we had completed our heavy work on the site we had a reshuffle among the team. David had gone back to his crayfish diving, Terry also had pressing work to complete; we were left with the two senior divers, Geoff Upton and Doug Rowe. One or two diving friends, who had been pressing us to allow them to dive when the sea was favourable, now took the opportunity to come out with us. One of these, a Scillonian gentleman, was to cause us the only anxiety we were to experience at the Gilstone. It was not his fault, it was entirely the fault of his equipment; a new valve, which he had received by post that day, let him down. At a depth of seventy feet this demand valve 'packed in', water leaked in and the diver's supply of air was suddenly cut off. We vetted our diver friends before they came with us, only the most experienced were allowed to dive; it was his experience that saved this man's life; he knew what to do in such an emergency. Naturally he leapt for the surface as quickly as he could, but his knowledge of diving told him to open his lips as he came up, a most unnatural proceeding. A submerged diver can liken his lungs to a reservoir of compressed air; compressed air expands rapidly as it comes to the surface. Had this man not opened his mouth, had not used his lips as a safety valve and allowed the expanding air to escape, his reservoir of air—in other words, his lungs—would have burst.

The divers in their exploratory work came upon many interesting articles, but these were invariably small in size; as had been forecast by us, no artefact of any size was going to be found on this wreck site. Small pieces of glass were found, some light green in colour and obviously from bottles; other pieces were dark and thick as if from wine-jars. Timber was scarce, some small pieces only being found; there was part of a wooden bung with a ridge showing the depth it had been hammered into a cask, this bung had a vent hole in it. Doug found a heavy sounding-lead, also a small brass avoirdupois weight; engraved on this was an 'A' surmounted by a crown. Geoff found a broken pair of wick trimmers; an interesting point about this latter find was that the little refuse box on it contained a small wedge of solidified wick trimmings. Also found were a leather handle such as would come from a kettle, part of a bronze lock, a pewter knob, a copper nail, sheet lead and piping, a glass stopper, spoon handles, pieces of metal and so on—all small broken remains. One exciting discovery was seven pieces of bronze which when put together like a jigsaw puzzle made up a half of the ship's huge bell, almost three feet high. Ships' bells usually bear the name of their vessel; if this one ever had a name on it then we must have the wrong half, it is devoid of any marking whatsoever. Two interesting finds consisted of pieces of stiletto hafts and guards, one in ormolu—gilded bronze—and the other in solid silver; these were both in a broken state. The ormolu one was in many pieces, with the solid gold plating flaking badly. As it was being carefully cleaned a grain of wheat was taken from its interior. This was placed in a phial of formaldehyde, but quickly though this was done it was not quick enough, the wheat grain lost a little of its bright yellow colour in the intervening period.

We were now well into the month of September, the summer was waning, a summer in which we had fought against strong seas at the Western Isles, during which time, but seven miles

Disintegrating cannon-balls, lead musket shot, silver coins and part of an ormolu dagger hilt at seventy feet down

away, the holidaymakers had basked in the sun, had bathed in the tranquil waters of the Islands of Scilly. This had been a summer never to be forgotten by us, it had been a summer tense with excitement; but soon our treasure hunt must end. Soon the winter gales would be upon us, soon the wind would veer sou'west and would remain in that quarter for the greater part of the time. The usually long queues of 'visitors', awaiting their day trips, were shortening; the hotels, cafés and restaurants were talking of closing, if not for the whole winter, then certainly for staff holidays. The launch owners were making plans for the winter hauling up of their boats. The smart cruising yachts, many of them flying the tricolour and one or two the stars and stripes, had departed. The harbour looked strangely empty. The *Regency* men had made an abortive attempt to depart for Falmouth, but off the Seven Stones they experienced technical trouble and had to return. The Fleet Air Arm men were due to leave within a few days.

The divers were not expending as much physical effort as they had done with the lifting of the guns, so they stayed down longer, sometimes for three dives of thirty minutes a day, or ninety minutes in all, at a depth of sixty to seventy feet. Their small finds of coins and silver pieces began to form a pattern; without our model this would never have become apparent. The location where every coin was found was tagged on the model. It soon became clear that there was one area near which the coins were more numerous than others, the further one went from that area the less numerous were the finds; it was not quite so simple as that but for security reasons that explanation will have to suffice. But here could be a clue as to what fantastic gimmicks the underwater currents can get up to at the Gilstone.

Take again our hypothetical treasure chest which had fallen to the sea-bottom intact. It had rotted away and had allowed its coins to slide out over a limited area. Could it have been possible that raging storms had sent fierce currents cork-screwing through the underwater subways and channels, currents powerful enough to have taken up loose coins in their grasp, coins as big as five-shilling pieces, and hurled them through the submarine corridors like a scattering shoal of terrified sprats? If the sea round about the Gilstone can, as we know, lift gravel from the bottom, it might well be powerful enough to lift money. From the evidence given by our model it looked as if the loose coins had come from one supply—one particular hoard. This could only have occurred when the coins were free of each other, during the first few years of immersion, before sea-growth, corrosion and fine deposits had cemented all together. Once this had happened the coins were trapped for ever; what we had to look for, we decided, was a hoard of trapped coins, a pile of coins cemented together by calcinous deposit. What would this cache look like? Although there might be a sprinkling of gold coins, we thought a weight of silver would predominate; silver is normally converted into black silver sulphide in salt water, so the outermost layer of coins would be totally blackened. When the coins are brought to the surface this corrosion can be rectified; by a treatment called electrolytic reduction a solution of zinc and caustic soda reconverts the corrosion to metallic silver.

By reason of this corrosion the coins adhere together. This was found to be the case in the sunken silver treasure of the Indian Ocean. The lost hoard was found in 1961 by Mike Wilson; this diver came across the remains of a twenty-two-gun mystery wreck on the reef near the Great Basses Lighthouse, which lies six miles off the south coast of Ceylon. A bronze cannon weighing 333 pounds was located in but thirty feet of water; round this gun lay all of a ton of silver coins; these proved to be Surat rupees in almost perfect condition. Some three hundredweights of silver were salved in a matter of four days' diving. An interesting point about these coins was that the silver had originally been packed into hessian bags, each holding a thousand coins and weighing thirty pounds. Although, surprisingly, some of the sacking had survived after its 260 years' submersion, the greater part of the material had, of course, rotted away. However, the sacks had held the silver together long enough for the sea to have welded the coins into lumps the shape and size of the original bags.

Not only would our divers have to look for coins corroded together in masses, there was also the calcinous deposit to

A William III half-crown, showing the damage inflicted by the sea

take into consideration. So what would the heaps of coins look like? They would be fantastically well camouflaged for a start—camouflaged by reason of this deposit of which we had come to know so much; a deposit which covers everything with a hard rusty-grey skin, as grey and as tough as elephant's hide. In fact the silver treasure would not look vastly different from the shale, rubble and rocks which carpet the sea-bottom at this hell-hole site. If divers, who have been searching for treasure at the Gilstone, have been looking for a mass of bright silver coins, then it is no wonder that they have been disappointed. The bright silver, which is found in small quantities, is made up of coins which have been taken up and put down by the currents. In the process some of these have become so polished, so worn, that they are but the thickness of paper.

Gold, a 'noble' metal, remains untouched by corrosion, even the all-pervading deposit seems to shun its surface. Every gold coin which our divers have located has come up as if it had just come from the mint. Gold then, unlike silver, can give a diver a welcome warning of its presence.

In our silver-treasure hunt the divers knew exactly what to look for, and this is terribly important; and thanks to our plasticine model they knew the approximate area in which to look. But even with these two important aids the task was stupendous. In their search they came across more large bronze pulley wheels from the running rigging of the wreck, some of these were spoked and others completely solid, but all had the Broad Arrow stamping on their inner bosses. But the divers found no other artefacts, no ship's fittings, no great copper spikes, no massive rudder pintles, nothing. Where was it all? In our opinion that which remains at the Gilstone lies buried in the stark granitic sediment which is lodged at the base of that huge pestle and mortar; the mortar-like Gilstone and Ledges, the pestle-like rocks—moving and grinding—rocks that have mashed the great flagship *Association* to pulp over the many years. Even some of the recovered coins are slashed and bent, proof positive that not even the smallest remnant is secure from the flagellation by the sea or debasement by the rocks.

12

A CACHE OF SILVER

The sea was an incorruptible blue; it had a guiltless calm which would have fooled anyone who had not seen it over the past few weeks; it was as limpid and as smooth as a clear conscience. The Gilstone itself squatted there guileless and childlike, with the wavelets lapping at its sides like lambs about their mother. As for the Outer Ledge, the water on the upper reaches of the Thames could not have been smoother, more penitent, more contrite, than there. The sea plays a deep game at the Western Rocks—fathoms deep.

The day was one of sun, for the sun predominated; there was no wind, no rough sea, there were no clouds in the sky—so the sun took over. At noon-tide it beat down from a clear, clean sky; its garish reflection pranced and darted across the sea in a wide stream of brilliance, flowing from the far-off hazy horizon, right up to our low-lying boat.

For week after week we had suffered the battering, the strain, of working on rough water; this calm was unbelievable; it was so strange, everything looked so neat and tidy. Nature could not have arranged things better—it was fitting to have fair weather on this day—our day of all days.

Geoff and Doug were both surfacing together, their bubbles had told me that they were coming up; I could see the colour of their yellow air bottles flickering way down in the depths, their brilliantly coloured hoods made streaks of orange in the limpid green water. They popped up side by side and handed up their underwater torches; together they took their demand valves from their mouths, together they uncoupled their bottle harness and one at a time I lifted their 'sets' inboard, for this day I was their only 'tender'. They both sat at the side of the boat; in silence, except for their heavy breathing, they took off their face glasses, their gloves and flippers. I said nothing—there was nothing to say. I waited for them to speak, I noticed that they were both looking at me.

'You tell him,' said Geoff, presently, still looking at me.

'No, no—go on, you tell him,' said Doug; he also was looking at me. I thought this was odd, they were talking to each other but were looking fixedly at me.

'Why! What's happened?' I asked. 'Is everything all right?'

'Fine!' said Geoff, laughing at my concern. 'We've found a hell of a lot of coins, that's all!'

'You haven't!' said I, or something equally fatuous.

'Yes!' said Doug. 'There's thousands upon thousands of them!' Each time he said 'thousands' he spread his arms out wide.

'The whole floor is covered with them,' said Geoff. 'We couldn't believe our eyes! I kept jabbing my torch in a different place, pointing out more and more coins to Doug—and he was doing the same to me.'

'Well—look,' said Doug, in his calm business-like way, as if he had a train to catch, 'we've both got enough air for another dive, I'll go down first while you tell Roland all about it, we can't both work in there together. I'll take that spike hammer down with me, I'll leave it there for you when I come up.'

'Take something with you to put the coins in,' said Geoff.

After Doug had disappeared with a splash I asked:

'Can't get in where together? What's he want the spike hammer for?' (A spike hammer is a slater's hammer with a long curving spike, ideal for underwater work.)

Jabbing his finger on the storm-boat's bottom boards, on which we were sprawled, each jab to emphasise some point he was explaining, Geoff told me of their amazing discovery.

It seems that the two divers were exploring the submarine tunnels and caverns in close company. These passages and caves are formed, in the main, by the spaces between rocks and under rocks; rocks lying in great derangement, one upon another; rocks, some of them, which reach the size of a bungalow. The visibility was almost nil, so each of our divers was armed with an underwater torch. The going, at best, was slow; every inch of the terrain had to be inspected, every likely-looking hump or lump had to be tapped with a small mason's hammer to see of what it consisted. Geoff came on a small opening in the rocks into which he shone his torch, but the interior was so devoid of light it was impossible to see far in. However, it could be seen that the opening widened out again just inside the entrance. Although the opening was too small for a fully kitted-up diver to pass, Geoff decided—'more or less on the spur of the moment'—to have a look inside. He unharnessed his air bottles from his back; pushing these in front of him with one hand, holding his torch with the other, he wormed his way—mainly by using his elbows—through the opening. It was a cave-like space under the tumbled rocks and had but one entrance. As he knelt on the floor of the 'cave', as he sorted himself out from his struggles in getting through the entrance, he felt the coins under the palms of his hands. They were stacked slantingly against each other, like slates on a roof. When he shone his torch on them, when he looked closely, he could see that the bottom was paved with coins, stuck together in a 'carpet' which stretched the full area of the floor space.

The cave had very little headroom, but, nevertheless, Geoff signalled for Doug to come in; Doug had watched Geoff's manœuvres in gaining an entrance, so on all fours he followed suit. With both divers occupying the confined space, like a couple of excited animals fussing about in a pen, the fine succulent silt rose up from under them like a black cloud. Their torches were worse than useless in the circumstances, in the Stygian darkness. Doug decided to make an exit, but when he came to move his air bottles he found they were entangled with those of Geoff's. Patting each other on the back as if to say, 'Don't move, stay where you are until this lot settles', they waited for the water to clear.

'There was a steady current passing through,' said Geoff, 'we watched the sediment flowing past the beams of our torches like smoke.'

The coins, the divers found, were well and truly stuck down. Here and there, glued and immovable among the coagulated mass, were many round shot, pouting up like bubbles of mud in a swamp.

After one or two tentative, but ineffectual, attempts to release a likely-looking lump from the parent mass, the divers gave up. They searched out several loose gold and silver coins, and put these to one side; but before they made their exit from the darkness of that hidey-hole they found it incumbent upon themselves to lay down their torches, and to execute—

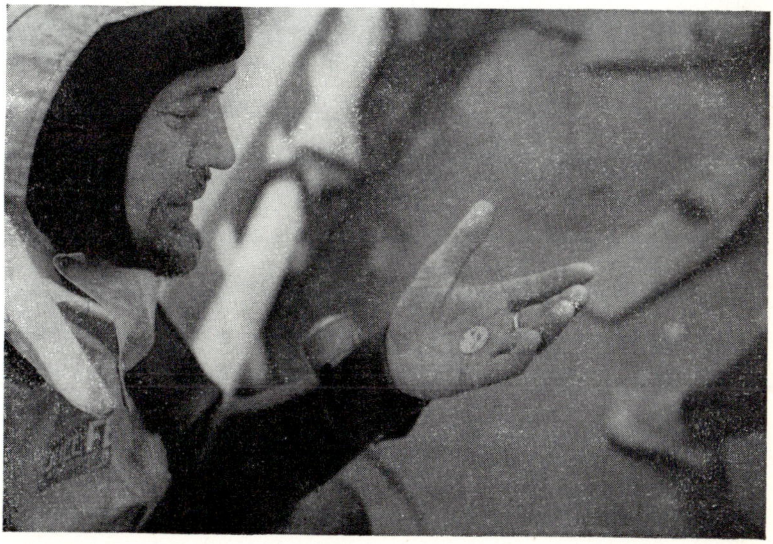

if I can so describe it—a sort of war-whoop of victory over the treasure trove. Squatting down on their haunches they jigged up and down on the silver coins, slapping the rough, fabulous 'carpet' with their flippers and the flats of their hands, all the time sucking away at their rubber umbilical tubes attached to their air supply, which they held precariously in their laps. Oh, that I had been a barnacle on the wall of that rocky igloo! After their short, exhausting, frog-like dance, they waited while the suspended grit drifted away, shook hands with each other and wormed their way out of the narrow entrance.

Any exhilarated reaction of mine to the news of the find was tempered a little by a feeling of admiration for the divers, and also a sense of anxiety for their safety. Manœuvres of the kind that Geoff had described to me call for the use of a 'surface demand' type of air supply. This is a supply of air which is carried in cylinders in the diving boat, the air in this case being taken, under pressure, from the surface down to the diver by a lengthy air line. Some divers do not mind this method—the only one I have ever experienced—other divers, owing to the tethering restriction of movement caused by the rubber pipe, will have little to do with it in any circumstances.

By the time Doug had come up with a large clump of blackened, encrusted pieces of eight and several golden coins, weighing several pounds in all, my words of praise had begun to resemble the blurb not unlike that which describes some epic of the screen: 'Stupendous!' 'Fantastic!' 'Amazing!' 'Sensational!'—and it was all of that!

With Doug up from his last dive of the day, Geoff dropped over the side for his third and final dive. I sat back against the sun-warmed timbers of the boat, I watched the ripples radiating out over the smooth water from the spot where Geoff had disappeared. I could not help but pause and wonder; just the depth of the sea away from us lay treasure; just seventy feet of water, but what an obstruction, what a prevention that had been over the years. Only today—after 260 years—had that watery barrier between treasure and discovery been breached. And now, here in the bottom of the boat, lay slim gold coins and chunky silver pieces of eight.

Doug sat on the floor of the boat with his legs stretched out in front of him; with a pencil as a lever, he was prising the coins apart. In addition to the pieces of eight there were English crowns, half-crowns and shilling pieces; the coins

After cleaning: English crowns, half-crowns and Spanish pieces of eight in varying states of preservation

of the outer layer of the lump of silver were, naturally, not so well preserved as those on the inside, most of the latter being in perfect condition.

'Look at this,' said Doug. He washed a coin in the tin of salt water beside him and handed it to me. It was a Charles II crown. 'DEI .GRATIA.—CAROLVS.II.', it read; on the date side was the inscription: 'REX.MAG.BR.FRA.ET.HIB.1666'. There was the proud King's profile—he resembled a Roman emperor complete with laureate head. It was in fine condition; there were many such crowns in the grimy lump of silver.

When Geoff came up he brought an even larger mass of coins.

'My goodness,' he gasped, 'that lot's going to take some getting out! We'll need a water jet or something to help us.' He dropped the silver lump with a thump on the bottom boards; I placed it in a bucket of sea-water so that the deposit should not harden further.

These were the first two treasure-lifting dives of the many which were to take place over the next six days, dives which occupied the divers from one and a half to two hours a day. It was slow work, so slow that we enlisted the aid of another skilled diver—John Rhodes, who was a friend of Geoff. John, who hails from 'up country', had brought down his own small Auster plane. As I was, now, spending half my time at Penzance and half at Scilly, I was constantly travelling to and fro, usually by the regular helicopter service. One fine and sunny day John had planned to fly his Auster from the mainland to the Islands; taking advantage of his offer of a 'lift', I squeezed myself into one of the passenger seats of this three-seater aircraft. We took off from Land's End airport with the stout little Gypsy Major I engine pulling us along in fine style. The airport at Land's End is so close to the sea that on take-off the aircraft literally shoots off the edge of the high cliffs. One minute the plane is but a few feet off the ground, the next minute one has gained a hundred feet of elevation; suddenly the cliffs seem to fall away and there is the sea: there is the Longships Lighthouse, standing alone amid a mass of white foam and serried black rocks, and there too, on our port side, is the isolated Wolf Rock light.

As I looked down from eight hundred feet the sea looked flat, the deepest of deep blue-green, and beautiful. Presently, away over on our starboard side we could see the white gash of the Seven Stones Reef; here the ill-fated, the ill-navigated, the black-oil ship *Torrey Canyon* came to grief; with its coming it brought death to thousands of our sea birds. Further away again, some distance from the reef, we could make out the shape of that floating sentinel—the Seven Stones Lightship.

With the Islands coming into sight ahead, I was just preparing my camera for some aerial shots when the engine cut dead; no longer was there that reassuring roar of splendid power, now there was but a revolting whistling of wind, the kind of cold, eerie noise one hears at the windows of draughty mansions. I am no aviator, but any fool could have judged that we were in trouble. I could not see the eyes of John, the pilot, who sat in front of me, so I looked at his ears; I took comfort from the fact that they seemed every bit as pink as usual, they had not blanched one jot. But the pilot was doing disturbing things with his hands; he was bending forward, fumbling under the dashboard; the nose of the plane dipped sharply, we headed down for the sea.

'Main tank has run out!' called John, crisply.

My mouth was dry, I watched the altimeter with watery eyes, 750 feet—700 feet—650 feet. Should I be brave, I wondered, and start taking photographs? The people who later developed my salvaged film would say, 'Just look at this!—would you believe it?—such *savoir-faire*! such audaciousness! This chap was taking photographs to the very end!'

At 600 feet—600 feet! We shall be in the sea in a matter of seconds now! At 600 feet the engine spluttered, roared into life, and we were back to normal.

'Had to switch over to auxiliary!' shouted the pilot.

The photographs I managed to take as we came in to land were all duff, they were hopelessly fogged, I wonder why?

I had a splendid experience some time later on a low-flying trip over the Islands. The Scillies from the air are indescribably beautiful. On a clear sunny day the visibility, down through the water, is unbelievable, for fully fifty feet of depth can be plumbed; the varying colours of the water, over sand, rock and weed, are entrancing. Flying over the Gilstone was a thrill in itself; to come swooping down over Broad Sound, to bear north a little—over the Gunners; west about over the Zantmans, the Crim and Tearing Ledge; then south over Flemming's Ledge, the Bishop, Flat Ledge and the Crebinicks, turn sou'east over the Retarrier Ledges and so to the Gilstone —to do this is to do something one will remember for a lifetime.

The 1967 autumn edition of the *Scillonian Magazine*, in its 'Diary of a Treasure Hunt', has this to say for the date 18th September:

'A summer of excitement and treasure seeking was marred

when the *Regency* salvage vessel, which had been in opposition to Roland Morris and the Fleet Air Arm men, caught fire and sank off the Wolf Rock when on passage to Lowestoft. The fire broke out in the engine room and spread rapidly. Soon her stern sank and her five-men crew took to the water in an inflatable dinghy. It happened during the night. SOS calls were received by St. Just coastguards who called out the Sennen lifeboat. Culdrose helicopters also went to the scene where the blaze could be seen for 13 miles. The first boat on the scene to pick up the men was a French trawler *Roi Mage* who took the men aboard just after 8 p.m. One man injured a knee. Instead of making for Newlyn where an ambulance was ready, the 150 ton Frenchman decided to make for St. Laurent because they had a full cargo of fish. St. Nazaire Radio said that the skipper had decided to make for France because low water would prevent him landing at Newlyn until the morning, with the consequential considerable market loss on his cargo. Other ships went to the *Regency*'s rescue, including the tug *Utrecht* and the French trawler *Relâche*. The leader of the *Regency* diving syndicate was Capt. Sutton, but he was not aboard. He left *Scilly* on the same day by the *Scillonian*. The mate was in charge when she left St. Mary's at 3.30. She was originally a twin-motor wooden survey ship built in New York in 1942. She was 183 feet long. In 1950 her name was changed to *Radcliffe* and in 1965 she became a dry cargo ship under the name *Regency Belle*. She was 265 tons and equipped with the latest suction and recovery gear. So this particular treasure bid ended in disaster.'

The sea is always triumphant, it cannot lose; on the east'ard side of the Islands it had gobbled up a 265-ton ship, on the west'ard side it had grudgingly unfettered just under a half-hundredweight of silver. For six days out of eight the divers had toiled at that silver mass; then the weather broke, we took it as a sign of gathering clouds, as an augury. All of three weeks of September had passed; the sea conditions during the summer had been capricious enough, but from now on they would become problematical in the extreme.

We decided to bring the treasure hunt to an end for the time being—to rest on our oars. We all lived near the Islands; at the first sign of fair and favourable diving conditions we could resume our work at short notice. At the Gilstone, bad sea conditions are the greatest hazard, so we decided that in the future we must take advantage of any fine spell that came along, even if it lasted for only one day. We had to wait a whole month for the sea to 'drop' sufficiently for safe diving to be resumed; even then the weather would allow us to work for no longer than that one day. However, as I shall relate—it was well worth it.

During those six days of hard diving—diving for silver—some 1,400 silver coins were brought to the surface. All this work had been carried out with the greatest of secrecy; while the fine diving weather lasted we kept the news to ourselves. If we had released the secret every diver in the locality would have been out there, it would have been impossible to have carried on. As it was, all sorts of ruses were resorted to; the boat was never moored over the treasure spot, invariably it was placed in a totally different location. The divers would drop straight down and then work their way along the bottom to the 'cave', always keeping a good look-out for other divers who were working nearby. Until the ownership of the wreck was made known to the public, until it was declared a private wreck, then the work of raising the silver would be fraught with many extra hazards. Judging from the weight of coins so far brought up, and the area they occupied, assuming the hoard was spread evenly, we calculated that the weight of silver in the 'cave' must be between eight hundredweight and half a ton. Our calculations of the time it would take to recover this amount of coins rather depressed us; it would take a long time if we stuck to the method of recovery we had, at the moment, adopted.

As events turned out, someone else was to have other ideas as to the best, and quickest, way of lifting that particular cache. That someone, having no Agreement to lose, saw no reason why he should adopt our slow and painstaking method of one coin at a time. On the contrary he was—literally—to plough up the sea-bed with dynamite and thus reap a quick and rich reward. There was no law in the land to say he should not do this thing, and thus add to the despoliation of the wreck—something which the sea has all but completed anyway.

Secrecy, then, was the order of the day—we told no one, not even the Receiver of Wreck. The evidence of my old chart, backed up by my Portuguese gold coin dated 1706, was good enough for me, the wreck, as far as I was concerned, could be no other that the *Association*. My Agreement with the Ministry of Defence said nothing of handing in any finds to the Receiver. It stipulated that he must be notified, within a reasonable time, of any such discoveries, these had to be described and it had to be stated where they could be seen. Nevertheless, even when my already strong evidence of the wreck's identity had been backed up by further proof, I made great play—*pour encourager les autres*—with the importance of handing everything over. Accordingly I wrote to the Receiver of Wreck at St. Mary's Island, I informed him that I had a large quantity of coins, I told him that I would be delivering these to him on a certain date.

By this time the Press had become unduly suspicious, especially the two resident journalists on the Islands, with whom we had a very amiable relationship. They had noticed the activity at the Gilstone, they had seen my comings and goings—they guessed that 'something was on'. When I told them the story they wanted to dash off straight away and phone their papers, but I placed an embargo on the news; it could not possibly break until I handed the coins over to the Receiver; in the past few weeks I had extolled the virtue of this procedure to such an extent I could do no other than adhere to it myself. Besides, I thought it would make a good story, the divers had done a marvellous job, we had com-

pleted our work as far as the weather would allow, now was the time to play.

In exchange for extravagant promises of still photographs, and snippets of 16 mm. film (which we never received), the three of us posed for the television cameras; we allowed the coins to run through our fingers, we said our pieces into the microphones. Geoff described how he had 'walked on a carpet of gold and silver'. Doug, when asked if he was afraid that others would discover the treasure, said: 'No, you see—we have not exactly signposted the place!'

Meanwhile, what more fitting place could the pieces of eight be than in safe keeping at the old Admiral Benbow? Here the parcel of coins was given a preliminary cleaning only, this to allay any risk of further corrosion. English coins predominated, and of these the greater number bore the date of 1696. So far, there are no Cromwellian coins, but there are Charles II, James II, William and Mary (gold only), and William III. The pieces of eight were found to be in splendid condition; what a fascinating coin this is, a coin which in its time was legal tender in any part of the world. British colonials referred to it as a 'cob'—a word meaning lump—these angular coins having a crude appearance compared with the slick-minted coins of the English, but their fascination, I think, lies in their angularity. No two coins are alike, each piece being chiselled from a flat bar of silver and hammered out into pieces of eight, pieces of four or pieces of two, according to weight. They were stamped by hand in the Spanish mints at Lima, Potosi or Mexico City. Their dates range from 1653 to 1690. On one side, beneath the quadrant of the Christian Cross, they bear the coats of arms of Leon and Castile. On the opposite side are impressed the pillars of Hercules—the gateway from the Mediterranean to the Ocean Sea—the Latin inscription 'PLUS ULTRA', with the embossed wavy lines, were the mark of Spain's overseas dominions.

On the day I handed over the coins to the Receiver of Wreck, I travelled to the Islands by the twenty-minute B.E.A. helicopter service. I must have an active imagination, for, as we travelled at a hundred miles an hour over the sea, at a height of a thousand feet or more, with the big rotor blades swishing round overhead, I could not help but ponder on the strange way of things. The old-time silver money I carried with me had been handled by seamen who lived at the time of the Merchant Venturers, the time of Robert Blake and Cromwell; men who fought with demi-cannon, culverins and sakers. Men who knew no other form of power than that of wind against sail—what, I wondered, would they have thought of the 'sails' of this sophisticated machine?

I was met on the St. Mary's tarmac by Geoff and Doug. As we settled back into the all-embracing seats of the heliport bus, those splendid seats upholstered in velvety plush with the floral design of blue and cream roses, the owner of the omnibus, Mr. Vick Treneary, gave us the news that the Press were awaiting us:

'They are down around the Custom House thicker than pilchards in moonlight weather!' he said.

One good facet of our treasure hunt was the fact that it had helped to enliven the tourist trade. Even on this day, towards the end of September, I will not say the pressmen were quite as thick as pilchards, but they were as plenty as blackberries, and that is quite a number.

We were hoping that when we alighted from the bus with a few choice words to the reporters, we might be able to squeeze past and gain the sanctuary of Mr. Saunby's office. But we had not bargained with the hospitality which is such a warm feature of the islanders. Not only were we invited upstairs to the sanctum sanctorum, so were the Press reporters and photographers. The small room became overcrowded, we stood yard-arm to yard-arm with big men in thick overcoats, all holding notebooks or cameras. We poured out the silver coins, some of them black and dusty, some bright and shiny, in a great pile on the office desk. We counted them and formally handed them over to Mr. Saunby, the official Receiver of Wreck, who, resplendent in his smart Number Ones, gracefully accepted them and gave us a receipt for them. We did not realise it at the time, but details of this rite, of give and take, were to be flashed round the world in a matter of hours.

Surprisingly, we were to receive letters from well-wishers from all parts of the globe; many people wrote congratulating the divers, praising their work and wishing them further success. Letters came in from France, Spain, America, Australia and even the Cocos Islands. I received a letter from the Philippines addressed to 'Hon. Roland Morris. No. 1. Tavern owner, England'. Inside was a newspaper cutting which bore the headline 'Diver finds 8 million dollar treasure'.

The article under this startling announcement explained in detail how this discovery had been made—Douglas Rowe was diving in a hundred feet of water off the Scilly Isles: ' "I saw a hole so small I couldn't get through it with all my gear on," said Rowe. "So I took it off, pushed it through the hole, and wriggled through after it. I slipped the gear back on and boy! There it was!" ' The letter enclosed with the cutting was from a little girl of fifteen, who was in her third year at a school in Manila, and wrote: 'As I know God is willing to help a poor girl, I thought of writing you as a believer in Him. I asked what I should do and I thought of dedicating this piece of newspaper to a great man and a request for some material assistance. I hope in my prayers that it is you who can live a long life and make more and more money . . .' H—mmm, I wonder—could that 'little girl' have been a middle-aged man, with a beard?

13

A SILVER-LINED TIDAL WAVE

As one newspaper stated: 'Much interest has been aroused by the recoveries now being made of the vast treasure long believed to have been on board Admiral Sir Cloudesley Shovell's flagship *Association*'. The *Guardian,* honouring us with a mention in its leader column, referred to our find as being 1,500 guineas. 'Yesterday', it said, 'the men of Penzance came up with them', then it corrected itself to say, 'or rather Mr. Morris confessed to having come up with them a week ago.' The writer stated that while no one will begrudge the Penzance team whatever they can get back from H.M. Receiver of Wreck, everyone would be rather pleased if the Navy men made the next big find. In several papers there was this faint undercurrent of regret that the Navy had not made the find. One or two papers carried articles which suggested that we might be classed as interlopers, not mentioning the fact that we had all been diving in our Cornish home waters for many years.

Most of the papers printed warnings such as the one which referred to 'A feared, feverish, underwater gold rush, with rival groups clashing in their scurry for the treasure'. They still fostered the hope that an underwater fisticuffs might materialise. We wondered how they would cover such a submerged assignment. One paper reported that I had said—in

answer to a question as to whether or not I was afraid others might stumble on the treasure—'We hide the entrance to the cave with a large boulder in between dives, no one could find it.' In reply to this gem, one of the other teams is alleged to have retorted: 'He can't fool us, that's just a blind!' Surely the very culmination of great journalism; quill-driving *par excellence!*

There were many reports of 'amateurs and professionals from all over Britain preparing to have a go at the Gilstone', while 'two foreign teams were planning to join the hunt'. Warnings to amateur divers appeared in most periodicals; one of the Naval Air Command Sub Aqua Club members stated: 'I cannot think of an easier place to make a mistake.' Another diver said: 'The reef is no place for the inexperienced. It is dangerous to dive there without full safety measures.' The Chairman of the Committee for Nautical Archaeology had the final word. He said: 'It will be almost certain that someone will be drowned soon down there'—meaning the Gilstone—'it's a bad area.'

The *Daily Mail* featured a cartoon by Illingworth depicting the Chancellor of the Exchequer, suitably attired in a frogman suit, swimming over the sunken Scillies gold about to scoop up the shekels with a shrimping net.

Still on the subject of diving, the Sunday papers carried sparse accounts of a group, led by a naval officer, who had been diving on the remains of a seventeenth-century Dutch East Indiaman. It seems that this vessel, the *Liefde*, sank in 1711 at the foot of a cliff at the Outer Skerries of the Shetland Isles. There was the briefest mention of the finding of a chest of silver ducatoons and a few gold pieces; the salvors, wisely, keeping the details of what they had found to themselves.

The mention of this Dutch Indiaman was more than interesting as I have lodged a claim with the Dutch Consul, through my solicitor, for the acquisition of the sole rights to dive on and recover articles of value from the wrecks of similar ships. Two East Indiamen were lost within a short time of each other at the Isles of Scilly; between 1740 and 1744 one of these vessels, laden '*with plate of considerable value*', while outward bound for the Spice Islands, came to grief inside the Scillies and was lost '*with all the People*'. Old records state that shortly after this vessel had foundered her owners arranged for a diver to go down, '*To ascertain by his Best*

Endeavour' if it was possible to '*Recover any Portion of her Vast Wealth*'. In those days salvors went down in 'diving engines'; these had been in use from about 1700. These 'engines' took the form of a wooden cylinder not unlike a lengthened watertight barrel, in which the operator lay face down. There would be two holes through which the arms of the diver would protrude, a watertight joint being made with oiled leather, and there would be a round glass window to look through. John Lethbridge, a Devon man who invented such an 'engine', describes it in the *Gentleman's Magazine* of September 1749. '*It is made of wainscot, is perfectly round, is about 6 ft. in length, about $2\frac{1}{4}$ ft. in diameter at the head, and about 18 ins. diameter at the foot, it is hooped with iron hoops without and within, to guard against pressure; there are . . . two airholes upon the upper part, into one of which air is conveyed by a pair of bellows, both which are stopt with plugs, immediately before going down to the bottom.*

'*At the foot part there's a hole to let out water sometimes; there's a large rope, fix'd to the back, or upper part, by which it's let down, and there's a little line, called the signal line, by which the people above are directed what to do, and under is fix'd a piece of timber, as a guard for the glass.*

'*I go in with my feet foremost, and when my arms are got thro' the holes, then the head is put on, which is fastened with scrues. It requires 500 lb. weight to sink it, and take but 15 lb. from it, and it will buoy upon the surface of the water. I lie straight upon my breast, all the time I am in the engine, which hath many times been more than 6 hours, being, frequently, refreshed upon the surface, by a pair of bellows. I can move it about 12 ft. square, at the bottom, where I have stayed, many times, 34 minutes. I have been ten fathom deep many times, and have been 12 fathom, but with great difficulty.*'

It is possible that these old-time divers exaggerated a little, for it is doubtful if they actually reached such depths. In J. T. Desagulier's *Experimental Philosophy* (London 1744) a Captain Irwin, diving in a similar machine, said that at a '*Depth of 10 Fathom he felt a strong Stricture about his Arms by the Pressure of the Water; and that Venturing two Fathom lower to take up a lump of Earth with Pieces of Eight sticking together; the Circulation of his Blood was so far stopped, and he suffer'd so much, that he was forced to keep his Bed six weeks*'. He goes on to say that others who had ventured to a depth of fourteen fathoms had died within a matter of three days as a consequence. Whether the coins were recovered is unknown.

But to come back to the East Indiaman, at the Scillies, to which a diver had been summoned, it seems that he met with little success. Robert Heath, writing in 1750, in his *Account of the Isles of Scilly*, describes the dive and the 'engine', Heath being stationed at Scilly at the time of the actual salvage attempt. The 'engine' is almost exactly identical with that invented by Lethbridge:

'*The Figure of the Diving-Engine*', writes Heath, '*was a Tapering-Vessel in which the Diver was plug'd up, with as much Air as could be blown into it, with a Pair of Bellows, at the Time of his going down. His naked Arms went out at a Couple of round Holes, next the biggest End; being exactly fitted to them, wrap't round with Neats-Leather, to keep out the Water. Lying flat on his Face, with his Legs buckled down with Straps to keep him steady, he looked through a Piece of round Glass, fix'd right before him, in the Side of the Engine, of about six Inches over, and two inches in Thickness. Thus he descended by the Force of Weights fixed to the under Parts of the Engine. He carries a Life-line in his Hand, which he pulls hard upon when he feels too Much Pressure, or wants to be drawn up.*'

It is very probable the depth of water round the sunken East Indiaman was excessive for this type of diving, the diver would quickly have found the pressure on his exposed 'naked arms' to be unbearable. But, whatever the reason, the project was abandoned, Heath explaining that: '*The Tide running strong at the Bottom, and the Sea appearing Thick, the diver could not see distinctly through the glass of his Engine, so returned without success.*'

So the wreck of the East Indiaman, with its '*plate of considerable wealth*', has remained undisturbed over the years; if the Dutch Authorities see fit to grant me an Agreement, maybe we shall have better luck than the intrepid gentleman in his audacious 'Diving-Machine'.

It might be wondered why we bother with other wrecks when there are hundredweights of silver waiting to be raised from the *Association*. To run a successful diving team at the Scillies one should have two, three, or even four different wrecks on which to work. It is all a matter of wind and seas. I would not like to have a repeat of what happened in the

Terry Parr and Mike Hicks admire a gold coin just brought up from the depths: see the 4,000 reis opposite and the James II guineas on p. 185.

summer of 1967; the long spells of waiting for a calm sea were frustrating and demoralising. In the end we took a chance. We worked, at times, in sea conditions totally unsuited for diving. Instead of asking ourselves, '*Can* we work today?' we should have been saying, '*Where* do we work today?—if the sea is bad at the west'ard rocks then let us go to so-and-so wreck out to the east'ard.' At least one sheltered wreck should be 'signed up' so that diving can continue despite the weather.

There are many wrecks—or, I had better say, remains of ships—lying on the floor of the sea round about Scilly. The archaeologists, who dive for themselves, will be quite content to browse amongst these, as and when they find them. But for the leader of a team of divers, who can and must earn their living at the trade, the exploration of wrecks is an expensive business. If this type of underwater activity makes a profit—something I have yet to achieve—then—and here I speak for myself only—that means more, and better, equipment for the next wreck. If it just pays its way, then—again as far as I am concerned—I am content; for in that case the artefacts from the sea, those which I am allowed to retain,

will represent the profit. In the vicinity of the old Admiral Benbow I propose to open a museum of nautical art, something I have had in mind for a long time. I have the building, I have many exhibits, but the needs of a museum of this kind are insatiable; it can never have enough if it is to be worth its salt.

At the Gilstone a prudent diver should work no more than three dives of twenty minutes' duration in one day, being a diving time of one hour, with suitable rests in between. But he might have to wait for days on end to get in that one hour of diving. So alternative wreck sites must be found. True, there are the three other wrecks from Sir Cloudesley's squadron; my old chart shows me their positions, and I have not one shadow of doubt but that we could find them. However, if one could not dive on the Gilstone, because of rough seas, then neither could one dive on any of these, for they are all among the Western Rocks.

Both Douglas Rowe and I own wrecks at the Scillies. These are old-time steamers or steam-and-sailers; with bronze and copper now fetching the highest ever prices it might well pay to look at these. But this is no longer my interest, no longer can I get a thrill out of a 'modern' steel wreck. Can one develop a refined taste in shipwreck? What on earth would Cap'n Phil Nicholls have said, had he been alive, if I had told him I was a connoisseur my wrecks must be antiques!

Every evening we phoned the Met men for the following day's weather. 'Suitable for diving at the Scillies?' we asked, and the answer was monotonously the same. 'Force four to six' or 'six to eight' or 'sou'west gale pending', and so on. But came the evening when Plymouth Met Office said: 'I can promise you a suitable day tomorrow, but after that it looks a bit dicey.' Since we had left the Islands there had been gale after gale, which, after all, is only to be expected in Cornwall in November. Now, nearly at the end of the month, we had the promise of one day's 'fairly calm' sea. With that silver just waiting to be prised free we decided to make a day trip of it. There would be Geoff, Doug, a newcomer called Colin Gregory, but, because of his luxuriant beard, known as 'Viking', and myself. Our transport for the crossing to the Islands was to be an ex-personnel-landing-craft called *Raider*. This magnificent but shoe-box-like craft is owned by the marine engineering firm of which Geoff is a partner. This craft is practically all engine-room, with a small bridge-like superstructure and room forrard for the personnel. The engine-room is crammed to overflowing with two Rolls-Royce 250 h.p. marine engines. Our time for sailing was fixed for five o'clock the next morning. We phoned Mike Hicks, over on the Islands, to watch out for us at 7.30 a.m.

The following morning was cold and dark, there was a light wind from the east. An ample moon, riding high, appeared fitfully through the heavy clouds. As I walked the shadows of the Penzance waterfront the town clock was striking the hour. I heard the voices of the others before I saw them, they were waiting for me in a group at the quay-head. The boat was alongside—below in the darkness of the quay-side, one small light glimmered in her bridge, her navigation lights were eye-catching jewels of colour in the blackness.

'There's just enough water to get her out,' said Geoff, alluding to the state of the tide.

The boat's performance was impressive; we thrummed our cautious way out of the harbour, but once out in the Bay, with clear water ahead, Geoff opened up the big engines. The bow rose, the stern dug in and we roared out into the obscurity of the early morning.

The roof of the bridge, or wheelhouse, slid back in the form of three big hatches; with the helmsman sitting at our feet the three of us stood half in and half out of the boat. We did this as it had begun to rain, making it difficult to see ahead from within the wheelhouse. The land from Newlyn to Mousehole, that land which forms the western side of Mount's Bay, was a pitch-dark mass unrelieved by any light other than that at the mouth of Newlyn harbour.

'Don't go and cut Mousehole Island in two!' said Viking.

'No—where is it?' asked Geoff, twirling the wheel and heading the boat away from the land. We all peered into the murk for a sign of the little 'island' which protects the entrance to Mousehole harbour.

'Now you're heading for the Lizard!' said I, making out the flash in the sky in that direction.

'I'll take her well out,' said Geoff, 'and then put her on a fixed course for the Scillies.' He held a small chart close to the binnacle light. 'Tell me when I'm clear of the land.'

The rain had ceased now, but, heading as we were side on to the seas and wind, we took a lot of water over the bluff bows, the spray of this made us dodge down behind the low wind-cheater. As we cleared the Bay the pale moon crept from behind the clouds; the bow was turned towards the Islands and, with the wind behind us, we worked up to full speed.

Our crossing was uneventful; our speed was exhilarating; we left behind a wake, in the dark haze astern of us, equal to that of a 7,000-ton ship. We rode the sea as a well-sprung lorry would take a rough road. The moon rode with us, slicing through the vaporous clouds in company with a huge encircling halo. In the half-light our speed had others guessing; in one instance we saw a fishing boat's green and masthead light on our port bow, she was some distance from us and on a course that would cross ours. By rights we should have kept our course and speed and she should have given way; obviously her helmsman had no idea of what a rate of knots we were doing, for he kept on. He must have wondered what manner of craft it was that swooped towards him out of the dawn, and then, taking evasive action, roared past him under his stern.

As daylight streaked the sky astern of us we began to pick up the lights of Scilly ahead. On our starboard bow the red stab of Round Island Light and, presently, to the south of this, the flash of the Penninis Light. Looking astern, over our port quarter, we could still pick out the light of the Wolf Rock.

Now the Islands were clearly visible; the big mass of St. Mary's, the jumble of islands to the north and the hump of Round Island showing prominently. As we came nearer, Geoff asked:

'Which way shall we go in—to the north of Hanjague?'

'A better way,' said Doug, 'is through Crow Sound, look—keep down south of Manawethan there.'

As we came up to the Islands Doug said:

'This is where the Blue Sea Divers lost their boat last month, round about here.'

This had been the second diving boat to sink within a matter of weeks. The 1968 winter edition of the *Scillonian Magazine* reports the happening:

'The lure of Sir Cloudesley Shovell's treasure at the Isles of Scilly has already claimed two ships. Shortly after 5.0 p.m. on Friday, October 13th. the 42ft. landing craft *Salvor* overturned and sank like a stone close to Trinity Rock, two miles east of St. Mary's. The three men aboard took to a rubber dinghy and were picked up by a launch from St. Martin's.

'In September the survey vessel *Regency*, base-ship of a team diving for the *Association*'s treasure, sank off Wolf Rock Lighthouse.

'The landing craft was travelling to the islands in connection with an expedition being mounted by a firm, Blue Sea Divers, to search for the treasure of H.M.S. *Association*. The landing craft had left Penzance on the Friday morning. The weather was fine, but a big swell was running. Coastguards at St. Mary's saw the craft making heavy weather of the passage towards Crow Sound and informed the Master of the M.F.V. *Queen of the Isles*, which was leaving for Penzance. Capt. L. D. Davies went near the craft but the crew did not ask for assistance, and the *Queen of the Isles* continued on her way.

'About 20 minutes afterwards a distress rocket was fired and the craft sank very rapidly. All the men, including Mr. J. Ridgway, who cannot swim, after a period in the water, managed to get into a rubber dinghy. A B.E.A. service helicopter was shortly afterwards flying over the dinghy, and remained until the men were picked up.

'Mr. Alan Goddard, of Sunnyside, St. Martins, was working in one of his flower fields when Mrs. G. L. Goddard shouted to him that she had seen a boat go down. Soon six men were on St. Martin's Quay and they set out in Mr. Alan Goddard's launch, *Busy Bee II*. In the boat were Messrs. Alan Goddard, Derek Perkins and Vincent Collins, who are all members of the island's Auxiliary Coastguard Service rescue section. They picked up the men after about a quarter of an hour. The St. Mary's lifeboat arrived on the scene five minutes later and took off Mr. Ridgway who was suffering from the cold. He was kitted out in dry emergency clothing carried in the lifeboat.

'The other two men remained in the *Busy Bee II* to retrieve some of their belongings. They were able to recover three bags of personal luggage, diving suits, sleeping bags and other items, but a considerable amount of equipment was lost. The St. Martin's boat then took the men to St. Mary's where they were met by Mr. Donald Simpson, local agent for the Shipwrecked Mariners' Royal Benevolent Society. The three men were given dry clothing and accommodation for the night at a St. Mary's hotel.

'The divers spent most of their stay in Scilly unsuccessfully trying to raise their sunken vessel instead of searching for H.M.S. *Association*'s gold—the real purpose of the exercise—and left Scilly empty-handed before Christmas.'

It was broad daylight as we entered Crow Sound, with the island of St. Mary's close to our port beam and the islet of Little Arthur on our starboard side.

'That's Little Biggal,' said Doug, pointing to a submerged rock, just awash. 'There's lots of Biggals around here.' As we foamed our way through Crow Sound we ate our sandwiches, and longed for a cup of coffee. We began to realise how cold we were, our teeth were chattering.

As we skirted the Cow and ran into St. Mary's Pool the time by my watch was 7.30. We had done the crossing in two and a half hours, certainly my fastest ever trip by sea. On the quay waiting to greet us was Mike Hicks:

A James II silver crown and a golden two-guinea piece

'I heard you coming five minutes ago,' he said. 'The missus has got breakfast waiting for you, so come on!'

Fried eggs, bacon, sausages and mushrooms, washed down with scalding coffee, in the snug warmth of a Cornish cottage, with the divers protesting and saying:

'We shouldn't—but just try and stop us!'

This was the welcome that Mrs. Hicks put on for us that morning. As we ate, we talked of our plans; they could not have been more simple; to raid that cave for more lumps of silver, that was all.

The *Raider*, of course, though aptly named, was no craft for the Gilstone; so we transferred our gear to Mike's father's boat the *Swordfish*; this was smaller and slower than Mike's *Sea King*, which was at that time undergoing her winter overhaul. However, the stout little thirty-two-foot *Swordfish*, with its Kelvin Ricardo engine, was not to be depreciated, she was an 'able' craft that had proved her worth time and time again, for had not she been with Mr. 'Gee' (for George) Hicks on that exacting run—the 'relief' of the Bishop Light—since 1952?

With Mike at the helm we set off; his dog Sandy, on his four amazing sea-legs, straddled the tiny foredeck, where he barked alternately at the sea birds and snapped at the spray that was flung up over the bow. The sun was bright, the air was cold and crystal clear; the sea was smooth; the big, oily swells were far apart. Halfway to the Gilstone the divers commenced to change; owing to the nip in the air they did this hurriedly, they were pleased to get into their thick neoprene suits. As this was Viking's first trip to the Gilstone, Geoff and Doug briefed him carefully as to what they wanted him to do. They would raid the cave; he would explore, but not too far afield.

It was pleasantly calm among the Western Rocks; the glassy sea undulated in slow motion as the big swells came rolling in from the sou'west—impressive reverberations from some ocean storm, way out in mid-Atlantic. As the leisurely sea heaved with languid energy, so the pale sunlight flickered with mincing steps across its mighty sinews. The tubby, heavily built *Swordfish*, riding easily and silently at her mooring, rose and fell at regular intervals; at regular intervals the swell would ride up the glistening sides of the Gilstone Rock, with a splash—and a trickling back of bubbling waters.

Complete with brilliantly coloured 'hood', self-inflating life jacket, hammer, chisel and under-water torch, Geoff tilts backwards into the water

Geoff and Doug, pleased with the idyllic conditions, had gone overboard on their second dive, their tell-tale bubbles, carried by the gentle tide, plipped and plopped, on the surface, some distance away from us. Coming up from their first dive of the day, they reported that a large amount of rubble had been washed into the cave, it lay several inches thick over

the whole area. They also had noticed that several large boulders had moved, some by many feet, since they last saw them five weeks ago. Where one of our mooring wires had been trapped by a rock weighing several tons, it was now free, the rock having been rolled some distance away.

Viking stood at the side of the boat preparing his second set of bottles; Mike was busy helping him. I had been photographing the antics of the sea in the region of the Outer Ledge; the giant swells, riding over the submerged rock shelf, formed themselves into spectacular founts of water which rose high out of the calm sea. These huge peaks of water—within fifty yards of us—would rise higher and higher, until their weight would curl them over, slowly, magnificently, flashing in the sun; then with a resounding clap of breaking water the whole towering edifice would collapse, away from us, in a thunderous, ostentatious fuss of foaming surf.

Camera in hand, I watched Viking and Mike as they fiddled with the twin air bottles, and the harness; the talk was of straps and buckles, and of 'quick releases'. Then we all became aware of a sound—a sound we all knew so well—but, unexpectedly, this sound was becoming louder, much louder; we all looked over our stern to see a boiling, roaring, wall of white water tumbling towards us. It was so unexpected we

just gaped at it in amazement; in seconds it seemed to tower over us. It will swamp us! I thought, the boat cannot possibly rise to it! It is too close to us! But, as quick as thought, we were flung skywards, so suddenly our knees were not ready, we staggered and sprawled about in the boat while the foaming torrent passed under us, and finally returned us to our original level, with the sea sizzling and hissing about us with heady spume.

We picked ourselves up in silence. Dumbfounded, we looked about us, the sea was as it had been five minutes before —calm, oily, the up and down of the swell lazy and gentle.

'Well, I'll go to sea! Would you believe it?'

Who said that? Not Viking, nor I, but Michael Hicks who has known the west'ard rocks all his life.

'Thank God,' said I, 'that we were stern on, and not broadside on to it!'

'If we'd been broadside,' said Mike, 'we'd all be down with the divers by now!'

When Geoff and Doug surfaced and clambered into the boat, they were so preoccupied (and so were we) with the lumps of silver they had recovered, that no one mentioned our 'near go'.

By the time the divers had come up from their third dive of the day sixty-eight coins had been separated from the lumps of silver. Many of the coins were pieces of eight. Of these Viking had found one, he had thus broken his duck on his first day.

With the coins spread over the top of the engine housing, we sat around and ate chocolate-covered biscuits and drank hot coffee. It was then that we told of the freak sea that had menaced us but a short while before. The divers looked at the unruffled water, at the flasks standing steadily upright in the peacefully rising and falling boat, they looked at us questioningly.

'All right!' I said, 'I shall be able to prove it! I took a photo of it as it was coming towards us!'

And so I had, some instinct had made me raise my camera at the crucial moment.

14

GUNS, GOLD AND—WHAT THEN?

The silver coins are undergoing a complicated cleaning process, they are being examined and catalogued. Many hundreds of them lie spread before me as I write. Before these coins arrived from out of the deep blue sea I knew little or nothing of numismatics. Now I can appreciate what a fascinating subject this must be. Take the obverse side of a coin; the very manner in which the curls of the monarch's wig fall is of the utmost significance. Are they draped across his chest? Is his hair 'high'? Has he a lovelock, or is his brow exposed? A small dot between the letters of the legend, an initial letter, or sign, below the monarch's bust—all these, and many others, are details of paramount import to the numismatist. All have a vital bearing on the worth he will set on the piece he is eyeing so meticulously.

As has been mentioned before, the greater portion of the English silver coins recovered bear the date of 1696. In this year, during the reign of William III, a special recoinage was taken in hand; this was undertaken to replace the hand-hammered silver that went to make up most of the coinage then in circulation; a great deal of this had become badly worn, or had been clipped by silver pilferers. To assist in gathering in the old coinage, and issuing the new, branch mints were set up in Exeter, Bristol, Chester, York and Nor-

wich; the initial letters of these mints appear on their respective coinage. It is interesting to note that silver coins, bearing a rose motif between the coats of arms, were made from silver obtained from the West of England mines.

For a while, before they were finally called in, unclipped hammered silver coins were allowed to circulate freely, provided they had been officially branded by having a hole pierced in their centres. However, in spite of this massive recoinage, there are many of the old coins to be seen amongst those recovered: Charles II (1660–1685) crowns and half-crowns abound, also shillings and sixpences; James II (1685–1688): the coins of this short reign are, naturally, not so numerous; William and Mary (1688–1694): only gold coins of this reign have been recovered; William III (1694–1702): crowns, half-crowns, shillings and sixpences, all are plentiful; Anne (1702–1714): there are no coins of this reign. It was in Queen Anne's first year on the throne (1702) that the *Association* was engaged in Admiral Sir George Rooke's Vigo Bay action, this was on the 12th October. The ship was commanded at that time—not by Shovell—but by one William Bokenham; Sir Cloudesley did not join the fleet until the 16th. But, as we know, on October 19th Rooke sailed for England, and so it fell to Sir Cloudesley to undertake the pleasant, and rewarding, task of refitting the captured galleons and recovering as much treasure, and as many guns, as was humanly possible.

A great part of the bullion thus seized was sent to be minted into coin; hence the Queen Anne coinage, made from this captured metal, is impressed with the word 'VIGO', this cryptic code name being placed just below the bust of the queen.

As one toys with the heavy, medal-like, silver English pieces, one cannot but pause and wonder at the countless human hands that must have handled them. What manner of goods have they bought? What joy—what sorrow have they given? Some, obviously, have not been in circulation at all, but many of these, otherwise perfect, coins have been spoiled by uneven wear caused by movement on the sea-bed.

One wonders also, as one allows the silver to drip through one's fingers, to whom did it all belong? An answer can be found in the *London Letter* of 9th July 1910. An article avows that the *Association* was carrying: '*A vast treasure—the*

Queen's Plate; several chests of money, besides ten chests of Sir Cloudesley's own, with great riches of the Grandees of Spain'. As we saw earlier from Sir Cloudesley Shovell's letter regarding the delivery of the '*considerable quantity of Tin in cask*' which was shipped by the fleet to Italy, a large trade was carried on by the Commanders both with and without the knowledge of H.M. Lord High Treasurer. Consequently a great deal of money from private trading could have been in those chests.

And now, unbelievably, a portion of this vast wealth lies on my writing desk; I look at the spread of silver, still with the same thrill as when I first saw it collected together, and gazing at it I cast my mind back over the past few months. The coins dissolve into soft focus as I see again, as if in a mist, the turbulent 'boil and bubble' of the Gilstone, I sense again the hapless 'toil and trouble' of that unblest day, the day when everything went wrong and the trawler hit the Outer Ledge. Certainly the sea did not treat us kindly that day, but then, we never expect it to do so, at any time; all the more reason for us to be grateful for being let off so lightly. Possibly this was our narrowest squeak of the treasure hunt; as we guessed at the time, as we now know for certain—having seen the scar on the iron keel—the blow was taken on the least vulnerable part of the trawler's anatomy—the keel itself. Had the point of impact been just twelve inches to one side, we should have been missing one garboard strake.

Sitting in the warmth and comfort of my office, I can see again—what is more I can hear again in my imagination—that which took us by surprise, the sudden onrush of that freak sea, and by 'sea' I mean a wave or comber.

This was the kind of giant sea that, in the past, has swept a keeper to his death at the Longships Light, at Land's End. The sea being calm the man was outside painting, he had been working far from the water, high up on the rock on which the tower is set, but the sea took him nevertheless.

This is the type of sea that caught the fishermen unawares as they talked, and lounged in the sun, on the lifeboat slip at Sennen Cove, it came up out of calm waters and sucked them back like so much flotsam.

We have been lucky twice; we must keep a sharp look-out for the inevitable third time, for surely it will come; the Gilstone Outer Ledge never lets up.

Most of the English silver coins are of the reign of William III, but many of the old Stuart coins are among those recovered

replaced by Mr. Eric Browne. Now a new Customs official has to tread warily, especially where the knotty subject of treasure trove is concerned, private Agreements only add to his troubles, he is concerned with just one basic ruling—the ownership of the wreck concerned. Tell him to whom the wreck belongs and the Receiver knows exactly how to act. So far no one had taken it upon themselves to state that the wreck is indeed that of a British naval ship. In the, understandable, circumstances, H.M. Receiver of Wreck at St. Mary's, Mr. Browne, informed me sadly that, he in his turn, must seek advice elsewhere, he would have to contact his superiors at the Board of Trade.

And so, while toxic chemicals impaired the splendid embellishment of these weapons, while oxidation, corruption, and erosion made inroads into the metal ostentation of these ancient guns, we must hang fire, while the officials wrangled among themselves.

When we got the go-ahead our troubles would not be over by any manner of means; transporting nearly ten tons of valuable bronze would be no joke, cleaning them would be a prodigious task. We only hoped that permission would come soon, for already we were making plans for the next season's diving; soon we should have no time for cleaning cannon, soon we should be busy on our continuing treasure hunt.

What will happen, eventually, to these bronze monsters? What are they worth? Who will buy them? These questions are difficult to answer. A bronze gun found in Mount's Bay many years ago, and brought up from the same mystery wreck as that from which we recently raised an iron gun, was purchased by the local council; it was mounted on an oaken carriage and can be seen to this day at the entrance to the Public Library. That is where they should be, on show, a museum is the rightful place for these ordnance pieces; they should be cleaned and polished so that one's face can be seen in them. They should be placed indoors away from the elements which they have resisted over such a lengthy period.

The value of these guns has been very much exaggerated in the Press; I have been quoted as saying that they are worth

£15,000 each, but I have never said this. In my view it is quite impossible to hazard a guess as to what their value might be. If they had no historic worth at all, if they were merely lumps of bronze, their metal value would be in the region of £1,000 each. That is £3,000 for the three, a figure well below the cost of recovering them. When they are put up for auction at Sotheby's they may well attract world-wide attention. The buying price will certainly top their metal value, but I can hardly think the price will reach £15,000 each, or anything near it. After the bronze guns had been in H.M. Customs bond for almost twelve months I received a notification from the Ministry of Defence to the effect that they had carefully considered the question of legal ownership. The outcome, to the satisfaction of all parties concerned, was that the guns had been identified as belonging to the Secretary of State. This meant that the giant cannon became my property by virtue of the Agreement I owned. This decision was, of course, subject to the usual pre-emption clause which I quoted on page 27.

It is not so difficult to place a value on the coins. From any bookshop catalogues of coins may be obtained; from these some idea of the value of almost any coin, in an average state of preservation, may be calculated. As the books explain, the value of any particular piece depends on three things: its exact design, legend, mintmark or date; the demand for it on the market; and, what is of prime importance, its state of preservation. By much patience, and careful study, one may gain a fair idea as to what the English silver coins may be worth. Their values vary enormously and depend on many factors. The 'ocho reales' or pieces of eight are more simple to assess. By their very crudeness, and roughness of making, a complete coin can never be found. As has been explained, the coin blanks were cut from roughly rolled silver bars with a hammer and chisel, the blanks were flattened by hand hammering. Possibly very few of the blanks were thin enough and flat enough, to become clearly impressed with the complete lettering and design. In fact the mints were turning out these pieces of eight in such enormous quantities that coins bearing the complete legend and design are probably not in being. Quality went by the board, time was saved in hammering out the blanks. Instead of a slim coin an inch and five-eighths in diameter, thick one inch and three-eighths diameter coins were produced. By the time enough metal had been cut off the roughly flattened planchet to bring it to its correct weight it had become smaller than the dies themselves. Even when the legends do show they tend to run off the irregular edge. So the New World coinage is never perfect.

Spain's coinage began in the year 1535, forty-three years after the voyage of discovery undertaken by Columbus. Cortez captured Tenochtitlan (Mexico City) from the Aztecs in 1521 and established it as the seat of the vice-royalty of New Spain. The mint was set in operation during the reign of Charles and Joanna (1516–1555) and this handled the huge flow of coinage from the fabulous mines of Mexico.

Other mints were at Lima and Potosi: take a coin at random,

Pieces of eight—'ocho reales'—owing to their crudeness and roughness of making, a complete coin can never be found

its legend says 'CAROLVE II DG HISPANA' (CHARLES II, by the grace of God, King of Spain), the reverse legend states, 'POTOSI ANO 85 EL PERV'. Potosi, now in Bolivia, was then a part of the vice-royalty of Peru.

Most of the pieces of eight recovered by us are in excellent condition, having withstood the long immersion in salt water very much better than the English silver coins. The eight reales of Philip IV's reign (1621–1665) with a Shield and Quartered Arms are valued at fifty dollars. Those of Charles II (1665–1700) could be worth thirty-five dollars, this without taking into account their historic value. In the self-same letter, from the Ministry of Defence, which gave me possession of the guns, I received news of the coins; news, I must admit, which was not entirely unexpected. Always I had felt that it would be impossible to identify the actual *owner* of the specie. The letter confirmed this view: 'even on the assumption that the coins could be proven to have come from *Association*, it would be totally impossible for the Navy Department to put forward a claim to ownership'. This means that the specie will have to be dealt with as 'unclaimed wreck' under part IX of the Merchant Shipping Act of 1894, which provides for determination by the Board of Trade of the amount of the salvage award.

During a period of calm weather in the second week of March 1968 one evening, in the Admiral Benbow, Geoff and I were chatting over a glass of beer.

'Let's take the 'copter over in the morning,' I suggested, 'and have a go at Porth Hellick.'

Geoff knew immediately what I meant; I had often talked of putting on a search at the Cove where Sir Cloudesley's body had been found.

'All right!' said Geoff, 'I'm game!'

There were no available seats on the morning helicopter so we crossed over to the Islands on the 3.0 p.m. flight.

As we swept over Mount's Bay the water was so still and clear we could look down and make out the wreck of a minesweeper that lies just off the mouth of Penzance harbour; a wreck of a ship that had blown up during the last war on a mine that she, herself, had trawled up. There she lay, a dark blue shape in the pale green water. Just after she had sunk, all those years ago, I had been directed to break her up and remove her; then the order had been countermanded, it had been decided that the wreck was a useful underwater, wartime, obstruction and should be left as such as part of the defence of the harbour. Now, very much flattened down, she is still there, with a wreck buoy marking her grave.

Arriving at St. Mary's heliport we were given a firm handshake by Mike Hicks, and a welcoming bark and a lick from his dog Sandy. As we rattled down the road in Mike's green van he said: 'What's on? What's to do?'

I explained that there were three things I would like to do; one was for Geoff to make a preliminary reconnoitre of the reef at Porth Hellick Cove, this with a view to putting on a big search of the site in the summer. Then I wanted, urgently, to recover an iron gun from the Gilstone; this could perhaps help in our endeavour to prove that the ship was British. The third task was more in the way of a luxury, I wanted more timber from the wreck of the *Chieftain*, near St. Martin's. These two latter jobs would require the trawler and two more divers; the *Ros Guill* was now at Scilly once again, having been at Newlyn all the winter undergoing an overhaul and repaint. The divers we could call on at a moment's notice if we required them—it depended, as usual, on the weather; our Plymouth Met forecast hinted at winds from the west.

As Mike's van beat a devil's tattoo along the island's uneven roads, as we startled the echoes in Hugh Town's narrow streets, we talked it over and decided to tackle Porth Hellick right away, that very afternoon; and, weatherwise, it was a good thing that we did.

Without further ado we loaded up Geoff's equipment; neoprene wet suit, fins, mask, lead-weighted belt, emergency life-jacket, demand valve and twin set of compressed-air bottles as well as gloves and other incidentals. Geoff lay among his equipment in the back of the van, I sat in the passenger's seat with Sandy breathing heavily down—and occasionally licking—the back of my neck.

We arrived at the Cove via a series of very narrow, rough, lanes and through a succession of farm gates all of which had to be opened and closed to allow of our passing. One of the narrow lanes was so overgrown that the springy branches of the bushes that lined the track stuck out so far they almost met in the middle. As we crashed through at speed, with the branches flaying the sides of the van, Sandy barked ecstatically and Mike shouted:

'When it's raining I come through here for a car wash!'

Presently we rolled down on to the sandy-grassy edge of the Cove beach; we passed the grave of Sir Cloudesley with its rough granite memorial, a memorial made by the cementing of one moor stone on top of another. There was a legend that the grass never grew on this grave, many Cornish writers in the past confirming this by their personal inspection of the place. In an article on Sir Cloudesley by Mr. S. R. Pattison, in the *Journal of the Royal Institute of Cornwall*, October 1864, he says:

'On a recent visit to the site of Sir Cloudesley's first burial place, on the inner shore of Porth Hellick Cove, we were informed by our guides—fishermen and pilots—that the body of the unfortunate Admiral when washed ashore was on a grating, on which was the dead body of his faithful dog. They are said to have been found, early in the morning after the wreck, by a woman named Thomas, then living at Sallakey farm—a short distance from the Cove. Mrs. Thomas immediately gave information and procured assistance from Sallakey, and the body of the unfortunate hero was buried at the innermost part of the Cove, near the junction of the shingle and the herbage, but within and at right angles with the latter. And here it remains, conspicuous from no inconsiderable distance, without a particle of verdure to obscure the brilliancy of the white shingle which occupies its space, in marked contrast with the dense herbage by which it is surrounded on three of its sides. Our guides asserted that this strange appearance of the grave is due to an imprecation uttered upon Sir Cloudesley a few hours previous to the wreck, and (as they, with other Scillonians, superstitiously believe) with more than human power of prophecy. The islanders assert that ever since the body of that cruel tyrant, as they deem the hero as quoted, rested in this grave, grass has never grown upon its surface, and they are confident it never will grow there.'

All I can say is that, either the weed-killer has run out, or whoever it was who crept out in the small hours of the morning to do a bit of clandestine hoeing has passed on, for now the grass grows freely among the grave's 'white shingle'.

Now we passed through the shadow cast by that amazing rock formation called 'The Loaded Camel'; this is a huge formation of lichen-covered granite, just out of reach of the sea; nature has carved this laden animal far more cunningly than any modern sculptor could have done. We came to a halt by a cache of salvaged timber; I had noticed other piles of similar timber along the beach, proof positive that the tide flows into the Cove at certain times of the day. While Mike sorted out the gear, while Geoff changed and Sandy barked at the seagulls, I walked down to the water's edge, to a point just below the Admiral's grave. The late afternoon was sunny but a cold wind blew off the ruffled sea; small wavelets curled and splashed eagerly ashore. I looked around me at the untidy wintry beach; it was strewn with dried, broken and blackened seaweed, there were bottle corks by the dozen. The beach itself was composed of white sand, fine and even enough for any hourglass. Here it was, within a few yards one way or another, that the Admiral had been murdered. James Herbert Cooke in his *The Shipwreck of Sir Cloudesley Shovel* says:

'Many years after' (the finding of the Admiral's body) 'a terrible confession was made by a dying woman to a clergyman of St. Mary's Island. She said that the Admiral had been cast ashore exhausted and faint, but still living, and that she had squeezed the life out of him for the sake of his clothes and his rings. She produced the long missing emerald hoop, and gave it to the clergyman, saying she had been afraid to sell it lest it should lead to a discovery of her guilt, and she had added that she could not die in peace until she had made this full confession. The disclosure was made between the years 1732 and 1736, after the death of Lady Shovell. The ring was sent to Lord Dursley, who became Earl of Berkeley in 1701, and from him it descended to his grandson, Sir George Cranfield Berkeley, and in the possession of one of his descendants it still remains, but has unfortunately been converted into a locket.'

I walked up the soft white sand to the 'dense herbage' which forms the boundary of the beach. Here, too, must be buried many people, for a number of bodies, other than the Admiral's, were found in the Cove; these included those of Lady Shovell's two sons by Sir John Narborough—Sir John and his brother James. Edmund Loades, the captain of *Association*, was also buried here, as were the crew of the

Admiral's barge. Like hundreds of others, at the time of the wrecks, they were stripped of their clothing and buried without identification.

Among the 'gentlemen of good family' who were aboard *Association* was Henry Trelawney, son of Sir Jonathan Trelawney, Bart., Bishop of Winchester. One would have thought that young Trelawney's body would also have been found at Porthellic, but this was not the case. In a letter dated 16th November 1707, addressed to the Bishop, and later printed in the second volume of the Penzance Natural History Society, a Mr. John Ben of St. Hilary describes the finding of the body elsewhere. It is quoted in modern spelling for the sake of clarity: '*My Lord*', goes the letter, '*Your Lordship's commands having been signified to my brother at Scilly, he immediately made the strictest inquiry that was possible of all the bodies that had been thrown ashore and buried, and being told of one buried at Agnes about Mr. Trelawny's age, was resolved to have him taken up in order to view him, whether it was he or no. He had seen the young gentleman at Torbay, but not willing to depend on his own judgement, desired the captain of the "Phoenix" fire-ship that was stranded there, who knew Mr. Trelawny intimately well on the voyage, to go with him. As soon as they had the body up, they found it actually to be the same, though somewhat altered, having been buried eleven days, and in the water four; however, the captain presently knew him, and my brother took care to have the body brought over to S. Mary's, and interred it in the chancel of the church there the 8th instant, with all the marks of respect and honour the island could show on such an occasion, some captains and the best of the inhabitants being present at the funeral.*'

The letter goes on to say: '*There is a great quantity of timber all round the islands and abundance of sails and rigging just about the place where the ships sunk, and a mast, one end a little above water, which makes them conclude an entire ship to be foundered there, because all the force they can produce is not able to move the mast. The "Eagle" most certainly is lost too, and I wish no other of the squadron may be wanting; besides those, though I am heartily sorry for the loss poor England has sustained of so many men and in a most particular manner for the share your lordship has.*'

In a postscript to the letter, Mr. Ben has this to say: '*The "Hound" came from Scilly yesterday, and was very near being taken, having three privateers behind and two before her, but she escaped by creeping along the shore, where they would not venture.'*

And now my attention was attracted by the barking of Sandy; Geoff was ready, he and Mike were walking towards the big rounding granite rocks which, it had been decided, would be the take-off point. Porth Hellick is a typical Cornish sandy cove, it faces south, it has a curving, half-moon shaped, beach. In the centre of the mouth of the small 'bay' there are rocks, these extend as a tidal reef right across to the western side of the cove. The eastern half is open to the sea and it was the eastern side on which we stood, it being impracticable to get near the reef by car in any other direction. Naturally, a boat would be used when a serious 'dive' took place here. Our being on the 'wrong' side of the Cove meant that Geoff would have to swim some hundred-and-fifty yards across to the reef; he slid off the rocks like a seal, and swam slowly, his brilliant orange-coloured hood showing up plainly against the blue of the sea.

'What do you expect to find?' asked Mike, chewing at a grass stem and backing down against a rock to get out of the cold wind.

'Look,' said I, 'I've always maintained that if Sir Clow had time enough to bring his dog along, he had time to rescue some of his precious possessions.'

'Well—such as?' prompted Mike.

'His jewels, perhaps; his gold certainly; surely he would have put at least one chest of gold aboard? Anyway, it's in the records that a part of a chest was found in this cove.'

We kept our eyes on the diminishing orange speck with the chopping fins behind it. There was little danger. The water was shallow, if Geoff got into trouble he had been told to make for the other side.

'The real idea of this exercise,' I said, 'is for Geoff to find out what the reef is like. Will it have retained anything that was spilt on it 260 years ago?—that's the question. The most promising side of a reef is that to the le'ward, where things can drop and stay.'

'He's gone down,' said Mike; Geoff's legs had appeared for an instant like the waving antennae of some glossy black sea-monster, then they had disappeared. We settled ourselves for a long wait; Geoff had enough air to last him one-and-a-half hours but we hoped he would return before then. The warmth had gone from the sun; the wind had freshened slightly; it was cold. We stumped up and down a flat sloping rock while Sandy explored the watery channels and chambers beneath us. Mike and I talked of Sir Cloudesley and that, last, long trip of his in the Admiral's barge.

'Many's the time I've lain awake at night and thought about it,' said Mike.

'Same here,' said I; 'he had to keep south of the islands, he would never have ventured to come through them in the darkness.'

'Mind—it's a long way,' said Mike, 'they had the wind and the tide with them, but my golly, it's a long way; they must have been all in by the time they got here.' He turned and pointed out to sea.

'They could have seen this opening,' I said, 'chanced their luck and made for the Cove, they could have come in between that rock'—it was my turn to point—'there! just about where Geoff is now!' The orange hood had bobbed up by the reef.

'Yes, he's spending quite a bit of time just about there,' said Mike.

It was forty minutes by our watches before we saw Geoff returning, by now we were 'nigh frozen'. Geoff swam up alongside us into a shallow gulley in the rocks, all Mike had to do was to bend down and help him ashore, while I took photographs.

We waited patiently while Geoff sat on a rock and caught his breath:

'Phew—it's cold!' he said, 'It's only my hands, I had to jettison my gloves.'

'Did you find anything?' asked Mike, unable to hold back the question any longer.

'I found some sheet lead with copper fastenings in it,' said Geoff.

'Was it square or oblong?' I asked, hopefully, thinking of the lead lining of a chest.

'No, there was a small roll of it, like rolled-up paper, but I didn't trouble with it as I found these . . .'

He fumbled at his neoprene cuff while a sense of expectation clanged about in my breast; Geoff pulled out first one, then another, of two brown objects covered in barnacles, he handed them to me; in spite of their thick encrustation I could identify them immediately, they were pieces of eight; on the edge of one the silver metal gleamed white where it had been scratched.

'Pieces of eight!' I exclaimed, in bewildered gratification.

'Well, I'll go to sea!' said Mike; he bore the disconcerted look of a man who has lived all his life amid a sea of wealth, and no one has taken the slightest trouble to tell him anything about it. By the time we had returned to the grass plot, on which stood the van, we had used all the expressions of astonishment we could think of.

'There can be only one of two explanations for this,' I said, 'either we've had the luck of the devil or there must be a lot of this stuff down there.'

'They were in a crevice in a rock,' said Geoff, 'I had to take off my gloves to get out the one that's scratched, it was jammed in so tightly.'

Further conversation became difficult for, suddenly, we were surrounded by a herd of cows; they examined our equipment minutely, they thrust their heads into the back of the van, they looked at us unblushingly from under their long white eyelashes. Presently a voice from the middle of the herd said:

'We couldn't believe it! It was the last thing we expected to see! Divers in this cold weather!'

The cows opened up to allow a young couple to step forward; obviously they were on their honeymoon. Talk about 'shoes and ships and sealing wax and cabbages and kings'; here we had a skin-diver talking to a honeymoon couple in the middle of a herd of cows on an island in the Atlantic, with them was a man with two pieces of eight while nearby stood a gigantic 'loaded camel': surely even Lewis Carroll would have been hard pressed to have contrived such a combination.

That evening, in the warmth of our hotel dining room, Geoff and I discussed the implications of his find. If we were going to be lucky enough to find anything at all, we had expected to find gold; to come across silver was a littleshattering. I could not visualise Sir Clow troubling himself with pieces of eight when his Great Cabin chests must have been stuffed with gold galore. True, Geoff had given the reef but a forty-minute search; true, also, that had he not known what to look for we should not be in possession of these intriguing pieces of eight; they resembled nothing better than two flat, oval, brown stones; most divers would not have given them a second look. Long ago we had talked of the possibility of finding gold on Porth Hellick reef, that is—if the barge had been wrecked there—if the old time Scillonians had not dived and taken it all—if the sea, over the years, had not washed it into the sandy cove, and we had admitted to ourselves the odds were very much against our finding anything. And now, just to prove that anything may happen in underwater exploration, the gods had presented us with these two barnacled coins from the way-back days of pirates and privateers. Geoff's description of the reef rather suggested that silver could be trapped and retained, especially so as silver takes the same growth as a rock; gold, free of growth, would slither and slide. Anyone who knows anything about reefs is aware that it is the far side, that is the side away from the open sea and over which everything spills, which is the place to explore.

Taken all in all, bearing in mind the duration of the dive, and the small spontaneous way in which we had gone about it, we decided that this small venture was our most lucky of all, to date.

That night, I was awakened by the rattling of my bedroom windows, it was moonlight, the curtains were billowing out like t'gallant sails, the wind had got up to gale force. As I closed the windows I looked out over St. Mary's harbour; the moon was full, as was the tide; the sea was spilling over the harbour wall—of a certainty there would be no diving on the morrow.

We decided to make public our small, but spectacular, find, even at the considerable risk of dozens of other divers descending on the reef. We could do no other than report the matter to the Receiver of Wreck, he in his turn would, in duty bound, have to post up the news on the Customs notice board.

This very real hazard of 'other divers' muscling in on our discovery was increasingly worrying us. As we ourselves made extensive, and expensive, preparations for our continuing treasure quest, news reached us daily of other teams preparing to dive at the Gilstone. Some openly boasted that it was their intention to vie with us in salvaging the silver we had discovered.

By permission of the Eastern Counties Newspapers Ltd. I

quote this article which appeared in their *Eastern Evening News* for 24th February 1968:

'WANTED: Local business men with £10,000 to finance an underwater treasure hunt that could pay off £3 million in gold and silver coins.

'Two Lowestoft divers and a friend plan to try to recover it from 70 feet down on the Gilstone Reef, in the Scillies.

'The men, Mr. H——, aged 31; Mr. B——, 34; and Mr. G——, 28, are so sure of success that they are putting every penny they have in the venture.

'Mr. H——, the leader, claims to be one of the three men who know the exact whereabouts of the treasure. It is from the *Association*, the flagship of the English Mediterranean Fleet, which sank with all hands on the treacherous reef on October 22nd. 1707.

'Last year, the three of them, in an expedition backed by a syndicate of London businessmen, brought up enough gold and silver coins to pay for their efforts.

'Bad weather stopped them searching further and they are now having difficulty in getting the money.

' "This time we are working for ourselves," said Mr. H—— "A fourth diver will be going down with us."

'The three intend to start in April, hoping to beat a rival team which had some success last year. Divers from the Fleet Air Arm Sub Aqua Club may also try their luck.

'Last year amateurs tried to get in. Now they have been warned by the Board of Trade and the Admiralty to keep away. Dangerous currents make it no picnic. Mr. H—— said: ' "It's pretty dangerous."

'At the moment the three men are fitting out the *Vigia*, a former pilot cutter, on Mission Quay, Gorleston. They are asking for local money because they know the area. And they freely admit that they are not financiers but divers and engineers.

'The money will help them supplement their already extensive equipment and pay for the long hard months of diving through to September or October.

' "We are going to make a bomb out of this," said Mr. G——. "Anyone who backs us is going to line his pockets."

'The seabed is not flat and easy to search but is twisted into underwater valleys and mountain peaks. The unwary diver, swimming out of a cave, could easily be dashed against rocks by a current of up to four knots.

'The gold and silver is hidden under giant boulders which they will lift with jacks.

' "We will be working at a depth of about 60 feet, in pairs, doing about 90 minutes a day," said Mr. H——.

'Even if the weather gets too bad to dive off the reef they will not be wasting a day. Scores of wrecks lie round about offering valuable salvage work.

' "Last year I helped to lift a nine-ton propeller worth £1,600," said Mr. H——.'

I quote this 'prospectus' in full, for we shall see many such in coming years, as more and more people take up diving. But what a whimsical, rhapsodical world in which to undertake salvage! A world of the Flying Dutchman and the Great Sea-Serpent, of the Man in the Moon and the Castle in the Air, a world where divers can work here, there and everywhere and '*they will not be wasting a day*'!

Treasure! what a word of magic this can be! What an incantation to be breathed as one rubs the lamp, waves the wand or casts a spell!

Treasure! this word can bedevil, enchant, obsess. It can command genii: it can call up spirits from the vasty deep; it can mesmerise the hardest-headed of businessmen into pouring out sufficient funds to undertake the most debatable of quests, and for the most shadowy of loot. One has but to mention Captain Kidd, or the Cocos Island, Tobermory Bay or the Spanish Main, and staid men stir from their humdrum existences and go adventuring for those ironbound chests of buried gold. Not—mind you—in person, to go adventuring all they have to do is—pay.

15

THE SOLID SILVER CLUE

During the winter months that followed our treasure hunting summer, more especially during the long dark evenings when the sea ran high in the cove below, and the sou'westerly wind shook the four corners of the house, the divers and I met regularly at the old Admiral Benbow. In the snugness and warmth of our favourite seats in the Wreck Bar we passed the time pleasantly enough.

Geoff was always the optimistic and cheery one; Doug, on the other hand, was often silent and preoccupied. His long-awaited salvage award for the tons of copper and bronze—which he handed in to H.M. Receiver of Wreck some twelve months previously—had been paid, and had proved to be disappointingly low. There had been some slip-up, too, over the giant propeller on which Doug had worked for so long, on which we, and the *Ros Guill*, had expended so much time and energy on his behalf.

As the winter progressed, as the days became longer, Doug finally left us; he had other plans, plans which included his diving at Scilly, but not with us. Our team for the continuing treasure hunt—1968 version—was to be composed of Geoff Upton, Colin Gregory and Mark Horobin, and a fine body of divers they proved to be.

And so we talked the winter evenings away; with Mike

Hicks—now with his swarthy face adorned with a full black beard—at times bursting through the doorway with a wide grin, and a giant hand outstretched in greeting:

'Well—you know—thought I'd just nip over in the 'copter to have a noggin, and see how you're all faring.'

On these occasions the talk would be of the Islands; of boats and engines; of such things as tide-rips and currents and submerged rocks:

'Yes, well, you've got to watch out for that one, she just about shows at low water springs.'

And the talk would naturally veer round to wrecks:

'When she went ashore Lloyd's Agent was taken out to her to assess the damage, and whilst he was standing on her deck with a couple of Customs blokes, the crew of the launch were busy handing out canned beer from her cargo through a port-hole—almost from under the Customs' feet. There was enough beer aboard that launch to put her down by a foot, it must have been well stowed for the officials never noticed a thing.'

Without any doubt we never wearied of our favourite topic—of wrecks, both old and not so old—you see, there are so

One of those who paid the price. The skull and bones of a young man in his twenties recovered from the wreck site during the summer of 1968

many of them and each has a story of its own. Before the evening was done someone was sure to mention the *Association* and certain it was that one or another of us would up and say:

'If only we could positively identify our wreck by name, what a darn thing that would be!'

It seemed we had not a Chinaman's chance of convincing the Authorities by our finds up to date. To our minds the clues were overwhelmingly in favour of its being a British Naval ship. The sheaves from the rigging blocks, with their British Naval Broad Arrow stampings, the round shot with similar markings, the gold rings with their British inscriptions—a second ring had been brought up bearing the legend, 'Not the value, but my love'—and the fact that the bulk of the silver coin recovered was British.

Clues there were, too, that she was actually the *Association*—no coin was so far later than 1706 (a vital point in view of the *Association*'s having sunk in 1707), and the silver spoon-handle, embossed with the crest of a mailed fist rising from the waves, recalled the similar crest used by both Captain Loades, the *Association*'s Flag Captain, and Captain Whitaker, her Sailing Master. Last, but by no means least, I had the evidence of my faithful old chart of Edmund Gostelo: *With the Soundings and Barings And ye Exact Places where the 'Association' . . . was Lost.* Yet we had still nothing that could have come without doubt from the *Association* and from her only.

At least, that was how matters stood until the Great Day. It came about while I was engaged in the intriguing task of cleaning the bronze triplets. At long last I had been allowed to ship these three guns over to my workshop for urgent attention. I had bathed gun Number One in a special cleaning solution for hours on end, this in order to remove the sea-growth. Then with specially soft brass-wire brushes, which lasted no time at all, I worked painstakingly on the raised decorative motifs. The metal responded well enough but how slowly it did so! The task took six weeks of my spare time, but—by the powers!—it was well worth it. By the time I had finished I had brought back that gun to its former glory; from the wriggling little salamander on the swell of its muzzle right aft to the lion's-mask touch-hole at its breech it shone like gold.

One thing is certain—something which the cleaning has

brought to light—at some stage in its chequered lifetime that gun had been in action. The complexion of the metal, in way of its breech, bears the coppery hue of bronze which has sustained prolonged overheating; this in contrast with the bronze-gold of the rest of the gun. Not only that, there is evidence that the gun has been, itself, under fire. Of the several injuries obviously caused during the break-up of the ship, two are very different, and are scars which show plainly where it has been hit by round shot travelling at high velocity.

My efforts during the final, very pleasant, phase of buffing up the gun were interrupted by a phone call from Mike Hicks:

'The boys have found something pretty good,' he announced simply, 'something very much to your liking I should think.'

'What is it?' I asked, my mind reeling under a sudden visionary flash-past of countless possibilities.

'Well, the boys found it, so it's only right for them to tell you themselves—I'll hand you over to Geoff.'

There was a long pause, whilst the phone clanked and my mind raced through a mental ship-chandler's catalogue.

'Hello!—Roland?'

'Yes!'

'Geoff here!'

'Yes!—yes?'

'We've found a plate!'

'A plate?'

'Yes! a solid silver plate!'

'A *plate*!'

'Yes! We've partially cleaned it—it's got a crest!'

'A *crest*!'

'Yes! a beautiful crest! Of course we don't know whose, but it's a wonderful piece of work, and in first-class condition.'

'Send it over!' said I, my fingers all of an itch. 'Put it on the next 'copter!'

'We haven't finished cleaning it . . .' complained Geoff.

'Never mind!' I yelled, now very much agog. 'Wrap it up and bung it over, this may be vitally important!'

In a matter of an hour or so I collected a dingy parcel from the heliport. The outer wrapping was composed of a flattened cardboard carton that had, at one time, contained pre-packed vegetables; a faded green-printed 'flash' could be deciphered—'SURPRISE'—it said; under this Geoff had scrawled: 'To be called for'.

Lips and eyes puffed by pressure, Mark Horobin, youngest of the divers working on the treasure and finder of the crucial silver plate

The plate was round, heavy and slightly battered; it was coated thickly in a hard, grey, sea-growth. At first I was for leaving this coating *in situ*—would the great white (archaeological) chiefs rather have it this way? After examining the plate more closely I decided not, the hardening growth was causing a blackening of the silver. Carefully I removed the calcinous deposit; the plate was revealed as a thing of beauty, the metal satin-soft and warm to the touch; the crest was perfect and undamaged.

With all haste a messenger was despatched to the local library with instructions to locate Sir Cloudesley Shovell's coat-of-arms, but it was a Saturday, the reference section was closed. *Was* it Sir Cloudesley's crest? If not, then whose?

My first clue came during the week-end. I looked up a photograph of Sir Cloudesley's tomb at Westminster. There, on the left-hand side of that indescribably ugly monument, I could make out a shield depicting three sheaves of corn—or, in heraldic terms—three garbs. We were on the right tack, for this was similar to the right-hand half of the shield in the plate's crest. Inquiries at the library on the Monday clinched

The plate was revealed as a thing of beauty

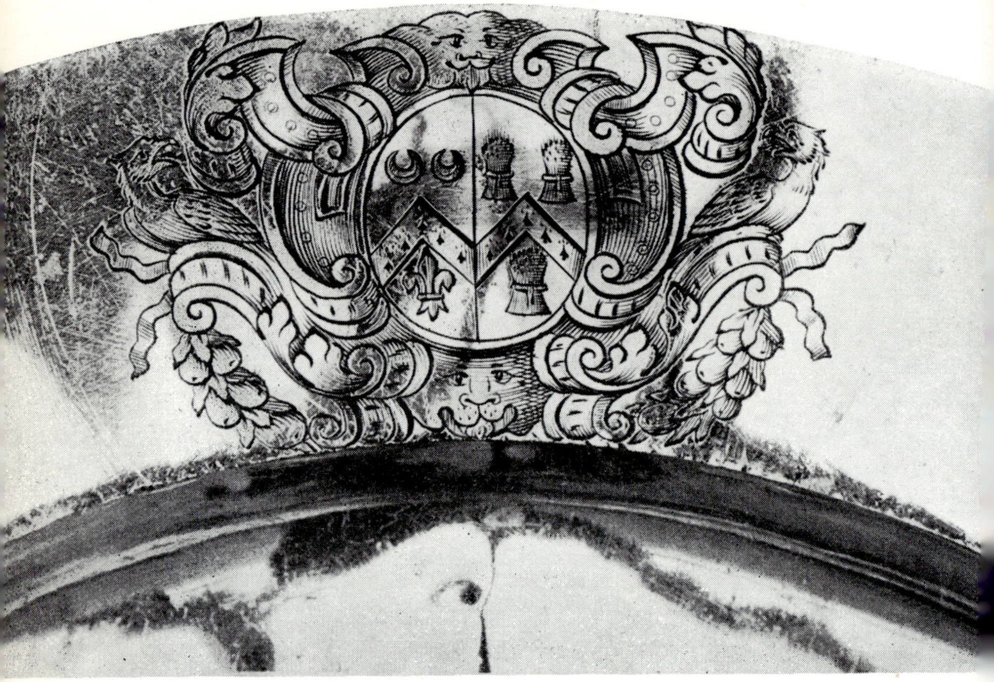

Sir Cloudesley Shovell's personal Coat of Arms: on the right-hand side of the crest are the arms of the Narborough family, Sir Cloudesley having married the widow of Admiral Narborough; those to the left are an augmentation of honour—Gules, a Chevron Ermine, in chief two Crescents Argent, and in base, a Fleur-de-Lis Or—commemorating Sir Cloudesley's victories in 1692, one over the Turks and one over the French

the whole thing. The arms of the left-hand side of the crest represented 'an augmentation of honour' awarded to Sir Cloudesley in honour of his victories over the Turks and the French.

We had made it! Here was proof indeed that our wreck was that of the famous *Association*, the ship on which we had the full permission of her owners—the Ministry of Defence—'to dive and recover therefrom gear, tackle, equipment and accoutrements'!

This was our most important find so far and great credit must go to the divers. Mark Horobin found it and a great diver Geoff Upton has made of him. His courage is unbounding, his skill will soon be on a par with that of Geoff and Colin

Gregory, and when he reaches that stage he will be one of the finest divers in the land—or, rather, the sea.

No matter what we discover in the future, nothing can be of greater import than this plate, for it is the one vital clue for which we have longed. It is a direct link with the élite of the *Association*, for assuredly the Admiral himself had eaten from it, as had Sir John Narborough and his brother James, and certainly Captain Edmund Loades. It is even feasible that the gallant Duke of Savoy had taken wine-steeped peaches from it with bejewelled, beringed fingers.

At my request Mr. W. J. G. Verco, M.V.O., Chester Herald of Arms of the College of Arms, London, gave the final verdict on the find:

'The achievement of arms . . . displays in appropriate heraldic marshalling the Arms of Sir Cloudesley Shovell and those representing the paternal Arms of his wife, Elizabeth (daughter of John Hill, Esquire, and widow of Sir John Narborough). Sir Cloudesley Shovell and Elizabeth were married at Allhallows, Staining, London on the 10th March 1690/1.

'The Arms of the dexter half of the shield (i.e. on the left as one looks at the shield) are blazoned; Gules a chevron ermine between two crescents in chief argent and a fleur-de-lis in base or. This Coat, together with its accompanying Crest (not depicted in the achievement) namely, Out of a mural coronet gold and demi lion gules holding a sail argent with an anchor sable, was granted direct to him and his descendants by Letters Patent under the hands and seals of the then Garter and Clarenceaux Kings of Arms, bearing the date 6th. January 1691/2 and wherein it is simply stated that the Grant was made in consideration of *the many eminent services performed at sea by the said Sir Cloudesley Shovell, Rear Admiral of the Blue Squadron of Their Majesties' Fleet, as for his good affections to Their Majesties.*

'Unfortunately, neither Sir Cloudesley Shovell nor any other member of his family ever registered particulars of genealogy here, but considerable detail of his career and family history is to be found in numerous printed works of reference such as the *Dictionary of National Biography*, and from this source evidence of his marriage was obtained which, together with the result of the search in the College records whereby the Arms on the sinister side of the shield have been identified as those pertaining to a number of families of Hill of the West country, leaves but little doubt as to the identification of the achievement as mentioned in the first paragraph above.

'The Arms of Hill, namely; Gules a chevron ermine between three garbs or, were registered during the Herald's Visitation of Cornwall in 1620, and the same Coat appears from printed works of armorial reference to have been borne by the Hill family of Taunton in Somerset, and presumably Elizabeth Hill claimed descent from one of these families.'

As luck would have it I was being visited by an official of the Ministry of Defence, Miss B. J. Day, at the time of the discovery of the plate. Miss Day admitted at the time, and later in a letter of confirmation, that it was a reasonable inference that the plate and the other 'finds' brought up from the wreck site came from the remains of H.M.S. *Association*. It was as if the Secretary of State had gone out to break a bottle of champagne over the Gilstone saying:

'I name this wreck *Association*, may God bless her and—provided they have permission to do so!—all those who work on her.'

Later I was to receive a letter from the Ministry which tidied up the treasure hunt in no uncertain way. They informed me that it had been decided to award me all those artefacts which had obviously come from a British Naval ship, *and to which the Ministry could thus lay claim*. This meant that the three bronze guns, the muzzle-loaders, cannon balls, lead shot, bronze sheaves, and the like, were mine to do with as I liked. If I had not obtained that Agreement, which allowed me to work on the *Association*, all these would have had to be handed in to the Customs. It pays to sign an Agreement with the owners of a wreck before starting serious diving operations.

As I well know, unhappily better than most, the sea never bestows, invariably it seizes; through our combined effort we have snatched back from its grasp beautiful, valuable and historic things. Nothing can give me greater satisfaction than this—and you may lay to that.

This, then, is our adventure—our treasure hunt—so far as it has run. An adventure of a thousand memories.

The obverse of this piece of eight (left) shows the Coat of Arms of Leon and Castile, the lions and castles contained in the angles of the large Jerusalem cross, the assayer's initial 'F' is on the left. The reverse (right) shows the two pillars of Hercules crowned, at one time the motto 'NE PLUS ULTRA' *appeared on the Spanish Coat of Arms and alluded to these pillars—the Straits of Gibralter. But the Spaniards having reached America,* 'NE' *was omitted*—PLU/SUL/TRA—*implying that Spain could indeed 'go further'. The initial 'P' stands for Potosi mint, the 'F' is the assayer's mark. The date is indicated by the last two digits—1699.*

I shall always bear in mind our fat, bewildered trawler 'chuff-chuffing' her spectral, uncertain way through the vapour-bound channels, on that soggy night of the fog and the mist.

I shall never forget the quiet day of brilliant light and crystal-clear water, when the sea and the sky were as one; when our boat and the effervescing divers seemingly swam in space; and when the frolicking, friendly seals nibbled at the divers' heels as they flipped their way down.

Never shall I lose the thrill of seeing glistening bronze and precious metals drying in the sun, after two-and-a-half centuries of lack-lustre submergence in the Atlantic Ocean.

Memorable, too, is the glow of the sunset on bearded, suntanned faces, and the velvet-black of the starkly silhouetted rocks as the sun drops behind the horizon in a slow-motion rampage of scorching colour.

But to my dying day shall I have in my mind the sound of the surf booming along the shores—and about the reefs and the rocks—of the Islands of Scilly.

INDEX